W9-DBK-512

Pedagogy Left in Peace

Pedagogy Left in Peace

Cultivating Free Spaces in Teaching and Learning

DAVID W. JARDINE

Continuum International Publishing Group
The Tower Building
11 York Road
London
SE1 7NX

80 Maiden Lane
Suite 704
New York
NY 10038

www.continuumbooks.com

ISBN: 978-1-4411-1372-6 (hardcover)
978-1-4411-6329-5 (paperback)

Library of Congress Cataloging-in-Publication Data

Jardine, David William, 1950-
Pedagogy left in peace: cultivating free spaces in teaching and learning/David W. Jardine.
p. cm.
Includes bibliographical references and index.

ISBN-13: 978-1-4411-1372-6 (hardcover: alk. paper)
ISBN-10: 1-4411-1372-X (hardcover: alk. paper)
ISBN-13: 978-1-4411-6329-5 (pbk.: alk. paper)
ISBN-10: 1-4411-6329-8 (pbk.: alk. paper)

1. Education–Philosophy. 2. Education–Aims and objectives. 3. Ontology. I. Title.
LB14.7.J367 2012
370.1–dc23
2012003061

Typeset by Deanta Global Publishing Services, Chennai, India
Printed and bound in the United States of America

CONTENTS

Introduction: "Left in peace"

War tends to make cultures alike whereas peace is that condition under which each culture flowers in its own incomparable way. Peace cannot be exported. Its attempted export means war.

. . . .

At the center, the emphasis is on "peace keeping"; on the margin, people hope to be left in peace.

— Ivan Illich (1992, p. 17, 16) from "The De-Linking of Peace and Development."

"To find free spaces and to learn to move therein"

I want to begin these meditations on *Pedagogy Left in Peace* by citing an extended passage by Hans-Georg Gadamer. It is from "The Idea of the University—Yesterday, Today, Tomorrow," part of a speech he gave at the age of 86 in Heidelberg, Germany:

> We should have no illusion. Bureaucratized teaching and learning systems dominate the scene, but nevertheless it is everyone's task to find his free space. The task of our human

> life in general is to find free spaces and learn to move therein. In research this means finding the question, the genuine question. You all know that as a beginner one comes to find everything questionable, for that is the privilege of youth to seek everywhere the novel and new possibilities. One then learns slowly how a large amount must be excluded in order to finally arrive at the point where one finds the truly open questions and therefore the possibilities that exist. Perhaps the most noble side of the enduring independent position of the university—in political and social life—is that we with the youth and they with us learn to discover the possibilities and thereby possible ways of shaping our lives. There is this chain of generations which passes through an institution, like the university, in which teachers and students meet and lose one another. Students become teachers and from the activity of the teachers grows a new teaching, a living universe, which is certainly more than something known, more than something learnable, but a place where something happens to us. I think this small academic universe still remains one of the few precursors of the grand universe of humanity, of all human beings, who must learn to create with one another new solidarities. (Gadamer 1986, p. 59)

I have two reasons to begin here. First, now that I have ended my 61st year, that it might possibly be able to think, experience, and recognize such a hopeful sense of what education can be at age 86 is both heartening and wonderfully humiliating of my own sometimes overwhelming exhaustions and frustrations about my chosen profession. Anyone in education has most likely experienced something of the seemingly perennial chill of our circumstances, about which we should have no illusions. Writing a book entitled *Pedagogy Left in Peace* seems, even to me every so often, an oddly doomed endeavor.

Echoing with Gadamer's images of a chain of generations and the ongoing task of remaking solidarities and shaping of our lives, Hannah Arendt (1969, p. 192–3) cautioned that

> To preserve the world against the mortality of its creators and inhabitants it must be constantly set right anew. The problem is simply to educate in such way that a setting-right remains actually possible, even though it can, of course, never be assured.

We might be fleetingly able to protect the conditions under which such "setting right anew" might be *possible* in the future. It might be possible, in this next venture of teaching and learning, to forge new solidarities in a free space of possibility and to shape our lives accordingly. However, under the contingent circumstances of schooling and its surroundings, with this class and/or that student, we can never assure that *this time* a free space will open up and something might happen to us—teachers and students alike.

It always *depends*. This, too, is part of the chill of the circumstance of education, good news in its own way, but tough news as well. We can prepare and invite, but preparation and invitation do not *cause* arrival but simply strive to set out some of the conditions of its possibility. Ours is, in part, an adventitious profession. This does not make education "unaccountable" but begins to define, in a deep and difficult way that is true to its nature, precisely what pedagogy is accountable to, for, and about. False assurances ring hollow against this often-suppressed, difficult, and, in the end, joyous, earthly, and deeply human insight.

It is important to understand that the bureaucratized teaching and learning systems to which Gadamer alludes (and which have long since been the object of study for those in the reconceptualist movement in curriculum theory [see, e.g. Pinar et al. (1995), Kincheloe and Steinberg (2006); see also Callahan (1964), Friesen and Jardine (2009); see Chapters 1, 2, and 4]), are bent, at their core, on trumpeting *precisely such assurances*. Such systems are bent on the belief that if we only select the right standardized procedures, enacted the right institutional structures, get the right funding, forms and assessment regimes, and so on, teachers' and students' futures will be finally secured and assured and peace will reign. However, as Ivan Illich contends in the passage cited above, this exportation from a center of a sort of *Pax Romana* throws many schools into what feels like a state of war—"the trenches," as goes the euphemism of some high school teachers and students (see Smith 2006f, 2008, Naqvi and Smits 2011, Naqvi and Jardine 2008; see Chapters 1–4).

These bureaucratic assurances are empty, but not because they may have, by chance or lack of diligence or information, selected the wrong structures or procedures and might just select the right ones in the future. (This is the terrible and often unspoken promise that too often comes with such assurances, that *this time* we've finally "got it right," thus oddly linking such assurances with a sort of market-driven sense of promise, subtle deceit, and eventual inevitable enervation.)

These assurances are empty because the belief that we can, if bureaucratically diligent enough, assure a future with no risk or uncertainty, no need for further thinking or negotiation or venture, mistakes our lives and our living circumstances and those of our students, with some sort of error that can be and needs to be fixed, a "problem to be solved and subsumed under a condition of mastery or explanation" (Smith 1999b, p. 139). The often harrowing, deeply dependent and interdependent work of confronting the mortality of the world that must be set right anew in concert and solidarity with the young, is not an error that needs fixing. Its contingencies and dependencies—viewed, to use Illich's image again, as simply "marginal" from "the center" (see Chapters 2 and 3)—are not avoidable, revocable, or expugnable. The ongoing need to set things right anew and the intergenerational task of opening, protecting, and cultivating the free spaces in which this just might happen is, as John Caputo (1987) coined it, a sign of the irremediable "original difficulty" of being alive that should not be betrayed by false promises (see Jardine 1992a):

> Living with children means living in the belly of a paradox wherein a genuine life together is made possible only in the context of an ongoing conversation which never ends, yet which must be sustained for life together to go on at all. Homes, classrooms, schools wherein the people in charge cannot lay themselves open to the new life in their midst, always exist in a state of war. (Smith 1999b p. 139)

Wanting to eradicate this paradox as is the wont of bureaucratic teaching and learning systems, is akin to wanting to eradicate what Hannah Arendt (1969, p. 196) identified as the correlate of the mortality of the world: "the fact of natality: the fact that we have all come into the world by being born and that this world is constantly renewed through birth." Thus David G. Smith's (1999b p. 140) still inexhaustible insight of the "monstrous states of siege" that then arise between the young and the old, the new and the established, natality and mortality. Thus, too, James Hillman's brilliant work (2005a, 2005b) on what occurs when the old and the young become estranged: the senatorial becomes senile and fixed, youth, vigor, and energy become flighty and puerile. Thus, too, the shift in ecological consciousness where we're coming to realize the deep affinity between "the wild" and our own renewal, and how the Earth must be part of the ongoing conversation necessary for "life together to go on at all."

We should have no illusion about the profound consequences of falling for such false assurances, betrayals, and attempted (and, more often than not, well-meaning and full of intentions of "for your own good" [Miller 1989]) eradications. Such assurances amount, however unwittingly and unintentionally, to a desire to eradicate the fact of natality ("savage childhood," one might say [see Chapter 3]—parallel, ecologically, to a desire to protect ourselves from and finally fully tame "the wild" [Berry 1986; Bordo 1987; Illich 1980; Jardine 1992b, 1997, 1998b, 2006b, 2008b, Miller 1989; see also Chapters 3–6]).

Cutting ourselves off from the wild troubles of living a life in the midst of the living interdependencies of the world does not provide for a pedagogy left in peace. It undermines it, imagining that peace will come when the future is fixed once and for all and the achievement of that fixed future is itself set out in developmental stages (see Smith 1999a, 1999b, 2006a, 2008; see Chapter 3 for the parallel between a fixed future and stages of development [see also Jardine 2005]; note, too, that Ivan Illich's work cited at the head of this "Introduction" is called "The De-Linking of Peace and Development"). Under such false assurances, education becomes akin to a sometimes overt, but more often subtle, war on the very possibility of unanticipated "uprising." Free spaces and those who cultivate them become suspect. Natality becomes experienced as a perennial insurgent threat to security that must be planned for and secured against. Education becomes cast as akin to a counterinsurgent war on terror (Smith 2006f; see Chapters 1–3 and 10)—a perpetual war (Postel and Drury 2003), given the perpetuity of the world's mortality. After all, a war against our response ("terror") to the very existence of uprising is, of necessity, perpetual. It is also profoundly Thantic—a longing for the end of this roil, for finality, fixity and death (see Jardine 1992a, 1992b)— but I'll leave this thread loose for now and for others to follow.

A pedagogy left in peace does not have a death wish in the face of the roils of the world, but its peace is had, not by pursuing falsely assured but illusory permanences, but by learning to live well under this perennial, deeply human chill of venturous, risky possibility without false assurances. This is its powerful fragility, that it *might* change everything and that it also might not occur at all.

Pedagogy Left in Peace, therefore, sets out an image of education, not as the pacified outcome of a bureaucratic system, but as a perennial, personal, and intimate task, which, at 86 years old, Gadamer was still able to envisage as always and inevitably needing to be taken up here, now, once again, and anew—this is the gathering and regathering in a whiling experience of time (see Chapter 9) and the perennial raising anew of the question of what is worth our while in this limited life, what possibilities might help us go on together. There is thus a terrible intimacy to a pedagogy left in peace. It is, after all, my life, the only life I will have, that is being or failing to be shaped, and thus, too, for every student and teacher (see Chapters 5 and 11).

"It is everyone's task," for the lives of teachers and students will be shaped one way or the other. Education's only prospect is that we might have some hand, some however small say in the setting right of the world and the shape of our learning to live therein.

We *might*.

Almost ironically, then, this personal and intimate task that is everyone's provides a way of transforming our understanding of the nature and life of the knowledge entrusted to teachers and students in school. Despite the best efforts of bureaucratic teaching and learning systems to render knowledge and our relationships to it into something secured and fixed, its life in the world eludes such dominance. Thinking, exploring, coming to know, setting things right, questioning, searching out possibilities and solidarities—these are ancient, multifarious, and convivial tasks, ones that are hidden right here, in the often meager curriculum mandates inherited by teachers and students in schools. The topics "covered" in school link teachers and students not just to each other but also to great arcs of mixed, contested, and sometimes quite troublesome ancestries, rife with possibilities of engagement and transformation, with successes and failures, heroes and villains and great contests over who is who and what is what. It burdens us with a deeply human burden of remembering (see Chapter 8) as a link to belonging, membership, but then, of course, also to threads and traces of exclusion and alienation (see Chapters 1 and 10). Every shred of grammar, every articulation of a circle's arc—all these wee curriculum topics—are, in their deepest reality, sites where setting right has once accrued and is still accruing in the continuing living of such matters in the world. Seeing through the thick encrustations of curriculum "bullets," finding such free spaces (recall, where Gadamer reminds us that not everything is possible. Freedom, here, is not "vague licentiousness" [Smith 1999b p. 139] but the convivial struggle to find truly open questions and possibilities), and learning to live therein—this struggle to become who I am in the midst of this convivial world—is a task that is always abundantly full of ancient voices and signs of ancient ventures and contradictory counsels right at the very moment and in the very same gesture that it is also singular and brand new.

After all, right now, while writing these words, Grade six classrooms in Alberta are venturing into the "mandate" curriculum topic of ecosystems and their life and sustainability, as well as into work on watersheds and their ways, right as news is arriving of the arrival of debris from the recent Japanese tsunami on the Western shores of Vancouver Island, bidding teachers and students alike, in "following" and "covering" these mandate curriculum bullets, to open up free spaces for thinking, for knowledge, for coming to know the world, around the real events of our lives and their possibilities.

Even in these simple examples, the cultivation of an open sense of time and its gathering (see Chapter 9) is linked to an awakening and cultivation of memory as something of my own, something that makes me who I am (see Chapter 8). After all, what are we to think and do about these matters? What are we to make of the irradiated materials heading toward the so-called Garbage Island in the Pacific? These are not rhetorical questions. They are questions posed *to* this old world by new events. The hermeneutic event of opening up free spaces, therefore, is not a radical attempt to eradicate the old, established, and ancestral (this is simply puerile). But neither is it just the mute repetition of traditions (this is simply senile). The old, rather, is *called to account* by the new, by the "fecundity of the individual case" (Gadamer 1989, p. 37) and is therefore called to face the possibility of its own renewal, transformation, "set[ting] right anew" or, perhaps, abandonment, rejection, or condemnation.

Part of the stunning nature of this is that these living threads exist *whether we know it or not*. They are always already at work shaping our lives *anyway*. We can retract from this convivial reality and tout our autonomy, but this only represses the reality of our actual situation and the responsibility that we are called to in the act of education: taking up our entangled embeddedness in the world and its ways, and taking responsibility for questioning the locales of our living.

This, then, is the second reason for me to begin by citing this passage from Hans-Georg Gadamer's speech. These images of opening free spaces, the tough and eminently practical and day-to-day work of building solidarities with the young and coming to learn how to live well with the living myriadness of the past—all this has been a reliable and ongoing refuge of my own work. I have had the privilege of being a very small part of countless classrooms where the convivial, difficult, contested, and vibrant life of the world has been engaged, enjoyed, understood, critiqued, and transformed into ever-new solidarities.

Left in peace, each has flowered in its own incomparable way.

"We should have no illusion"

> School (1): "place of instruction," O.E. *scol*, from L. *schola*, from Gk. *Skhole* "school, lecture, discussion," also "leisure, spare time," originally "a holding back, a keeping clear." (OED)

We should, however, have no illusion. Free spaces are rare and hard won, and learning to live well within them is hard work that requires stillness, generosity, and perseverance. Left in peace means being left to and challenged by what Gary Snyder (1980) called "the real work" of the places we come to inhabit—these curriculum topographies, these *topics* (see Chapters 5–9)—and all this ventured all over again, here, this year, these students, this time, in the surrounds of these causes and conditions.

Just in these past few months, 22 out of 26 of my undergraduate students in a mathematics/science curriculum class had practicum placements that allowed nothing but photocopied worksheets to be passed out, filled in, and handed back, all day, every day from Kindergarten to Grade six. When one student desperately begged for help in her Grade Five practicum situation where students could not fathom long division, I suggested talking to them about . . . and was interrupted:

> "My teacher said that there is no time to *talk* to them. There's too much to cover. He wants me to make a sheet."

School. From the Latin, *schola*, "leisure." Imagine. "School" and "leisure" said in the same breath. Imagine, too, that other etymological image of "holding back and keeping clear," an image of work that needs to be done, a task that is set out for us as teachers and students, that will, if not ensure, then at least invite and protect such ventures. It seems a bit like a cruel etymological joke.

"We should have no illusion." Over and over again, circumstances that make schools, teachers, and administrators retract from any such suggestions of free spaces and the work needed to learn to live therein, arise ever vigorous and new. In fact, such suggestions often seem outright ludicrous, the very sort of thing that an Ivory Tower might issue when it is seemingly totally unhinged from the lived realities of the world.

Several times over the last few years, in professional development seminars I have given at many local schools, the issue has been put like this. Although it has an attractive face and sound like a "nice idea," many teachers are not simply afraid to pursue this sort of venture. They are often unable to see, in their present circumstances, how it would even be *possible*, let alone warranted by the powers that be. The stakes are too high. They and their students are already overburdened and don't need something added to the mix of expectations. They are exhausted, worn out, caught in what is experienced as an ever-acceleration rush of one thing after the other (see Chapter 9; see also Jardine 1997, 2008; Ross 2004; Ross and Jardine 2008b). Add to this school-board level expectations, varying and sometimes unreliable administrative support, worsening economic conditions, decreased funding, larger and larger class sizes, student apathy and disengagement, increasing diversity and difference in the classroom, a proliferation of "special needs" and ever-increasing, ever increasingly urgent reams of paper work, and we have a deep mire that makes quite sensible and sane the retraction from what can only be believed to be the false promises of abundance (Jardine, Clifford and Friesen 2006) and a pedagogy left in peace. Add to this the ways that institutional and political structures are able, sometimes purposefully, sometimes unwittingly, to manipulate and exaggerate these low-level fears and potential threats to security for the purpose of maintaining enough low-level anxiety to produce obedience and compliance in teachers and students (see Chapter 4 for the root of this organizational feature in the work of F. W. Taylor [1903, 1911]; see also Callahan 1964; Braverman 1998; Friesen and Jardine 2009, to cite only a few, limited examples) and we have but a small glimpse of the roil and squirm of our troubled circumstances. We get a glimpse of the surfaces of suffering. What's worse, these very same circumstances distract us from the prospect of breaking through that surface. I find myself often simply skittering from one thing to another in a sort of side-long distractedness and business that eat up energy, time (see Chapter 8) and diffuses and wearies attention and portends a fading of memory and its significance, and the terribly burdensome freedom it allots, if well-tended (see Chapter 9). I know, in a terribly personal way, how voracious, greedy, and insatiable this perennial suffering is and the vainglorious pursuit of proffered remedies that promise to cure it and thereby, often unwittingly (but, under market logic, often quite deliberately and repeatedly), simply feed it.

Thus splays open, over and over again, a genuine and painful field of lament, of "if only" and "I'd love to, but . . . ." Worse than this, here is the site where too often starts a weird in-fighting which casts one part of the city against another ("I could do this if I worked *there*"), one grade level against another ("Maybe you can do that in the earlier grades where there is less at stake"), and on and on. And I will admit here, now, and loud and clear, that I end up, over and over again, as exhausted as anyone when I step into this fray of causes and conditions.

An old story, told over and over again:

> "Education is suffering from narration-sickness," says Paulo Freire. It speaks out of a story, which was once full of enthusiasm, but now shows itself incapable of a surprise ending. The nausea of narration-sickness comes from having heard enough, of hearing many variations on a theme but no new theme. (Smith 1999a, p. 135–6)

It has been difficult for me these past few years to keep the nausea at bay when this story rises up, again and again. The faces change, the voices fluctuate, the specifics of circumstance and blame flutter and twist, but the story seems to stay the same. To use Gadamer's images, it is like an old and exhausted solidarity that was forged beyond our control and to which we are now simply subjected, one that sucks new teachers and new students into its orbit, into its repetition without seeming renewal. It dominates the scene even in its very act of naming the dominant scene as the problem it laments, the "if only" it rues. Inside of this tight-wound circle, there is an intergenerational story told to new teachers about the hopelessness of intergenerationality, the hopelessness of setting things right anew—"Just like you, I, too, was once full of enthusiasm when I started teaching." This old story has remained, with some variations, nauseatingly the same for the decades I have worked in education and, as shall be demonstrated in some detail in the chapters that follow, far beyond and before that. And when my own familiarity with this story starts to breed contempt (which, frankly, I've deeply felt welling up in some situations related to my teaching and my work in schools), that contempt *itself* tethers me to that cycle and we become each other's deluded tormentor, each the other's "reason" to continue with unabated anger and determination (see Chapters 1–3).

But right here is the point of this book: *right in the midst of these very same difficult causes and conditions*, free spaces keep being opened and kept clear in real classrooms and real schools. Spaces are opened up where things can happen to us, and our lives can be shaped with some graciousness and mindfulness.

Somehow, a pedagogy left in peace is not the outcome of having quelled or conquered the burgeoning and threatening circumstances that "dominate the scene." *Somehow*, "right there, in the midst of things," (Wallace 1987, p. 111), something "lets go," (see Chapter 11) and free spaces flower and unfurl.

An ontological delusion

I am no slayer of dragons, and lack much of the courage and conviction of many scholars in education who take on the causes and conditions of bureaucratic teaching and learning systems, or the work of articulating and righting the wrongs of economic, cultural, linguistic, gendered, racial, or other disparities, injustices, and inequities. I don't know how to "change the system" and have too often exhausted myself at that breach, and seen too many dear friends and colleagues, too many beautiful ideas and ventures, ruined by that pursuit. This book, *Pedagogy Left in Peace*, is not a prescription for how to cure the world—and, in particular, the world of education—of its woes and its myriad embattlements, because its focus is on what can and has arisen in schools and in the hearts and minds of teachers and students *despite* such woes.

As will become evident to readers, the scholarly, experiential, and practical refuge of my own work has long been an odd mixture and admittedly skewed reading of convivial links between hermeneutics, ecology, and Buddhism (see Chapters 4–9 and 11). These three inheritances provide two interrelated sources of refuge for me and, indirectly, have given me a way to articulate and keep clear the sometimes downright miraculous classroom work I have witnessed and that has arisen right in the midst of and in spite of our real, common, and perennial suffering.

First of all, these three inheritances allow for a multifaceted identification of what can be described as an *ontological delusion*, a real, terrible, and pervasive trap into which thinking, practice, and experience devolve. Much of what follows in this book will begin unwinding detailed, often ancient, threads of this powerful and false-promising trap. Here, as an introduction and alert for readers, I will simply sketch this ontological delusion in skeletal form (for a filling out of this, see Chapters 4 and 11). I portray it here as sequential steps but in fact each of these steps dependently co-arises with the rest. Each seemingly separate "step" illuminates what appears to come before and after:

- We understandably "retract" from adventurous work and the risky venture of experiencing and understanding our convivial being in the world because of the woes we face that make us feel threatened and embattled. We revert to what is tried and true and relatively secured and securable (see Jardine 1992b; Smith 1999b). Such retraction produces a sort of "hardened identity" (Huntington 2003, p. 266)—an exaggerated and often then trumpeted sense of an autonomous, self-secured, and independently existing "I am" that is seemingly separate from any sense of or reliance on our worldly conviviality (see Chapters 1–4 and 8). The monstrous shape and size of these exaggerations and the loudness of this trumpeting are themselves ways to keep the threat at bay—feigned and marshaled monsters meant to be equal to the monstrosities we fear (see Jardine 1998c).

- From this locale of threatened retreat, we then treat things in the world as if they are also full of potentially threatening, unsecured, and suspect convivialities that must themselves be retracted and secured. On behalf of securing our surroundings in order to further secure our threatened "selves," the world becomes fragmented into separate, self-existing objects whose convivial relations to and dependencies upon one another have either been inquisitionally purged (see Chapters 1–4 and 10) or reduced to those that can be put under securable, standardizable control, and surveillance (akin to David Smith's "conditions of mastery and explanation" cited above). A commonplace of common sense, that one thing is different than another, gets hardened into what is, in the Western tradition stretching back at least to Aristotle, a logic of substance (here as inherited by Rene Descartes [1955, p. 255]): "a substance is that which requires nothing except itself in order to exist." We can sense here seeds of ecological disaster, as the world is put under the threat of methodical doubt that underwrites the advent of modern European science (see Chapters 4, 6, and 8). Also here are the nebulous origins of colonial issuances from a secured and univocal center (see Chapters 1–3 and 6), as well as the first tethers between colonization and constructivist images of knowledge (see Chapter 3). Here, too, the seeds of how the industrial model of efficiency and sequential assembly of separate parts boded for its holus bolus adoption into our images of education (see Chapter 4; see also Friesen and Jardine 2009; Callahan 1964).

- We then get caught in a sort of forgetful ontological projection. What was in fact the often-understandable *outcome* of embattlement and threat (e.g. Descartes' threat of methodical doubt that renders the world into mathematically secured and manageable objects; F. W. Taylor's desire for increased industrial efficiency that fragments things into sequentially assembleable bits and pieces under regimes of surveillance, deskilling, and standardization) becomes understood as simply *the way the world exists*—or, as I've often heard it expressed by teachers as they pull back from suggestions of abundance and free space, "*this* is the real world." What were understandable retractions under threat become no longer experienceable as often suitable and warranted responses to troublesome causes and conditions. A sort of ontological amnesia sets in, a neurosis, where we can't remember what has been done to us, or that there might be any perpetrating causes and conditions at all. We become deluded into believing that hardened identities and a fragmented world that are the *outcomes* of threat are, instead, an *intractable ontological given*: things *are* retracted, separate, isolated, autonomous, and fragmented. I am a separate, autonomous, self-determining "I." Each of my students is a unique, autonomous and self-determining individual (see Chapters 1–4). These supposedly autonomous sites then become understood as the secured platforms from which constructivism and even social constructivism are launched (see Chapter 3). At the cultural level, they become the sites out of which multiculturalism is often unwittingly cobbled together through the bringing together of hardened ethnic "identities" and "differences." Thus, in one of our deepest delves into trying to overcome the singularities of race, gender, culture, and the like is encoded a hidden "hardness" that blocks our access to the difficult, mixed, contested, and lived convivialities that antedate such hardening (see Chapter 1 and en passim).

- Against this deluded ontological background ("things are what they are independently of everything else"—what is called in Tibetan Buddhism the delusion of inherent self-existence), we get what Edmund Husserl (1970, p. 48), the father of contemporary phenomenology, called a "surreptitious substitution," a sort of weird, suppressed *inversion.* What is in reality an in-the-end delusional outcome of threat (acting and thinking as if things are inherently self-existent) gets codified as more "basic" (see Jardine, Clifford and Friesen 2008a) and more "real" than that convivial, dependently co-arising life left in peace *from which* threat induced a retraction. Opening free spaces, experiencing the conviviality of the world, and creating new solidarities with the young in the face of the mortality of the world—all this becomes understood, under this inversion, as secondary, post hoc, optional, a "frill," something we might get to once and if the hardened realities are dealt with. Convivial life (the "life world," to use the phenomenological term) becomes understood and treated as epiphenomenal. It and our experience in and of it become subjectivized (see Chapters 2 and 5), and most assuredly *post hoc* to the separate and hardened "realities" of "the real world."
- This secured reality of separate selves and separate things, borne of this ontological delusion precipitated by threat, becomes linguistically, culturally, and institutionally encoded into the very structure of schooling itself and into the fragmentation of the living disciplines of the world's knowledge. Once thus codified, of course, Gadamer's images of entering into the convivial life of knowledge and exploring its possibilities with the young seem to be pointing to something that no longer exists, perhaps never existed, some old Romantic, subjective, liberal, unaccountable dream. As is not unexpected, given how it dominates the scene, out of this ontological delusion is borne the belief that those who don't accept these "facts" are, well, *deluded.*

- In one final inversion, suggestions pointing to the exploration of free spaces with the young, intergenerationality, risk and venture, and creating solidarities aimed at "setting right anew," become experienced as not only based on a misunderstanding of the "basic" and secured reality of things . The proposal of a pedagogy left in peace becomes understandable as precisely *the key source of threat to that security*. Peace becomes a threat.

So powerful and hidden is this ontological delusion that it ends up feeding its own hiddenness under the guise of something like a conspiracy theory: anyone questioning it is clearly deluded. This, of course, is a sign of its dominance, that it is in a position to negatively characterize, name, and marginalize any questioning of that dominance. In this way, many good hearted, well meaning, and thoughtful attempts to ameliorate the difficult circumstances that surround teachers and students in school, or to "reform" education or to instigate more inquiry-based learning in the classroom (or whatever the new catch-phrase will be once these have worn out), get unwittingly enacted from a hidden-but-dominant site (a site that need not, because of its dominance, given an account of itself [see Chapter 10]) that *has already been deeply encoded with the ontological seeds of their own inevitable failure*.

Differently put, until these hidden seeds of affliction are unearthed, attempts at imagining a pedagogy left in peace are often deployed from a site already constructed and construed under threat.

Hermeneutics, Buddhism, and ecology, each in their own ways, can be brought to bear on this threat–retract–project mechanism and all the three approach it at its ontological root: hermeneutics in its critique of substance (see Chapter 5) and its avowal of a hermeneutic experience in which the convivial, interdependent "worlding" of things beyond the feigns of self-enclosed self-identity can be cultivated and studied (see Chapter 5 and *en passim*; this is the root of the "critique of Cartesianism" that defines interpretive work in education); Buddhism in its understanding of how things are empty (Sanskrit: *shunya*) of self-existence (Sanskrit: *svabhava*) and are, instead, in their deepest reality, dependently co-arising (Sanskrit: *pratitya-samutpada*; see Chapters 4, 6, and 11); and ecology's insistence that we are part of the Earth's fabric, its weaves, its texts, and textures and that this can be experienced, understood, and we can learn to live with this reality out from under the delusions of unearthly independence and autonomy (see Chapters 6 and 7).

This, then, points to the second way in which these three inheritances have provided a refuge for my own work in education. All the three also proffer an image of abundance and a certain vivid mindfulness and steadying peace that comes from experiencing the dependent co-arising of things and the dependent co-arising and shaping of our selves in light of this insight. All three give ways to articulate these truths, to study them, to become experienced in their ways, and to invite others into these insights. These three inheritances provide ways not only to name and decode our ontological delusions but also to release our attention and devotion from this exhausting cycle and release us into ways of experiencing our lives, our world, and the task of teaching differently. They offer images of and insistences about the need for practice, cultivation, patience, and perseverance, as well as rich descriptions of the joyousness to be had in such courageous pursuits right in the midst of the very same causes and conditions that afflict.

These three inheritances can therefore give heart and wisdom and encouragement to those who feel that vertigo rush of the opening of free spaces that define a pedagogy left in peace. These three inheritances can give refuge and reassurance to our struggles to cultivate free spaces in teaching and learning.

"Everything around us teaches impermanence"

Hermeneutics, Buddhism, and ecology, however, don't offer an easy path. All the three also and unavoidably let us begin to feel the chill that describes our real ontological circumstance, the real circumstance of being left in peace. All the three point in different ways to the root affliction that sets off this threat–retract–project mechanism, a root affliction that harkens back to Arendt's invocation of the mortality of the world and the fact of natality:

> "Everything around us teaches impermanence." (Tsong-kha-pa 2000, p. 151).

> Insight is more than the knowledge of this or that situation. It always involves an escape from something that had deceived us and held us captive. What [we] learn through suffering is not this or that particular thing [but] insight into . . . the experience of human finitude. The truly experienced person is one who has taken this to heart. (Gadamer 1989, p. 357)

Or, as Gary Snyder (2003, p. 29) elegantly put it, in deeply Earthly, ecological terms:

> I have a friend who feels sometimes that the world is hostile to human life—he says it chills us and kills us. But how could we *be* were it not for this planet that provided our very shape? Two conditions—gravity and a livable temperature range—have given us fluids and flesh. The trees we climb and the ground we walk on have given us five fingers and toes. The "place" (from the root *plat*, broad, spreading, flat) gave us far-seeing eyes, the streams and breezes gave us versatile tongues and whorly ears. The land gave us a stride, and the lake a dive. The amazement gave us our kind of mind. We should be thankful for that, and take nature's stricter lessons with some grace.

With some grace. A pedagogy left in peace surely requires something like this. The deepest and most heartbreakingly beautiful lesson learned in shaping my life is that none of us is in full or final command of this living, convivial world. Truly understanding the world is truly letting go of this grip and letting ourselves experience our deeply human, convivial, worldly make up. This shaping, which has long since gone on "beyond our wanting and doing" (Gadamer 1989, p. xxviii), is not a threat to who we are. It is who we are (see Chapters 5–9 and 11), the broad place of becoming human, this human, and becoming aware, in the process, of the radiant and translucent emptiness-interpretablility of this world and our lives in it.

And, of course, we should have no illusion. This is not how much of our world understands itself. Much of our world is frightened and full of afflictions that obscure itself to itself. This, for me, makes all the more miraculous, that a pedagogy left in peace can be found in this world, in classrooms bearing multiple afflictions, deep troubles, and woes.

There is, I believe, no real refuge, no real solidarity to be made or had, no free space to be cultivated, inside of the whirl of or in devil's bargains with these perennial afflictions and delusions. And yet *there they are*, these free spaces blossoming again this year, right in the midst of all the very same causes and conditions that are our shared grief; near-miraculous, imaginative, innovative, funny, challenging, enlivening, sometimes even enraging: places, broad, spreading, populated with myriad voices, and multiple, sometimes contradictory, witnesses; topics in that old, archaic sense that is at the heart of hermeneutics (see Chapters 5 and 8).

Those three legacies of Buddhism, hermeneutics, and ecology point to a pedagogy left in peace that just doesn't simply happen. Our concerted efforts at cultivating such free spaces are necessary conditions for their emergence, even though they are not by themselves sufficient. It takes work and it takes practice to become practiced in such practices. It involves, inevitably, the task of *cultivation*. A pedagogy left in peace takes a thoughtful, careful, convivial, difficult work. Free spaces need to be freed up in concert with our attention and devotion to them. The Buddhist tradition links the stillness, wisdom, and openness to the need for deliberate, difficult practice in concert with others who are devoted to this pursuit (*Sangha*). Hermeneutics speaks of the old humanist idea of *Bildung*, which hinges on the insight that, in coming to know about the world, opening free spaces, and shaping our lives accordingly, one's identity, one's "character" is shaped and cultivated in the very act of shaping and cultivating an understanding of the world(s) we inhabit: you *become someone* in the difficult cultivation of free spaces in teaching and learning. And, of course, cultivation is an old ecological image of our conviviality with the Earth, how that might be sustained and nurtured, and how it requires "continuity of attention and devotion" (Berry 1986, p 32), a "pedagogy," one might say, that links my well-being to the well-being of the fields I inhabit, explore, and transform by my living. As goes the old Buddhist adage, in aspiring to look after the welfare of all beings out from under the delusions of inherent self-existence and permanence, my own life—the life that itself dependently co-arises with those very beings—is cared for.

Finally, as readers will see in the pages that follow, the task of the cultivation of free spaces also requires unearthing and facing some of the histories, ideas, and ancestries that have distracted our attention and devotion to a pedagogy left in peace. A pedagogy left in peace entails cultivating a detailed understanding of the circumstances, ideas, images, assumptions, and desires we have often unwittingly inherited, so that when these ghosts rear up, we don't arrive at them unprepared. Those pursuing a pedagogy left in peace need to take seriously and seriously practice the cultivation of their own understanding of this living, difficult world and the work needed to keep it open for the arrival of the young. Unprepared, unlearned, we will simply retract all over again, and set the cycle of delusion off into another round. This is the deep and difficult message hidden behind the sometimes-too-happy message of "life-long learning." Differently put, a pedagogy left in peace and the cultivation of free spaces in teaching and learning can help ameliorate our susceptibility to getting caught up in the vagaries of threat and the ways that distraction and delusion are manipulated to ends that are themselves full of delusion.

All praise, then, to those who have stepped aside from this delusion and felt what Patricia Clifford and Sharon Friesen always called the lift and buoyancy of the world that comes when things are treated well, and peace is sought and won. It is to them—all those myriad teachers and students and colleagues and co-writers whose perseverance is a great perfection—that I dedicate whatever meager merit might accrue around or arise from these words.

Acknowledgments

The author would like to thank those publishers who have granted permission to reproduce the following previously published work:

Jardine, D. (2006). "Youth need images for their imaginations and for the formation of their memories." *Journal of Curriculum Theorizing, 22*(3), 3–12 (Chapter 8).

— (2008). "'I Am' has sent me": Arguments with myself and others on the subject of certain suspected allegories regarding democracy and education. In J. Wallin, ed., *Democratizing educational experience: Envisioning, embodying, enacting*. Troy, NY: Educator's International Press, pp. 110–29 (Chapter 2).

— (2008). On the while of things. *Journal of the American Association for the Advancement of Curriculum Studies*. February 2008. Accessed at: http://www.uwstout.edu/soe/jaaacs/vol4/Jardine.htm (Chapter 9).

— (2011). "A hitherto concealed experience that transcends thinking from the position of subjectivity." In S. Steinberg and G. Cannella, (eds) *Critical Qualitative Research Reader*. New York: Peter Lang Publishers (Chapter 5).

Jardine, D. and Batycky, J. (2004). Filling this empty chair: On genius and repose. *Educational Insights*, 9(1). Accessed July 21, 2009 at: http://www.ccfi.educ.ubc.ca/publication/insights/v09n01/articles/jardine.html (Chapter 7).

Jardine, D. and Naqvi, R. (2008). Learning not to speak in tongues: Thoughts on the librarian of Basra. *Canadian Journal of Education*, *31*(3), 639–66. (Chapter 10).

Jardine, D., Naqvi, R., Jardine, E., and Zaidi, A. (2010). "A zone of deep shadow": Pedagogical and familial reflections on "The clash of civilizations." *Interchange: A Quarterly Review of Education*, *41*(3), 209–32 (Chapter 1).

CHAPTER ONE

"A zone of deep shadow"

DAVID W. JARDINE, RAHAT NAQVI,
ERIC JARDINE, & AHMAD ZAIDI

. . . men are all neighbors and brothers.

*— al-Zubaidi (accessed 2007), tutor of al-Hakam II,
Tenth century CE*

I

In December 2007, Aqsa Parvez, 16, was strangled by her father Muhammad in the family home in Mississauga, Ontario, Canada:

> Police were called to the Parvez's home around 8 a.m. Monday morning by a man who told 911 operators he had killed his daughter. Paramedics found the girl motionless on her bedroom floor. Paramedics detected a faint pulse and rushed her to hospital where she died several hours later. Friends have said Aqsa left her home about a week before the attack because she had been fighting with her father and brothers about her refusal

> to wear the *hijab* and other traditional clothing. The teenager often would change into Western clothes when she got to her high school, then put the *hijab* back on before she went home, friends said. Investigators later charged her father, a taxicab driver from Pakistan, with murder. (Offman 2007)

The range of responses to these heartbreaking events was, for the most part, unexceptional. Items ranged from Muslim clerics' denunciation of the death along with reiterations of the hijab's importance (Offman 2007) to suggestions that this was just like any other abusive family dispute but for its tragic outcome (Henry and Mitchell 2007), to scattered portraits of Aqsa as "just like any other girl," to claims of this being nothing more or less than another example of female oppression (White and Mick 2007).

The court in Brampton, Ontario, on June 16, 2010, found her brother and father guilty of second-degree murder. In his decision, Judge Bruce Durno found it "profoundly disturbing that a 16-year-old could be murdered by a father and brother for the purpose of saving family pride, for saving them from what they perceived as family embarrassment." He deemed this a "twisted and a repugnant mindset" (Aqsa Parvez. 2010).

Amidst this heated array of voices back in late 2007 and early 2008, there was another, noticeably frequent thread. El Akkad and Bascaramurty's (2007) article was entitled "The Religion-Culture Clash." Eltahawy (2008) spoke about being "Caught in the Clash of Civilizations." Although other reports took on this language of "clashes," they, too, served to spread this way of speaking:

> Media reports in the *Star* and other newspapers and broadcasts, were quick to focus on Aqsa's friends' comments, which immediately framed the story as a cultural clash, in line with the "clash of civilizations" thesis – the idea that there is inherent conflict between Western values and Islamic faith. Seeing this as a clash of cultures provides an easy way to attempt to come to terms with the tragedy of a father accused of murdering his adolescent daughter. (English 2007)
>
> A spokesman for the Canadian Council on American-Islamic Relations (CAIR-CAN) said he is dubious of opinions that the girl's death resulted from a "clash of cultures" and "a relative" said "it's not about culture." (Robert 2007)

Some conversations that one of the authors participated in and overheard in local Toronto Mosques right after these events focused simply on this family, this man, this girl, and how things can get out of hand and how, in the ensuing media blitzes, one could feel even more "visible" a minority, as if one's very complexion bore the reason or excuse or culpability for the ever-exaggerated claims and real or perceived dangers that some felt to be in the air around this event.

One television commentator interviewed a Muslim woman who called this family's troubles, not a "clash of civilizations" but a "clash of ignorance." Suddenly, out of the midst of these (in retrospect, rather mildly) threatening and disturbing events in a suburb of Toronto, Canada, the language and imaginations of those thus caught up, spurred on by media-driven incitement, have moved into the realm of Samuel Huntington's *The Clash of Civilizations and the Remaking of World Order* (2003, originally published in 1996 as a follow-up to a 1993(a) article in *Foreign Affairs* with the same title). We mention these bibliographic details because Edward Said's article, "The Clash of Ignorance" was posted online, tellingly, on October 4, 2001, in response to events that had occurred about three weeks earlier and that had, at that troubling and threatened time for America, taken up, in media-frenzies, Huntington's images of civilizational clashes as a way of thinking through the events of 9/11 (see also Ferrero-Waldner 2006; Huntington 1996; Muller 2008 [whose article is called, on the cover of *Foreign Affairs*, "The Clash of Peoples" and, on the inside, "Us and Them"], for just a few more of a vast number of ongoing conversations in this conceptual orbit).

It would be foolish to ignore the fact that these events and their consequences happened post-9/11. We, in Canada, are living through a weird admixture of thoughtfulness and fear these days regarding Islam and its current self- and other-exaggerations (see, notably, Steinberg, Kincheloe and Stonebanks 2010). In the midst of all this, and as a response to Aqsa's murder, Jonathan Kay (2007), in his article "The true enemy: Human tribalism," provided an articulation of our current lot in language that is as full of clarity and confidence as it is full of unarticulated and presumptive images that are laden with interpretive opportunity:

> The clash of civilizations we're living through is widely seen as a battle between Islam and Christendom. I'm convinced it's more basic than that. The reason Iraq and Afghanistan remain

unsettled battlefields isn't that our two civilizations can't agree on the nature of God. It's because we can't agree on the nature of man. In the West, we take it for granted that human beings are autonomous individuals. We decide for ourselves how we dress, where we work, whom we marry. Our political system is an atomized democracy, in which everyone is expected to vote according to their own idiosyncratic values and interests. Our pop music and moves are about misunderstood loners. The ethos of individual empowerment fuels daytime talk shows. Individualism has become so fundamental to the Western world view that most of us cannot imagine any other way of conceiving human existence. But in fact, there are billions of people on Earth—including most of the world's Muslims—that view our obsession with individualism as positively bizarre. In most of South Asia and the Middle East, humans are viewed not primarily as individuals, but as agents of family, tribe, clan, or sect.

II

Once started, [wars between civilizations] . . . tend to take on a life of their own. Identities which had previously been multiple and casual become focused and hardened [and ensuing conflicts] are appropriately termed "identity wars." As violence increases, the initial issues at stake tend to get redefined more exclusively as "us" against "them" and group cohesion and commitment are enhanced. Civilization consciousness strengthens in relations to other identities. A "hate dynamic" emerges in which mutual fears, distrust, and hatred feed on each other. Each side dramatizes and magnifies the distinction between the forces of virtue and the forces of evil and eventually attempts to transform this distinction into the ultimate distinction between the quick and the dead. (Huntington 2003, p. 266).

There can be no true friends without true enemies. Unless we hate what we are not, we cannot love what we are. These are the old truths we are painfully rediscovering after a century and more of sentimental cant. Those who deny them deny their family, their heritage, their culture, their birthright, their very selves! They will not lightly be forgiven. (Dibdin 1996)

> Either you are with us, or you are with the terrorists.
> George Bush (2001) on September 20, 2001, in his *Address to a Joint Session of Congress and the American People*

The authors variously found themselves caught up in these matters after December 2007, both in the realm of graduate work in international relations in political science and in the day-to-day, face-to-face matters of working in schools in the Calgary, Alberta area, where "multiculturalism" and "diversity" are the official order of the day and part of the lived-nature of schooling. Conversations had been had, a year earlier, in a Northeast Calgary High School with groups of Muslim young women regarding British Minister Jack Straw's insistence, on October 5, 2006 (see news.bbc.co.uk) that Muslim women "unveil" in his office (see Chapter 9).

It is very difficult to understand this shadowy spot that is occluded by Samuel Huntington's offhand phrase cited above: "once started." The work of articulating and unraveling these "multiple and casual identities" (Huntington 2003, p. 266)—those identities that antedate the hardening, dramatizing and magnification that occurs in times of threat—is not of concern to Huntington himself.

We begin in this locale of Huntington's "once started," but we are not interested in what then follows, but in something more ephemeral: *what has been left behind*. We are also interested in how what *follows upon threat* (Huntington's "hardened identities") is "read back" into the casual and multiple lives that antedate such threat.

We posit, along with David G. Smith (2006d, p. 75) that, under threat, the resultant "self-enclosure . . . deprives the self of the benefit of an encounter with what lies beyond the contours of its own imagination." All that can be encountered under threat is an equally exaggerated, equally deprived, inevitably capitalized "Other"—a "Them" for our "Us" on both sides.

What is this movement from a terrible local event in Mississauga to the dramatic and exaggerated reaches of apparent civilizational discord? What is it that is left behind once this movement is started? This movement is *away from* Huntington's "multiple and casual" sense(s) of local, contingent, interdependent, and codetermining identities, and *toward* what Edward Said calls the "vocabulary of giantism and apocalypse, each use of which is plainly designed not to edify but to inflame" (Said 2001, p. 4). Ivan Illich (with Cayley

1992, p. 127) almost playfully names the inflaming and exaggerating urge in these matters a sort of "apocalyptic randiness"—basically framed, "I have an even more horrible example to tell you! Let's imagine an even worse situation . . . !" (p. 127), spoken or written with a sort of energizing, arousing, inciting, conspiratorial glee coupled with a strange tinge of superiority, distain, and moral indignation. This, of course, is reminiscent of school staffroom conversations: "You think *that* kid is trouble? A couple of years ago, I had a kid in my class who . . . ." (Interestingly enough, speaking of apocalyptic randiness and threat, the "real world" of schools [especially high schools] is occasionally off handedly portrayed as "the trenches"—a lingering war metaphor captures a sense of the lived-experience of threat and embattlement in some schools and with some teachers and students [see Smith 1999b].)

Identity wars need identities to be of a certain character. They need to be purged, purified, and clarified (see Chapter 2). All the long entanglements that have defined our living with and alongside each other, all the, shall we say, soft vulnerability and susceptibility of mutual, admixed, and casually drawn and borne identity formation that goes on day to day in everyday life—all this, under threat, is put aside. Under threat (even under the effects of comparatively minor events like in Mississauga in December 2007) identity "contracts," reverts to the "tried and true," and cuts its tenuous and contingent tethers to anything remotely "other." This is an often mutual condensation "inwards" to a self-identity (where "we" become "us" and "them," so to speak) that has been purged of all that is "revocable and provisional" (Gray 2001, p. 36), all that is multiple and casual, all that is interdependent and mutually articulating, all that is perceived to be accidental and not essential:

> Huntington . . . wants to make "civilizations" and "identities" into what they are not: shut-down, sealed-off entities that have been purged of the myriad currents and countercurrents that animate human history, and that over centuries have made it possible for that history not only to contain wars of religion and imperial conquest, but also to be one of exchange, cross-fertilization and sharing. This far less visible history is ignored in the rush to highlight the ludicrously compressed and constructed warfare that "the clash of civilizations" argues is the reality. (Said 2001, p. 3)

This is an important passage from Edward Said, but we would read Huntington a little more delicately. Huntington *does* ignore this "far less visible history." He *does* focus on "compressed and constructed" identities whose exaggerated incommensurateness invokes "clashes." However, it is not clear that he is suggesting that these exaggerations are "the reality" and that the mutual and casual identities of everyday life, which Huntington himself mentions (with, we agree, terrible brevity), are *not real*. He is simply not interested in such matters. He is interested (2003, p. 266–98) in where the "fault lines" will emerge in times of threat—again, an interestingly cataclysmic term. As is the wont of political theorizing, Huntington's work wants to be usefully predictive regarding what could happen "once started," and there is a long tradition of scholarship since that has critiqued, clarified, or replaced this line of thought (see, e.g. Sen 2007).

However, as the daily media coverage of Aqsa's murder demonstrated, the language and images of civilizational clashes has had a sort of backwash effect. It has insinuated itself into everyday discourse, perhaps, in part, because of its imaginal clarity and incendiary potentiality. The issue of concern, in this chapter, is a more dangerous sort of backwash into everyday life. We are interested in whether this charged language of civilizational clashes actually has the effect of shaping how we are able to imagine, think about, and articulate "the myriad currents and countercurrents that animate human history." This exaggerated political theory language of clashes has a disturbing affinity to the "apocalyptic randiness" of everyday life, as noted by Ivan Illich. The language and images of civilizational clashes becomes like an invasive species, which takes up filial refuge with the worst of our everyday proclivities. However thoughtful may be Huntington's "clash of civilizations," its very exaggeratedness can give credence to the everyday paranoias of "you know what *those* people are like!" And this, in turn, can give rise to all-too-familiar instances of those in power taking advantage of precisely this proclivity. More on this below.

We agree, therefore, with Edward Said's underlying concern. Long and tangled threads of a living history become forgotten or occluded by the drama of a Clash of Civilizations. Echoing Edward Said's language, David Levering Lewis (2008, p. xxiv) calls this all-too-perennial phenomenon "the rise . . . of a reciprocally reassuring ignorance and of an addiction to war as the substitute for the complexities of co-existence."

Tellingly, Lewis' book is entitled *God's Crucible: Islam and the Making of Europe, 570–1215*. This retracting movement is ancient and familiar, linked to issues of survival and self- and familial-preservation. Under threat, anything that is casually presumed or contingently worked out, anything where the conditions of interaction are not fully secured in advance—all such casual and convivial matters are, under threat, foregone. Even those modest ways in which we might work out conflictual matters and come to an understanding with each other, or those ways that matters of dominance and power, minority and majority, ignoring, avoiding or just "getting by," have been suffered and worked through without precipitating identity wars—all this is forgotten.

Such a retracting movement is quite understandable and often fully warrantable. What is dangerous, however, is the false consciousness that can come with it. Once condensed—"once started"—our movement of exaggerated self-enclosure and what induced it is forgotten as are the multiple and casual interdependencies that are left behind. We pay "scant attention to complex histories that defy such reductiveness and have seeped from one territory into another, in the process overriding the boundaries that are supposed to separate us all into divided camps" (Said 2001, p. 4). In addition (and here again we echo Said's concern with Huntington), once these fault-lines appear between ever-exaggerating identities ("each side has incentives not only to emphasize its own civilizational identity but also that of the other side" [Huntington 2003, p. 270]) these identities are then projected as the hidden reality that has been there all along, hiding underneath the now-shown-to-be-false convivialities. Ironically, then, ordinary practices of everyday life, such as wearing the *hijab*, become understood as a way of hiding or veiling threatening, suspected, suspect, realities. "What have they got to hide?" has become a common plaint, not only about "them" and their veilings, but also about anyone who argues against increasing surveillance.

In light of the seemingly secured enclosures of threat-induced identities, any suggestion of boundaries being in any way overridden or "permeable" (Smith 2006d, p. 77) becomes understandable only as *a security threat*. Surveillance, paranoia, border patrols, increased accountability, and monitoring become the order of the day as by-products of the now-purified "identity" of "us" being increasingly susceptible to "contamination" by "them." Threat produces a situation where the very casualness and multiplicity of day-to-day situations of everyday life becomes identifiable as the *cause* of threat. The very brownness or whiteness of a face I pass on the street becomes excusably alarming and "racial profiling" becomes vaguely understandable. My retreat into a secured self-identity can now be blamed solely on this very Other whose exaggeration my retreat had a hand in producing.

The conviviality of multiplicity and casualness itself becomes understood as a realm of contamination (regarding the link of this to purification rituals, see Chapter 2)—as goes Said's concern, not who we "really" are. "Here," amidst these mutually interdependent retreats into self-enclosure, "can be witnessed what Dussel (1995) called the 'gigantic *inversion*' [where] 'the innocent victim becomes culpable and the culpable victimizer becomes innocent'" (Smith 2006d, p. 76). The one threatened is the one causing the threat. It is notable that, "once started," it is always *them* who started it and always *us* who are the victim.

As has happened post-9/11 in some quarters in North America, what follows is an educational nightmare: paying even scant attention to these complex histories of coexistence itself becomes vaguely suspect. Trying to act on the belief (inside or outside of schools) that the matters at hand need more intellectual subtlety than purged and clarified exaggerations-under-threat allow, starts to appear as an act of betrayal or sedition. Believing that there is more complexity to the story than the abstractions and idealizations allow is to be branded a conspiracy theorist. Thus, paranoia is projected on to those for whom simplified platitudes are not enough. Those wanting to know more, to explore and carefully think through these matters are experienced as threatening to security as a means of subjectivizing, pathologizing, and thus depotentiating, their concerns. Their concerns are "in reality" *about them*, not about something afoot in the world.

Thus couple the sometimes-overwhelming anti-intellectualism that is an occasioned proclivity in the public sphere (and in many schools the authors have individually and collectively experienced [see Callahan 1964, p. 8; see Chapter 4]) with issues of loyalty and patriotism. Wanting to know something more than the simplistic, threat-induced clarities about this "us" and "them" becomes egregious. *Knowledge and its pursuit become experienced as a threat to security* (see David G. Smith's [2006a] brilliant "Enfraudening in the Public Sphere" for more on this point and its telling consequences for pedagogy). And, speaking of enfraudening in the public sphere, suggesting becoming educated in such matters, suggesting that the simplified surface story is not adequate, becomes vaguely equated with a sort of liberal elitism that wants to coddle (capital "T") Terrorism by *thinking about things and how they have become thus* and *then* make now-informed decisions about what needs to be done, instead of simply exaggeratedly and simplistically reacting under threat.

One of the recent reasons for the emergence of these matters is that, of course, making people feel threatened can be manipulated and utilized politically as a form of social control—an old thread of Straussian thinking (along with another current Straussian favorite, Plato's "noble lie" [see Postel and Drury 2003]): Post-9/11, there seems to be a weirdly paranoid celebration of not-needing-to-know (Kincheloe 2006), because needing to know something more or different entails making permeable and vulnerable to breach the "borders" of my already self-enclosed understanding and self-understanding. Under threat, thinking becomes *unthinkable*.

This is where the nub lies of Huntington's presumptions and Said's response. As Huntington (1993, emphases added) replied to the critics of his Clash-hypothesis, *exaggeration is in the very nature of serious thinking itself*:

> When people think *seriously*, they think *abstractly*; they conjure up *simplified* pictures of reality called concepts, theories, models, paradigms. Without such intellectual constructs, there is, William James said, only "a bloomin' buzzin' confusion."

We suggest that serious thinking that wishes to pursue *unsimplified*, rich, multivocal, ambiguous, and complex details about casual and multiple lived-realities—an adequate description of interpretive work (see Chapters 5, 8, and 9)—might make us *less* susceptible to the dramatizations and exaggerations caused by threat and its simplified abstractions.

Here is the great irony: Complex thinking bent on pursuing the rich worldly complexities of "the unsimplified" is considered threatening because it wants to pursue a knowledge of the unthreatened nature of our casual, multiple, and convivial identities.

Thus results another gigantic inversion of sorts wherein, in schools, attempts to ameliorate public worries over "diversity" can sometimes simply play out simplistically "positive" exaggerations, and the complexities of our casual and multiple lives become reduced to multicultural celebrations involving "interesting" and "different" foods, costumes, dances, and customs. The complexities seem too difficult, too threateningly complex to raise, full of volatility, mutuality, difference, locatedness, perspective, mixed memories, and ancestries and heat. It is not that these "celebratory" practices are pursued disingenuously in schools. It is just that the ways in which "multiculturalism" and "diversity" are treated can all too easily *leave in place* an image of "different cultures" as constituted by the very sort of dumbed down, simplified "self-enclosure" that is in fact produced of and producing of threat. This then becomes ameliorated by relentless (but well-intended) positiveness about diversity and talk of honoring difference and tolerance, and the like. Consider:

> In every lexicon, tolerance signifies the limits on what foreign, erroneous, objectionable or dangerous element can be allowed to cohabit with the host without destroying the host—whether the entity at issue is truth, structural soundness, health, community, or an organism. The very invocation of tolerance . . . indicates that something contaminating or dangerous is at hand. Tolerance appears, then, as a mode of incorporating and regulating the presence of the threatening Other within. (Brown 2006, p. 27)

This sort of dumbing down of knowledge (a dumbing down which, in some ways, seems to pass, for Huntington, for "seriousness") is not restricted to such cultural matters, nor is it restricted to what goes on in Social Studies classes in schools. The vibrant and difficult conversations that constitute all of the living disciplines entrusted to teachers and students in schools have undergone such "reductiveness" (Said 2001, p. 4; see also Jardine, Clifford and Friesen 2008a). The clarities and platitudes that are left behind are a version of knowledge that is easier to manage, put under surveillance, and test (see Chapter 4). Remnant difficult and intellectually challenging conversations about the knowledge requisite of living disciplines are thus rendered through processes of "privatizing and individualizing" (Brown 2006, p. 21) into "frills." The complex, convivial, multivocal, lives lived outside of threat, lives "left in peace" (Illich [with Cayley] 1992 p. 16), are evacuated from the public sphere, and any articulation of these lives is subjectivized into opinions neutered of any public weight.

On speculation, Samuel Huntington's understanding of serious thinking, being bent on finding simplified order in what he cites from William James as a "bloomin' and buzzin' confusion," operates with an idea of knowledge that is itself threat-based, threat-reactive, and threatening by its very nature (as is the wont of its Cartesian origins [see Chapters 2 and 8]; see Chapter 4 for a hermeneutic alternative to these images of knowledge). Serious thinking *demands* simplification of its object (see Chapters 2–4), the shedding of all that seems "revocable and provisional" (Gray 2001, p. 36).

Perhaps Said was right, then. Perhaps Huntington *is* suggesting that hardened, abstract, simplified identities are more "real" than those of casual multiplicity, because only as such can identities become the (necessarily abstract and simplified) objects of serious thinking. Perhaps "once started" denotes both the threats leading to civilizational clashes and the parallel threat that serious thinking brings to and demands of such matters. Once started, serious thinking threateningly demands abstract identities and erases from seriousness any consideration of that which antedates such threats.

Incidentally, the exact phrase in William James' (1890/1981, p. 462) *Principles of Psychology* is "one great blooming, buzzing confusion," so even Huntington's making-casual, however-much-unintended, dropping of letters and adding of two apostrophes in their stead betrays something interesting: "bloomin' and buzzin'" become akin to a slangly uneducated casualness that the simplified abstractions of serious thinking might find uncivilized (see Chapter 3), wild (see Chapter 6 and 7), or contaminated (see Chapter 2).

III

> War, which makes cultures alike, is all too often used by historians as the framework or skeleton of their narratives. The peaceful enjoyment of [that which is not under threat, embattled] . . . is left in a zone of deep shadow. (Illich 1992, p. 19).

> The [Mississauga] tragedy comes at what is usually a joyous time for the Muslim community: A week from today marks the beginning of Eid al-Adha, a religious festival marking Ibrahim's willingness to sacrifice his son Ismael to God. (El Akkad and Bascaramurty 2007)

This passage regarding the beginning of Eid al-Adha reminds us of what Edward Said (2001, p. 6), three weeks post-9/11, called "the bewildering interdependence of our time." There is, surrounding Aqsa's murder, a living world of interdependencies and mixed lives and blood, admixed stories, names, faces, images, and agonies, all of which continues despite the gigantism and simplifications that threat induces. There is a familiar, convivial heartache in this Biblical tale of Ibrahim and Ismael" regarding God and his people, parents and their children, and what sacrifices are too much to ask. There is even some vague lesson, here, about teachers and students, and what we need to know and what we might have to sacrifice to become knowledgeable in the face of the world. These threat-induced identity-purgings of that which is revocable and provisional are, in effect, akin to a sacrificial *purification ritual* (see Chapters 2), an expelling of multiplicity, an expulsion of the "many" in favor of the One ("A = A" at the heart of Cartesianism [see Chapters 2, 4, and 5], "one best way" at the heart of both developmentalism [see Chapter 3] and the affinity between industrial assembly and contemporary schooling [see Chapter 4]). And this movement of purification (ironic, given that Aqsa Parvez's murder can be thought of as a purification of the shame of her family) and the fears that arose out of it regarding "Islam" and "the West," bears a great resemblance to the purifying and clarifying expulsion, beginning in earnest in 1491, of the Jews and Moors from the south of the Iberian peninsula as Spain condensed and purified its own identity (and its language [see Illich 1980]) into "the first modern nation state" (Reston 2005, p. xix) and then, from this clarified and exaggerated and purified self-identity, proceeded Westward.

IV

When speaking of apocalyptic randiness, Ivan Illich (with Cayley 1992, p. 127) also warns of falling prey to its opposite,

Romanticism, where, with equal exaggeration, simplification, and thoughtlessness, one sees good news everywhere. This is why we hesitatingly bring up an idea that comes from Southern Spain prior to the expulsions. Over the course of about 700 years, what held sway was something called, at the time and since (see, e.g. Lowney 2006; Mann, Glick and Dodds, eds. 2007), *convivencia*. From approximately 711 CE to 1492 CE, an admittedly sometimes exaggerated state of relatively peaceful coexistence or conviviality—great intellectual, cultural, and artistic flourishing—held tenuous sway (see Chapter 10).

Conviviencia, which translates simply as "conviviality" or "coexistence," has two meanings. The first has to do with living "left in peace" (Illich [with Cayley] 1992, p. 16)—"peace is that condition under which each culture flourishes in its own incomparable way" (p. 17). There is a second meaning of *conviviencia* that indicates something more than each culture or person incomparably flourishing. These flourishings are not simply self-enclosedly coexisting alongside one another. They are shaping, forming, and multiply determining, each other:

> Our specific human identities constructed through tribe, race or religion can never be ultimately secured, not only because they are always open onto the horizons of others but also, more important, because they are *always already everywhere inhabited* by the Other in the context of the fully real. (Smith 2006c, p. xxiv)

As Ludwig Wittgenstein (1968, p. 33) so deftly said, we can *draw* boundaries around such matters, but we can't *give* such matters a boundary. We *can* "simplify," or "abstract," but we cannot thereby *make* these matters thus. Even under threat, conviviality persists in shadow and silence. Even believing that we are completely other to them is an old, relived, multifarious tale, full of *versions*. Coming to understanding this "always already everywhere" requires "ignor[ing] the orthodox who labor so patiently trying to eliminate the apocryphal variants from the one true text. There is no one true version of which all the others are but copies or distortions. Every version belongs" (Thompson 1981, p. 11–12).

Threat produces a *false* (albeit occasionally expedient and circumstantially warranted) experience of uninhabited, singular, sealed-off identity, an experience which is an ecological and pedagogical disaster:

> One of the great and necessary intellectual challenges is to recover the 'lost' dependencies of so much of our coveted traditions, because without such work we become forgetful . . . and end up behaving in ways that assume that Others don't matter to who we think we are. That kind of assumption involves a hubris hiding from its nemesis, as 9/11 serves in reminder. (Smith 2006b, p. 40)

Paradoxically, *even under threat*, these lost dependencies persist, and exploring them can provide resistance to the lures of exaggeration and hardening. The knee-jerk response to threat that Huntington identifies occludes the difficult work that is needed: "to reflect, examine, and sort out what it is we are dealing with in reality, the interconnectedness of innumerable lives, 'ours' as well as 'theirs'" (Said 2001, p. 4).

V

> Here it is difficult as it were to keep our heads up and to see that we must stick to the subjects of our every-day thinking, and not go astray. We feel as if we had to repair a torn spider's web with our fingers. (Wittgenstein 1968, p. 46)

> A boundary is, in itself, profoundly disruptive. Its first disruption is in his mind, for having enclosed the possibility of control that is within his competency to imagine and desire, he has become the enemy of all other possibilities. And second, having chosen the possibility of total control within a small and highly simplified enclosure, he simply abandons the rest, leaves it totally out of control; that is, he forsakes or even repudiates the complex, partly mysterious patterns of interdependence and cooperation, controllable only within limits, by which human culture joins itself to its sources in the natural world. This attempt at total control is an invitation to disorder. And the rule seems to be that the more rigid and exclusive the specialist's boundary, and the stricter the control within it, the more disorder rages around it. (Berry 1986, p. 71)

We speculate that the richer and more unexaggeratedly detailed is one's understanding of these convivial and casual identities and their bonds to the sources of the natural world (and the bonds to each of our lives, our familial life and, for teachers, the lives of our students), the more likely it is that one will not easily fall prey to the temptations of exaggerated self-enclosures and the manipulative use of arousing but unenlightening simplifications. Otherwise, in school classrooms, teachers and students find themselves in a sort of "intellectual limbo" (Gray 1995, p. 25) and easily fall into a situation where, say, the wearing of the hijab is "discussed nervously in a strangulated Newspeak [from George Orwell's *1984*] of difference and otherness" (p. 25):

> In Orwell's [Newspeak] dystopia, emphasis was placed upon short, clipped words "which could be uttered rapidly and which roused the minimum of echoes in the speaker's mind." In other words, "ultimately, it was hoped to make articulate speech issue from the larynx, without involving the higher brain cells at all." This aim was frankly admitted in the Newspeak word *duckspeak*, meaning "to quack like a duck." (Daly 1978, p. 331)

This is not only an issue of "terrorism's affinity for abstractions" (Said 2001, p. 5—Said hints here at an affinity between terrorism and Huntington's "serious thinking"), but also of contemporary liberal democracy's kindred affinity for abstractions such as "Mission Accomplished" and Canada's "Highway of Heroes."

VI

As a beginning step out of this weird intellectual limbo, David G. Smith (2006b, p. 55) proposes that

> The real challenge is to face the truth that no one tradition can say everything that needs to be said about the full expression of human experience in the world and that what the global community requires more than anything else is mutual recognition of the various poverties of *every* tradition. The search to cure the poverty of one's own tradition works in all directions at once.

This brings us to a vital juncture regarding the complexities of conviviality. In a self-declared "multicultural" country like Canada, issues of dominance, power, and positioning still prevail in (mostly comparatively) modest ways. In fact (and this is an important point for educators to consider), Canada's dominant, White (capitalized so we can remember that this term is itself a site of exaggeration and simplification) culture has the luxury of not feeling at all compelled to understand or articulate *its own* traditions. This is precisely a *sign* of dominance, that an articulate self-knowledge (let alone an articulate knowledge of others) is not especially necessary to pursue and cultivate for "the winners of the world" (Nandy 1983, p. 47). In fact, even when *not* in times of explicit threat, it is always the minority who are asked to face the poverty of *their* traditions (see Naqvi and Jardine 2008; see also Chapter 10).

As a sign of dominance, then, one has trouble experiencing the poverty—one might say, the thinkability/interpretability/permeability—that shadows that dominance. For example, in the media coverage following Aqsa Parvez's murder, there was a marked *inability* to speak of the issue of modest that comes with the Muslim tradition of the hijab, and a fetish-like interest in and loud defense of the issue of choice itself. Aqsa's murder becomes experienceable only as another case of the "hijab [as] a symbol of oppression" ("Tarek Fatah, the outspoken founder of the Muslim Canadian Congress," cited in White and Mick 2007) coupled with talk of how, "in the so-called 'clash of civilizations,' Muslim girls and women are the biggest losers" (Eltahawy 2008):

> Aqsa Parvez . . . wanted to hang out with friends instead of obeying her 5 p.m. curfew. She wanted to listen to rap, hip hop and R and B, which her parents didn't permit. She wanted to be "free" and independent of her family's devout Muslim beliefs. Vivacious and outgoing, Parvez wanted to dress like a Western woman in tight-fitting clothes and show off her long, dark hair by removing her hijab. (Henry and Mitchell 2007)

Wendy Brown contends that the West's touting of "choice," like Aqsa reportedly desired for herself, itself hides a poverty. To the extent this touted freedom is not thought through carefully, to the extent that its insinuation in regimes of power, marketing, and political suasion are not unthreaded and questioned, "choice can become a critical instrument of domination in liberal capitalist societies" (2005, p. 197), a sort of marketing gimmick, such that we can easily mistake "elective surgery for freedom from coercive power" (p. 196). It becomes easy to equate not feeling compelled to think about what we choose, and why, and what forces are at work, with freedom of choice. After all, being compelled to think is too often experienced as an impingement on freedom itself.

This issue of who "really" chooses "freely" and what this means for school topics like "media literacy," is a complex and variegated one. One of the Muslim girls in that Grade Ten Social Studies class mentioned above (wherein Minister Jack Straw's actions were considered):

> Talked . . . about how she understands that her *hijab* is seen by many as a form of oppression. She explained how, in her tradition, if you wear a *hijab* simply because someone tells you to, you might as well not wear it at all, but she understood how some Canadians, some of her classmates, have trouble understanding how anyone would *chose* such a thing. She admitted, as well, and without hesitation, that, of course, some in her tradition simply do what they are told. We commiserated a bit over how this is a deep kinship that many traditions share, that we, here, share face-to-face, of mindlessly simply doing what you are told and remaining silent and silenced. (Jardine 2008d, p. 230–1; see Chapter 9)

Imagining that this girl's decision (or the decisions some of her High School friends make to dress immodestly, or Aqsa's decisions, or those of her brother and father, in fact) was done by an a-cultural "individual" for whom this "choice" bears no sense of belonging or obligation in and to the world (to imagine, then, that one's place in the world is "optional" [Brown 2006, p. 152]), is, of course, a remnant of the culture of liberal democracies:

> [The] conceit in play that the individual *chooses* what he or she thinks. This same choosing articulates the possibility of an optional relationship with culture, religion, and even ethnic belonging; it sustains as well the conceit that the rationality of the subject is independent of these things, which are named as contextual rather than constitutive elements. (p. 152)

In such school discussions, and throughout the media converge of Aqsa's murder, *choosing* remains insistently the topic. *That* something is freely chosen is what is deemed relevant. *What* is chosen, whether you have carefully considered this choice or considered it at all, whether it is peer-pressure related, or family related, or "just what people do,"—all this is "up to you." That is, *what is chosen* and *how it is chosen* are rendered into a personal and private matter. We are thus each "left to our own devices" (Arendt 1969, p. 196) to swap opinions that only have "personal" weight and no worldly recourse in the substantive, convivial, always-already-everywhere complex work of carefully considering *what* is chosen.

Therefore, conversations regarding the potential poverty of the presumably freely chosen *immodesty* of "the West" and its consequences rarely arose in light of Aqsa's murder. The poverty of choosing immodesty is trumped by something simpler and more abstract: "choice" and its consort, an image of "myself" as an individual untethered to the world. Choice in this abstract and simplified sense requires a sense of my own identity that is already on a war footing with the world.

Conclusion

> A principle of cultural complementarity points to the multiple ways that cultures turn to each other to heal themselves of their exaggerations (Smith 2006a, p. 12–13).
>
> [The] received logics [of exaggerated identities] prevent this perception, so the pedagogical and curricular tasks must involve a critique of those same logics, with the very means for such a critique available precisely through what until now has been so aggressively silenced and repressed. (Smith 2006b, p. 36)

What has been "aggressively silenced and repressed" is not, on the one hand, the Voice of Islam proclaiming "tribalism" and, on the Other, the Voice of the West asserted "individualism" and "choice." We've heard plenty of this Newspeak. What has been aggressively silence and repressed are the more modest voices that speak out of a difficult, tenuous, delicate, ongoingly negotiated, familial, potentially generous and convivial, place. Our pedagogical and familial concern is on behalf of cultivating this richer and more detailed, slower, more scholarly and intellectually rich understanding. It is on behalf of reflection, historical knowledge, thoughtfulness, and the seeking out of the sorts of encounters that Smith suggests as moments where unexaggerated, difficult, embodied knowledge may be had and in which our mutual and individual tethers to such matters can be thought through and worked out in concert and solidarity with others.

The modest freedom that such cultivation requires, as with the freedom that comes from such cultivation, is not abstract or inalienable, and it must be won, again and again, it must be cared for and nurtured, and it must be treasured as a rare gift when it comes. As authors, we admit wholeheartedly that our reflections, here, are borne of not ourselves feeling especially under threat. Compared to so much of the world, we have been, to varying degrees, left in peace. We admit, too, that we each are located—by gender, by age, by first language, by cultural background, by political leanings and interests, by experience and knowledge, by our surroundings, and so on—in different ways in this difficult work. We are not simply different, each flourishing separately. But neither are we somehow abstractly identical. Neither of these over-simplifications is what conviviality means. The logic of identity and difference (perhaps the core axis of simplification and abstraction) is not adequate to the matters at hand.

This "healing of exaggeration," is a site of opportunity and terribly difficult challenge for schools, and not just in the areas of cultural understanding, but also in the ways we take care of all of the living, convivial, disciplines entrusted to teachers and students in schools. The "desire to be healed" (Smith 2006b, p. 40)—to be made hale, whole, livable, convivial, once again—"recovering one's 'lost' dependencies" (p. 40)—can be a locale of great pedagogical, familial, and ecological flourishing that can, however fragilely and contingently and temporarily, lift some of the deep shadow we are under.

CHAPTER TWO

"I AM hath sent me unto you"

DAVID W. JARDINE

Abandon the fear that arises from the thought "I am."
from The Peacock's Neutralizing of Poison,
attributed to Dharmaraksita (tenth century).

— (Gyalchok & Gyaltsen 2006, p. 159)

I

3:13 And Moses said unto God, Behold, [when] I come unto the children of Israel, and shall say unto them, The God of your fathers hath sent me unto you; and they shall say to me, What [is] his name? What shall I say unto them?

3:14 And God said unto Moses, I AM THAT I AM: and he said, Thus shalt thou say unto the children of Israel, I AM hath sent me unto you. (*Exodus* 3:13–3:14)

3. Let him deceive me as he may, he can never bring it about that I am nothing, so long as I shall be conscious that I am something.

> 4. But I do not yet know with sufficient clearness *what I am*, though assured *that I am*; and hence, in the next place, I must take care, lest perchance I inconsiderately substitute some other object in room of what is properly myself. (Descartes circa 1640/1901, emphasis added)

II

> The thinkers of the Enlightenment . . . never doubted that the future for every nation in the world was to accept some version of Western institutions and values. A diversity of cultures was not a permanent condition of human life. It was a stage on the way to a universal civilization. (Gray 2001, p. 2)

Educational Conjecture: the more intensely we envisage students as autonomous, unique, and free individuals, at the same time a correlative movement occurs.

As we become autonomous, worldless, "individuals," the world becomes populated with autonomous, worldless objects. Objectivism and subjectivism are cousins, married to the same ideals that interpretive work (see Chapters 5, 8, and 9) is wont to critique.

As Enlightenment-origin democratic ideals of autonomous individuality become increasingly abstract, educational standards (like state- or provincial-examinations) themselves become increasingly abstract. As a correlate to the abstraction of "autonomous individuality," *that which standardized examinations examine* is objective knowledge and, therefore, *those whom standardized examinations examine* are only those who can live under such standards: standardized subjects ("a diversity of cultures [i]s not a permanent condition"). Any legitimate "differences" between these thus-examined student-subjects is only *vis-à-vis* their proximity or distance from the standard, and the measures of examination themselves are wrought as "one best way" (see Chapter 4).

The individuality of students is not only abstract but paradoxically universal. Each student becomes an indistinguishable instance of a universal "everyone is an individual." *That* each student is unique is more fundamentally pronounceable than *what it is* that makes any particular student is unique—"what it is" is secondary to "that it is." Who or what I am is secondary and accidental to the universal and necessary (Kant's terms for the *a priori*; see especially Chapter 3) *that I am*. All matters of gender, language, family, bloodlines, and vernacularity are thus rendered "revocable and provisional" (Gray 2001, p. 36), secondary, not primary, accidental, not essential.

Correlatively, then, standardized school examinations become populated with the knowledge that anyone must have. To pass such examinations is to gather the knowledge proper to "anyoneness" and to learn how to articulate such knowledge in ways that anyone would (i.e. ways fitted to the standardized examination). Any vernacular or convivial spin on such matters is a matter of *contamination* (a common enemy in objective research). Standardized examinations are thus allegorically related to objective experimentation. Students are "[put] under the question" (Reston 2005, p. 11) and such questions invoke from students what they know stripped of all provisionalness. All that is left of who an individual student is his or her proximity or distance from the measure, and they bear this as their "mark."

III

> Both a standardized mother tongue to be taught in the schools and the nation state were born in the same moment. (Spanish 2008)

The condensation "inwards" to a self-identical nation state (a nation as "I am" affirmed with pure self-sameliness [A = A, the root objectification-logic of modern science], purged of all that is revocable and provisional—anything "other" than the "I am") and standardization are twins. The condensation of the autonomous self out of its worldly, local attachments (the "accidental") and into an autonomous individuality (the "essential," the "not dividable" [L. *individuus*]—the "accidental" can be divided from the essential and is not required by that being [L. *esse*] to be what it is) proffers and presumes the same movement.

In a beautiful essay entitled "Vernacular Values," Ivan Illich (1980) speaks about a moment when this force of inward and upward (the essential is always metaphorically imagined as "rising above" the happenstance and accidents of everyday, vernacular life) condensation and standardization took hold at the level of language itself. In discussing the flourishing differences of vernacular language—localized, intimate to a particular place, in service of the immediacies of a life lived when "left in peace" (Illich 1992, p. 16)—he notes how a peculiar effort emerged coincident with the granting of license to Christopher Columbus to sail West.

Columbus sailed on August 3, 1492 (a Friday). On August 18, 15 days later, Elio Antonio de Nebrija petitioned Isabella. "Nebrija advocates the reduction of the Queen's subjects to an entirely new type of dependence. He presents her with a new weapon, grammar" (Illich 1980, p. 17). Nebrija convinced Isabella that, in order to take firm control of her own domain and to provide a solid foundation for its subsequent colonial ventures, a Universal, standardized language was required under the Crown (under, one might say, the "I am"). "[Nebrija] offers Isabella a tool to colonize the language spoken by her own subjects; he wants her to replace the people's speech by the imposition of the queen's *lengua* – her language, her tongue" (Illich 1980). The standardization of Spanish into a single tongue acted correlatively with the first steps of Spanish colonization in the New World.

> My Illustrious Queen. Whenever I ponder over the tokens of the past that have been preserved in writing, I am forced to the very same conclusion. Language has always been the consort of empire, and forever shall remain its mate. Together they come into being, together they grow and flower, and together they decline. (Nebrija, cited in Illich 1980)

Prior to Isabella's and Nebrija's efforts taking hold in the standardization of Spanish, Cristobal Colon ("meaning 'bearer of the Christ" and 'repopulator'" [Fischlin and Nandorfy 2002, p. 39]) latinized his own name to Christopher Columbus in order to move from being seen as a mere citizen of Portugal or Italy to being thought of as a "a citizen of the world" (Reston 2005, p. 127; see Smith 2006f, p. 7). Even though Latin bespoke such worldliness, the newly emerging nation of Spain required its own single tongue, its own "univocity" (see Jardine 1998a).

Bearer of Christ: "There is neither Jew nor Greek, there is neither slave nor free, there is neither male nor female: for ye are all one in Christ Jesus" (Galatians 3:28).

IV

> I resolved to assume that everything that ever entered my mind was no more true than the illusions of my dreams. But immediately afterwards I noticed that whilst I thus wished to think all things false, it was absolutely essential that the "I" who thought this should *be* somewhat. And then, examining attentively that which I was, I saw that I could conceive that I had no body, and that there was no world nor place where I might be; but yet that I could not for all that conceive that I was not. (Descartes 1640/1955, p. 29)
>
> A new age of centralized authority was beginning. (Reston 2005, p. 54)
>
> The point of departure in this process is the European ego, which is a constituent element of the historical event: "I discover," "I conquer," "I evangelise" (in the missionary sense) and "I think" (in the ontological sense). (Dussel 1988, p. 128)
>
> What [Descartes] left undetermined when he began in this 'radical' way was . . . the *meaning of the Being of the "sum"* [L., "I am"]. (Heidegger 1962, p. 46)

The *sum* of Rene Descartes' *cogito ergo sum* echoed that old Exodus issuance of the "I AM has sent me," wherein the great affirmation of the Creator is replaced by a whole new experience of an emergent European-Democracy-Individual-Science-Ego as the issuing center of all things. Right at the founding of modern science in Cartesianism (and right at that junction where the Democratic "I am" starts to become conceptually radicalized into a self-determining, autonomous individuality), we find a Mosaic Allegory.

Here is the logic. Through a process of methodical doubt, Descartes purged from himself every revocable and provisional attachment, every other "object in the room" that could possibly be doubted. This resulted in an affirmation of a worldless ("there is neither Jew nor Greek"), bodiless ("there is neither male nor female"), equally in sway beyond power and earthly circumstance ("there is neither slave nor free"), "I am" that is beyond doubt. It is this "I" than then chooses that to which it might have an affiliation (see Chapter 1).

But in Cartesianism (as in Christianity's urge to proselytize, as in colonialism urge to civilize), this choice is issued as a *demand* for only a certain type of affiliation (regarding this demand, see Chapter 3). The "I am" demands that the world live up to the clarity and distinctness that it has won for itself. The truth of the "I am" becomes the standard for the truth of the world.

The ontological logic here is simple, and it is an iteration of vernacular common sense: whatever an object is, it is what it is. *That it is* what it is (A=A, the principle of identity in Aristotelian logic) is beyond doubt; however, much doubt may be cast on our knowledge of this "what":

> An adequate knowledge is thoroughly clear knowledge, where confusion is no longer possible, where the reduction to marks and moments of marks (*requisita*) can be managed to the end. (Heidegger 1978, p. 62)

"The essence of truth," so this old story goes, "is identity" (Heidegger 1978, p. 39).

To be in truth therefore is *to be* independent of anything else. All connections and relations are thus revocable and provisional and *post facto* to the reality of autonomy and separateness. To be in truth is thus to be a *substance*: "A substance is that which requires nothing except itself in order to exist" (Descartes 1640/1955, p. 255).

Thus meet the purified, worldless subject and the purified, subjectless world, which is itself full of separate, worldless "objects" each one of which, according to the doctrine of substance, is "nothing but itself."

Descartes' meditations are thus a sort of *purification ritual* whose means is doubt and whose goal is clarity and distinctness, both of the self and of the world. These meditations do not leave things in peace, but threaten them with doubt, demanding clarity. Left in peace, things are presumed to be *contaminated*. Under threat, things render into their uncontaminated truth, their substance.

V

> Dr. Mary Douglas has recently advanced the very interesting and illuminating view that the concept of "pollution" "is a reaction to protect cherished principles and categories from contradiction."

> She holds that, in effect, what is unclear and contradictory tends to be regarded as unclean. The unclear is the unclean. (Turner 1987, p. 7).
>
> The 150 years that followed Nebrija's work was the so-called Golden Age of Spanish arts and literature. It wasn't until 1713 that Juan Manuel Fernandez Pacheco, Marquis of Villena, founded the *Real Academia Espanola de la Lengua Castellana*. Their motto, much ridiculed in modern days, was established as *Limpia, fija y da esplendor* – "clean, standardize, and grant splendor." The word *limpia* cannot but invoke the concept of *limpieza de sangre*, purity of blood, [used in] the Spanish Inquisition. The animosity against Jews, Muslims, and women, was represented in the dictionary's pages. (Spanish 2008)

In 1491, the expulsion of the Jews and the Moors from the south of the Iberian Peninsula began, and the great and sometimes difficult coexistence that had flourished in many shapes for centuries and that had helped end the so-called Dark Age of Europe was undone (see Chapter 10). "It is no accident that the expulsion of the Jews from Spain in 1492 in the name of Christian reterritorialization coincides with Columbus's fantasies" (Fischlin and Nandorfy 2002, p. 89). The outward expulsion of any revocable "other" (Jews and Moors) is the correlative movement to the inward condensation of the self-identical (Spanish) nation which then becomes a "foundation" for the propulsion Westward:

> The modern *ego cogito* was anticipated by more than a century by the practical, Spanish-Portuguese *ego conquiro* (I conquer) that imposed its will (the first modern "will-to-power") on the indigenous populations of the Americas. (Dussel 2000, p. 471)

From Friedrich Nietzsche's *Will to Power* (1975, p. 346):

> The will to power can manifest itself only against resistances; therefore it seeks that which resists it. Appropriation and assimilation are above all a desire to overwhelm, a forming, shaping and reshaping, until at length that which has been overwhelmed has entirely gone over into the power domain of the aggressor and has increased the same.

Ego conquiro requires the "I am" to, shall we say, conquer its own doubt and conquer its own vernacular dispersions and contaminations, and through such conquerings, come to experience itself as destined to master all things (the fulfillment of God's designating Adam's dominion; in Jean Piaget's work [1952, p. 372], such dominion over all things is had through mastering the methodologies in terms of which things are epistemologically constructed: children are "destined to master science" is itself an *ego conquiro* by being a maker of worlds). The "great work of purification," as Pope Sixtus IV called "the Inquisition" (Reston 2005, p. 103), required exactly the same correlative movement: *self-purification* (of the Vernacular Iberian lands to the modern Spanish State, from the vernacularities of speech to a codified Universal grammar, from the comingling of cultures to the expulsion of the Moors and Jews) and Ferdinand's self- and Church-appointed mission of the *purification of the world* (Reston 2005, p. 143). (Strange, then, that Reston [p. xix] finds the link between Spain's founding of the modern nation state and the Inquisition of all things "ironic.")

Tomas de Torquemada, the Grand Inquisitor, was thus the great clarifier, the great purifier. Just like Descartes, two centuries later, threatening the world with doubt until it objects into logico-mathematical self-identicalness (A=A), Inquisitional "torture was called putting the suspect 'under the question'" (Reston 2005, p. 11) until that subject, in an act of salvational or sacrificial self-purification, lets go of its ambiguous convivialities had when left in peace, and "objects" (see Smith's [2006f, p. 7] explication of the workings of Enrique Dussel's "myth of sacrifice" and "myth of salvation").

VI

> Modernity is a single condition, everywhere the same and always benign. As societies become more modern, so they become more alike. At the same time, they become better. (Gray 2003, p. 1)

"The multifariousness of . . . voices" (Gadamer 1989, p. 284) is "not a permanent condition of human life" (Gray 2001, p. 2). Thus, too, "difference" (multifariousness) becomes "a problem to be solved under a condition of mastery and explanation" (Smith 1999d,

p. 139), a condition whose initiating gesture, so this story goes, is self-mastery and self-affirmation. The key to such self-mastery is "the individual":

> For [Michael] Ignatieff [incidentally, a recent leader of the Liberal Party of Canada], racism and ethnically based nationalism are the effects of being "trapped in collective identities," the cure for which is "the means to pursue individual lives." Thus ... Ignatieff argues that "the culture of individualism is the only reliable solvent of the hold of group identities and the racisms that go with them." [He] also understands this way of seeing as . . . closer to the truth of what human beings really are. The more developed and rewarded this individual is *as* individual, the more that collective identity is eroded or undercut . . . and the greater the prospects for a tolerant world. (Brown 2006, p. 185)

So, if a diversity of cultures is not a permanent condition and we are becoming more and more alike as time passes (so goes the Enlightenment logic that underwrites the democratic "I am," and goes the logic of developmentalism itself [see Chapter 3]), it becomes not quite so strange when Francis Fukuyama (2006) proclaims that liberal democracy and the Market Economy (both of which are squared upon "the individual") can be considered the long-in-coming developmental *end* of a process of gradually alikening Universalization. "This makes the individual a distinctly Hegelian *a priori* in Ignatieff's analysis—ontologically true yet historically achieved" (Brown 2006, p. 185)—*there is* an individual self, but it must struggle through time and through the world. It must "achieve" itself over time, but its *truth* already *is*.

In a most brilliant inversion, this also makes our embodied, vernacular, cultural, and religious belonging in the world—the ways we are when not under threat, when "left in peace" (Illich 1992, p. 16; see Chapter 1)—the *outcome* of "procedures of abstraction" (Brown 2006, p. 185) and makes the purified "I am" the only concrete reality. Thus, culture becomes simply "a source of comfort or pleasure for the individual" and religion becomes, under the individual's "reign," "a choice and . . . a source of nourishment, moral guidance, and moral credibility" (Brown 2006, p. 153).

Coupling Fukuyama's *The End of History and the Last Man* (2006) with the Bush administration's apocalyptic, end-of-time Biblical fantasies regarding the Middle East, we find a (re)declaration of what every empire has declared of itself: we have a new and better means of expulsion, or, to use Ignatieff's term, we have the last and perfect "solvent" to difference, the final solution.

VII

> Lioniz[ing] individualism reproduce[s] . . . the "greatly truncated" postmodern community of the shopping mall, a community devoid of communality, where people come together to mind their own business. The progress of the group is linked to the progressive individuation of its members. (Dressman 1993, p. 259)
>
> They are the ideal consumers. By inducing in them little panics of boredom, powerlessness, sexual failure, mortality, paranoia, they can be made to buy virtually anything that is "attractively packaged". (Berry 1986, 24)
>
> The mere existence of an alternative mode of being, the presence of which exemplifies that different identities are possible and thus denaturalizes the claim of a particular identity to be *the* true identity, is sometimes enough to produce the understanding of a threat. [President Bush has] manifestly linked American identity to danger. (Campbell 1998, p. 3)

The most attractive package to sell to individuals that are thus untethered from the world is precisely *the idea of threat itself*. An untethered "I am" will quite literally "buy into" the idea of "being threatened" since this is precisely the hidden origin of the self-assertive, self-confident "I am" in the first place. The abstract "I am" thus produces an equally abstract, threatening enemy: *threat*.

Allegorical speculation: that the recent War on Terror is a war against threat itself. To play on Ignatieff's Hegelianism mentioned above, the fact that this War is currently linked to Islam and the Middle East is just one more revocable and provisional, historical achievement of a deeper ontological truth both required and produced by individualism itself. As such, the War on Terror combines the perpetuity of threat (which is ontologically linked to the idea of solvent individuality) with the need for "a state of permanent war" (Wood 2006, p. 16).

Postscript

There is a moment in Jane Yolen's *Encounter* (1992) where a young Native boy, having had lucid dreams of "great winged birds and voices of thunder" (p. 1), realizes that Columbus and his crew "touched our golden nose rings and our golden armbands, but not the flesh of our faces or arms" (p. 15). The new arrivals were not interested in dreams or flesh or faces or arms. They wanted The Standard: Gold.

I jumped up, crying, 'Do not welcome them'. But the welcome had already been given. (p. 15)

CHAPTER THREE

"The savage childhood of the human race"

DAVID W. JARDINE

We are an empire now, and when we act, we create our own reality. And while you're studying that reality–judiciously as you will–we'll act again, creating other new realities, which you can study, too, and that's how things will sort out.

— An unnamed White House advisor to George W. Bush (cited in MacMillan 2006, A19).

Accordingly, the spontaneity of understanding becomes the formative principle of receptive matter, and in one stroke we have the old mythology of an intellect which glues and rigs together the world's matter with its own forms.

— (Heidegger 1985, p. 70)

Introduction

The work of Immanuel Kant in his *Critique of Pure Reason* (1964, originally published in 1787) can be thought of as a filling out of the categories or *a priori* forms that shape *how* "I think." Descartes' contracted and self-contained "I am" thus proliferates, and each form of formal logic participates in and thus preserves the clarity and distinctness he had won. Thus, to the extent that these forms are used to think *about things in the world* (i.e. to the extent that they are understood as a transcendental logic—a logic whereby the subject understands that which transcends the subject, things in the world), those forms form *how* we demand of things in the world that they be rendered into their truth (i.e. into their separate, clear and distinct, "objective" character, purged of anything contaminating, accidental). The knowable world thus becomes a reflection of the universality and necessity that I presume myself to already embody, and the mission of knowledge becomes one of rendering that world into this universality and necessity.

As I've suggested in Chapters 1 and 2, this is the logic of colonialism and it hides in unintended ways in education's contemporary love affair with "constructivism" and its educational consort, "development." This thread comes down to us through Jean Piaget's characterizing of his own work (1965, p. 57) as "very close to the spirit of Kantianism."

In this and what follows, the pedagogical consequences begin more directly to unfold. Keep in mind what was just about to be visited on that young boy in Jane Yolen's *Encounter* (1992) alluded to at the end of Chapter 2.

"A light broke upon the students of nature"

The brighter the light, the darker the shadow. (Bly 1988, p. 1)

A light broke upon the students of nature. They learned that reason has insight only into that which it produces after a plan of its own, and that it must not allow itself to be kept, as it were, in nature's leading-strings, but must itself show the way with principles of judgment based on fixed laws, constraining

> nature to give answer to questions of reason's own determining. Reason . . . must approach nature in order to be taught by it. It must not, however, do so in the character of a pupil who listens to everything the teacher chooses to say, but of an appointed judge who compels the witnesses to answer questions which he had himself formulated. While reason must seek in nature, not fictitiously ascribe to it, whatever has to be learnt, if learnt at all, only from nature, it must adopt as its guide, in so seeking, that which it has itself put into nature. (Kant 1964, p. 20)

Immanuel Kant's *Critique of Pure Reason* (originally published in 1787) was, as its title suggests, intended as a *critique*, that is, as a *setting of the limits* of human reason. Kant was profoundly concerned about the potentiality for human reason to overstep its boundaries. It is precisely this potentiality for overstepping that has fallen into deep shadow in much of the contemporary love affair with constructivism.

The roots of this potentiality can be simply stated. In knowing objects, we cast them into relationship with our ways of knowing. Independently of human reason, things themselves, Kant allows (1964, p. 178), "conform to laws of their own," but human reason has *its own laws*, which, in knowing the world, it *imposes on that world*.

The above-cited passage from Kant's *Critique* gives us two clues to follow to explicate that are of especial interest to educators:

- Human understanding is a *demand* that is properly wielded free from nature's leading-strings and earthly constraints.
- The path to this freedom of human understanding is the road to *maturity*.

From these themes emerge a new figure in this cautionary tale, one much closer to the hearts and minds of educators: Jean Piaget.

Theme one: Human reason is a demand made upon things

Immanuel Kant's epoch-making *Critique of Pure Reason* conceived of knowledge as an active, orderly, and ordering *demand made upon things*. "To know," is not understood as passively receiving information from an object ("filling an empty vessel" or "writing on a blank tablet"). Rather, "to know" is to *do something*, to *act* in ways that *make* something of experience, or, in popular contemporary educational parlance, to *construct*.

Such action does not simply reveal an existing orderliness of things. It is, rather, *productive of order*:

> The order and regularity in [what] we call *nature*, we ourselves introduce. We could never find [such orderliness and regularity] . . . had not we ourselves, or the nature of our mind, originally set them there. (Kant 1964, p. 147)

This is why Kant insisted that this order and regularity in nature is not, as far as we can know, the order and regularity of things themselves as they exist independently of our attempts to know. It is rather the order and regularity of how the world *appears* when cast in relation to human reason. As conceived by and inherited from Immanuel Kant, human reason is a *synthesizing* faculty which, in the act of knowing something in the world, *actively constructs orderliness out of the chaos of experience* in accordance with human reason's own categories. Nearly two centuries later, Jean Piaget (1971a, p. xii) would call this "imposing cosmos on the chaos of experience." *To be an object in the world*, according to Kant, means *to have been constructed as an object* according to human reason's criteria of "objectivity."

The origin of this idea in Kant's work is very simple. He examined the type of knowledge found in logic, mathematics, and Euclidean geometry and determined that such knowledge cannot be *derived from empirical experience*. Any knowledge thus derived can only lead to *empirical generalizations* whose status is always only *probable*. However, Kant noted that in logic, mathematics, and Euclidean geometry, there is a type of knowledge at work that is not probable but rather universal and necessary—the grammar of logical deduction, the structures of mathematical reasoning, and the rules governing geometry. He therefore deduced that, *by its very nature*, human thinking has universal and necessary forms that are not derived from experience but rather antedate that experience. And, since thinking has such universal and necessary forms, thinking *about* something in the world necessarily becomes an act wherein the thing thought *about* must, *of necessity*, submit to the *a priori* forms of thought.

What occurs in Kant's work at this juncture is that a great divide opens up in our understanding of the nature of nature itself:

> That nature should direct itself [in] conformity to law[s imposed by human reason], sounds very strange and absurd. But consider that *this* nature is not a thing in itself but is merely an aggregate of appearances, so many representations of the mind. (Kant 1964, p. 140)

A divide opens up between nature "itself" (whatever this might now mean) and the *appearance* of nature in human experience and knowledge:

> The question arises how it can be conceivable that nature should have to proceed in accordance with [*a priori*] categories which . . . are not derived from it and do not mold themselves on its pattern? The solution of this seeming enigma is as follows. Things in themselves would necessarily, apart from any understanding that knows them, conform to laws of their own. But appearances are only representations of things that are unknown as regards what they may be in themselves. As mere representations, they are subject to no law of connection save that which the connecting faculty [of human reason] prescribes. (Kant 1964, p. 178)

Insofar as human reason sets the conditions under which anything might be experienced, it makes sense to say that "the *a priori* conditions of a possible experience in general are at the same time conditions of the possibility of objects of experience" (Kant 1964, p. 138). One of these *a priori* conditions is what was, in Aristotle's and Descartes' work, the old idea of identity as a property of objects: A=A. Another is the distinction between substance and accident. In Kant's work, these and the rest of his table of categories are no longer understood to be properties of things themselves but are properties of how human reason universally and necessarily *constructs* the *a priori* properties of objects-as-experienced.

Thus, nature-as-experienced becomes a closed system with humanity at its center. And, more troublesome, we become effectively cutoff from nature "itself," since to know it is to render it in light of our own demands—or, to use the contemporary phrase, to know is to *construct*. It was Kant's great and honorable intention to pronounce this light that had broken upon the students of nature regarding human reason as precisely a *humiliation* of its scope and power. Human reason is shown in his work to be *incapable* of thinking beyond its own constructions and therefore *incapable* of finding the measure of those things that come to meet us in our experience except through its own demands. However, this simply more deeply codifies the self-secured contraction into the "I am" and its "productions." *Within* the immanence of the "I am" there is now a constructed-as-objective world of its own making.

We can hear in this suggestion of immanence something more than mere epistemological speculation. Immanuel Kant's imagining of human reason as a self-limiting demand had a terrible consonance with the spirit of its times, right at the height of European *colonialism*. Issuing from Europe at this time was the unshakeable belief that "we" (a great and contentious identifier) have in hand the universal and necessary conditions of reasonableness, civility, culture, and morality, and it is our duty, in traversing the so-called New World, to *demand* that heretofore unreasonable, uncivilized, disorderly, primitive, savage, world be *made* to live up to its truth, the truth that we have already secured *a priori*. Part of the spirit of colonialism is thus salvational.

And so, something of the shadow cast by the bright light that broke upon the students of nature. We (who cleave to the essence of human knowledge, civility, freedom and reasonableness) embody that which is universal and necessary (*a priori*) and the world is spread out in an array of proximity to and distance from such a demanding, issuing center.

Theme two: Immaturity, maturity, and the developmental step-child of constructivism

There is another theme here that is much more immediately in the minds of educators. In the *Critique*, and also from a later essay entitled "What is Enlightenment?" (1983, originally published in 1794), Kant consistently links up the refusal to use your own Reason (and its ordering demands) with *immaturity*. Acting in accord with the *a priori* demands severing our dependence on "Nature's leading-strings" (Kant 1964, p. 20) (the "apron-strings" that tie us, if you will, to "Mother Nature"):

> *Enlightenment is man's emergence from his self-imposed immaturity. Immaturity* is the inability to use one's understanding without guidance from another. This immaturity is *self-imposed* when its cause lies not in a lack of understanding, but in a lack of resolve and courage to use it without guidance from another. *Sapere Aude!*: "Have courage to use your own understanding!"—that is the motto of the Enlightenment. (Kant 1983, p. 41)

Reason is pictured as the way in which humanity can overcome its animality ("leading-strings" names a cord used to lead and train animals) and dependencies ("leading-strings" were used to teach children to stand and walk).

On the face of it, this appears to be good news. *Sapere Aude*! Think for yourself. What happens next, however, is that thinking "without guidance from another" (if you are to cleave, i.e. to the *a priori* to that which is universal and necessary and not childishly "dependent") becomes linked to how even the youngest child, in the course of their development, is *destined to think*. More bluntly put, mature thinking, as universal and necessary, means that mature thinking is thinking where everyone thinks the same and differences become, not universal and necessary but rather "revocable and provisional" (Gray 2001, p. 35–6).

Jean Piaget, in "the spirit of Kantianism" (1965, p. 57), believes that human reason is an active, structuring *demand made upon the world*. However, the Kantian *a priori* categories, and their handmaiden disciplines, logic and mathematics, are only a late-arriving set of ordering demands in the course of both the development of the species (*phylogeny*) and the recapitulatory development of the individual (*ontogeny*). In Piaget's work (1965, p. 57), the Kantian categories are not the point *from which* knowledge emerges (*terminus ad quo*), but the *point to* which knowledge develops (*terminus ad quem*). The Kantian categories emerge as humans mature. Piaget's response to the Enlightenment call that we "grow up" is that this is not a matter of courage and resolve but a matter of *the natural course of human development*, one we are developmentally "destined" (Piaget 1952, p. 372) to achieve.

But how can the Kantian categories be a universal and necessary demand made upon things if they emerge as humans mature?

According to Piaget, *all of human life*—from the frail actions of a newborn infant to the abstract intricacies of logic and mathematics—*has the character of such a demand*:

> *Every relation* between the living being and its environment has this particular characteristic: the former, instead of submitting passively to the latter, modifies it by imposing on it a certain structure of its own. (Piaget 1952, p. 118, my emphasis)

There is, for Piaget (1952, p. 19, my emphasis) an "organizing activity *inherent in life itself*" and this inherent *activity* is "the fundamental reality about living things" (Piaget 1971b, p. 347). *This organizing activity or functioning*—not the Kantian categories or structures of reasoning—is the *a priori*, and it is how *all* relations between the living being and its environment function.

So what is it that makes the constructs or categories or forms or structures (all these terms become effectively interchangeable) of logic, mathematics, and Euclidean geometry (Kant's *a priori* in his *Critique of Pure Reason*) *seem* universal and necessary? Cashing out this semblance takes a few steps.

In Jean Piaget's work, what is *a priori* is not this or that set of constructs, but the inevitability, in all living beings, of the *functioning of constructing* (captured in Piaget's terms assimilation, accommodation, and equilibration). How construction functions is *a priori*. But more than this, this *functioning* becomes that *because of which* the maturing of reason occurs. The functioning of "life itself"

> orients the whole of the [developmentally] successive structures which the mind will then work out in contact with reality [culminating in the structures peculiar to the mature adult]. It will thus play the role that [Immanuel Kant] assigned to the *a priori*: that is to say, [this functional *a priori*] will impose on the structures [characteristics of each stage of development under consideration] a certain necessary and irreducible conditions.

> Only the mistake has sometimes been made [for example, in the work of Immanuel Kant] of regarding the *a priori* as consisting in structures existing ready-made from the beginning of development, whereas if the functional invariant of thought is at work in the most primitive stages, it is only little by little that it impresses itself on consciousness due to the elaboration of structures which are increasingly adapted to the function itself. (Piaget 1952, p. 3)

Thus, for Piaget, "the progress of reason doubtless consists in an increasingly advanced awareness of this organizing activity" (1952, p. 19). Structures, constructs, or categories must now be thought of, not as fixed and finished demands, but rather as

> particular form[s] of equilibrium, more or less stable within [their] restricted field and losing [their] stability on reaching the limits of the field. But these structures, forming different levels, are to be regarded as succeeding one another according to the law of development, such that each one brings about a more inclusive and stable equilibrium for the processes that emerge from the preceding level. (Piaget 1973, p. 7)

Development, now understood as a succession of structures oriented toward steadily increasing stability and inclusiveness, "*tends towards an all-embracing equilibrium by aiming at the assimilation of the whole of reality*" (p. 9). Life, according to Piaget, is *teleologically oriented* toward this particular end.

It will be of no surprise that it is precisely a version of the Kantian categories that constitutes this "all-embracing equilibrium." The functional *a priori* is embodied in the *functioning* of "established science" (Inhelder 1969, p. 23), its *methods*. As long as we cleave to the *methods* of objective science and the products constructed by that method ("objective knowledge"), we cleave to the inherent ordering character inherent in life itself (see Chapter 4, for sketches of what happens when this becomes codified into the "one best way" [Kanigel 2005] of industrial assembly and the adoption of this in schools). Even in the imaginative playfulness of the toddler, this functioning is *already fully there*, albeit embodied in unstable, easily disequilibrated structures. Thus, development is pictured as a progress toward a future that already exists *a priori*.

Therefore, development ("maturing," to use Kant's Enlightenment-call term) is a process of slowly adapting not to "things themselves" (Kant's work disabused us of this naivety) but to the *a priori* functioning of adaptation itself. The peculiarity of the Kantian categories is that they constitute "an extension and perfection of all adaptive processes" (Piaget 1973, p. 7) insofar as they are perfectly adapted *to this organizing activity*. The Kantian categories take on the appearance of universality and necessity (take on the appearance of being *a priori*) at the end of development because they are perfectly adapted to that which *is* universal and necessary. The developmental end of this process of adaptation—logico-mathematical knowledge—is a stage of "all-embracing assimilatory schemata [structures or categories, if you will] tending to encompassing the whole of reality" since it is an embodiment of that very organizing activity in terms of which reality itself is constructed. Logico-mathematical knowledge "proceed[s] by the application of perfectly explicit rules, these rules being, of course, the very ones that define the structure under consideration" (Piaget 1970, p. 15). The rules for *doing* the operations of logic and mathematics are precisely the rules *upon which* one operates. Logic and mathematics are thus perfectly equilibrated (i.e. perfectly adapted to the inevitable process of adaptation itself), for there is no longer any difference between

- *the operator* (the individual who *does* logic and mathematics) is not the vernacular, embodied "myself" but a purified, "epistemic subject" (Piaget 1973, p. 8) like Descartes "I think" who operates only in accord with the rules requisite of logic and mathematics, i.e. according to "processes common to all subjects" (Piaget 1965, 108),
- *the operations* that subject performs (logical and mathematical operations), and
- *that upon which we are operating* (things insofar as they have been constructed into possible objects of objective science, things, therefore, insofar as they follow the rules of logic and mathematics).

As Jean Piaget put it a century-and-a-half after Immanuel Kant, "the sciences are self-sufficient and alone guarantee their own reflection" (Piaget 1965, p. 225). They operate upon "an ideal, perhaps a hope, of intrinsic intelligibility supported by the postulate that the structures are self-sufficient and that to grasp them, we do not have to make reference to all sorts of extraneous elements" (Piaget 1970b, p. 4–5). Development thus culminates in an oddly Narcissistic self-consciousness akin to the unshakeable clarity and distinctness of Descartes' "I am," where the one reflecting and the one reflected are identical, that "one" having purged itself of difference and having come to cleave to the universal and necessary. A=A, and outside recourse is unnecessary, in fact contaminating, of this purified self-sufficiency achieved over the course of development.

We come perilously close, here, to a constructivism that has lost its Kantian hesitancy about its own limits.

"The savage childhood of the human race"

We are not dealing, here, with mere epistemological matters regarding images of knowledge and its makings. The language of "development" links with the Enlightenment image of reason needing to overcome its immaturity or primitiveness. We know that those subjected to colonial rule were systematically and deliberately characterized as "children" (see, e.g. Nandy 1983, 1987). When Piaget (1971b, p. 12–14) speculated, (following Haeckel [1900] and followed by Benjamin Spock [Spock and Parker 1957, p. 253]) that ontogeny (the stages of growth of the individual) might recapitulate phylogeny (the stages of growth of the species), it became once again feasible—now with in Jean Piaget's purportedly strictly *scientific* project of genetic epistemology—to think that our ancestors were like children, to think that those from cultures and ways other than Enlightenment Europe might be full of something like the naiveté, immaturity, and petulance of childhood, that they

> belong to a different mentality: savage, primitive, underdeveloped, backwards, alienated, composed of opinions, customs, authority, prejudice, ignorance, ideology. Narratives are fables, myths,

> legends, fit only for women and children. At best, attempts are made to throw some rays of light into this obscurantism, to civilize, educate, develop. (Usher and Edwards 1994, p. 158)

In Piaget's work, "the child is the real primitive among us, the missing link between prehistorical men and contemporary adults" (Voneche and Bovet 1982, p. 88; also see Malvern 1994; Nandy 1983; Jardine 2005) Jean Piaget's work thus emerged in the wake of ongoing colonial images of how the world works and how the peoples of the world are to be understood in light of the Crowning achievement of European Enlightenment: underdeveloped children.

Bluntly put, unfolding a developmental sequence (whether phylogenetic or ontogenetic) is only done by those who see themselves as *already developed*. You don't map out a developmental sequence in order to find that you are, say, "third" (world), but only to show what you already believe, that you are already "number one." Hints, then, of the old colonial spirit. However, developmentalism adds a profound new element to the colonialism that is part of the spirit of Kantianism. With colonialism, we were able to believe that we stood in the midst of the world as the best—the freest, the most reasonable, and the most civilized. With developmentalism, we get a new twist on the modernist spirit of universality and necessity (recall, Kant's criteria for the *a priori*): "we" (let's say, now, those who have the resolve and courage and requisite developmental ability) are not just "the best" among others in the world. "We" are that *toward which* the world is heading in its natural and inevitable progress toward maturity. "We" are not just in the world but are its natural *end* (see Fukyama 2006), and the failures of the world to continue to (naturally) develop into what we already are must be dealt with preemptively (see Chapters 2 and 3).

There is, of course, a great whiff of this in education itself, where educators are always at great pains to understand *in advance* what students' futures might be. We can think, for example, of developmentally sequenced curricula that map out in advance, always in universal terms, what language can developmentally become over the course of a child's education. We can think, too, about how deviance from the path toward this ordained future is treated in schools (see Chapter 4, for the industrial assembly-line recapitulation of this tale). It is little wonder, then, that "education seems like a preparation for something that never happens because . . . it has *already happened* [like Piaget's *a priori*, "at work in the most primitive stages" (1952, p. 3)]. There *is* no future because the future *already is*" (Smith 2006e, p. 25) (like Ignatieff's "individuality," "ontologically true yet historically achieved" [Brown 2006, p. 185]).

Just in case this seems to have gotten a bit out of hand, consider the following except from an interview with David Frum, a Canadian who was one of the authors of George Bush's "axis of evil" *State of the Union Address* on January 29, 2002. Frum was speaking with Evan Solomon, one of the hosts of the Canadian Broadcasting Company's (CBC) television program *Sunday Morning*. Frum was attempting to lay out his vision of the place of recent and future American preemptive actions in the Middle East, and images of childhood, adolescence, and adulthood—images of development—appear:

> *Evan Solomon*: It this a prescription for American imperialism? Is this the new empire? I know that you think it is a beneficent empire . . . .
>
> *David Frum*: No, no, Absolutely not. This is the adolescence of the human race. This is the moment when human beings are making the transition from a world governed by violence to a world governed by law. Just as the North Atlantic is governed by law, we hope that some day the whole world will look like that. But the instrument whereby humanity is going to make that transition from the savage childhood of the human race to law-abiding adulthood is through the instrument of American power. It is America who is going to . . . maybe someday it will be somebody else's . . . maybe someday it will be India's job, a while ago it was Britain's, but today it is America's power that is going to spread the realm of law and civilization and democracy. (Frum and Solomon 2004)

Our self-understanding is thus not simply that we are *the most developed* but that we (and, again, I leave this contentious signifier undefined) are *the destiny of the world*. Our interventions in the world are thus aimed at bringing out in others what we already know their inevitable destiny to be. And even if others usurp us—"maybe someday it will be India's job"—we already know what they must become in order to be properly allowed to do so. They must, of necessity and universally, become what we already are.

Conclusion: Developmentalism's repudiating embrace of childhood

> We are all familiar with the dominant Cartesian themes of starting anew, alone, without influence from the past or other people, with the guidance of reason alone. The specific origins of obscurity in our thinking are the appetites, the influence of our teachers, and the "prejudices" of childhood. The purification of the relation between knower and known requires the repudiation of childhood, a theme which was not uncommon at the time. For Descartes', happily, the state of childhood *can* be revoked, thorough a deliberate and methodical reversal of all the prejudices acquired within it, and a beginning anew with reason as one's only parent. (Bordo 1987, p. 97–8)

Images of "savage childhood" and its repudiation are nothing new and are, as Susan Bordo notes, at the core of Cartesianism itself. Much has been made, for example by Alice Miller (1989), of the late-nineteenth-century idea of children as wild and willful and in need of having their wills broken "for their own good." Her citations from mid- to late nineteenth-century pedagogy manuals are enough to send a chill. Here, for one small example, she cites (p. 42) an ominous passage from *The Encyclopedia of Pedagogy* from 1851: "pedagogy correctly points out that even a baby in diapers has a will of his own and is to be treated accordingly."

Jean Piaget's developmentalism, of course, was central in shaping our understanding of childhood away from these images of the child as simply a savage to be repudiated and broken. But this shaping has its own hidden shapes and shadows.

In 1915, Piaget wrote a peculiar piece entitled "The Mission of the Idea" (1977). Written in the midst of the ravages of World War I, he speculatively linked up what later became formulated as his interest in the *a priori* functioning of "life itself" (1952, p. 19) with

Christ and Christ with salvation. A few brief passages from this old text will help fill out these links:

> "In the beginning was the Idea," say the mysterious words of the Christian cosmogeny. (Piaget 1977, p. 27)
>
> The individual can only attain true life . . . by sacrifice, by force of the Idea, harmony with life (Piaget 1977, p. 30).
>
> It is the Idea, which is the engine of life, it is the Idea which will animate our corpse. Let us restore the Idea! (Piaget 1977, p. 32–3)
>
> The good is life. Life is a force which penetrates matter, organizes it, introduces harmony, love. Everywhere life brings harmony, solidarity in the new and vaster units that it creates. (Piaget 1977, p. 31).
>
> Life is good, but the individual pursuing his self-interest renders it bad. One day intelligence appeared, illuminated life, opened new domains to mankind, and through him God thought to attain his ends. But here again self-interest appeared, now armed with reason. Life is threatened, instinct evolves and is transformed into a sacred feeling which sets man on the right path again, and brings him back to God. But man, having tasted of the fruits of the tree of life, remains caught in this conflict between self-interest and renunciation (Piaget 1977, p. 29–30).

Piaget's life work thus originated in a mystical, near-ecstatic image of life as "the good" and an identification of "life" with Christ as the *eidos* of the Cosmos, there, abiding in and from the beginning. In his later claims regarding the "self-organizing principle inherent in life itself" (Piaget 1952, p. 19) are hidden evocations of a sort of biogenetic vision of the Living Word and a vision of humanity and human development as a progressive, developmentally sequenced shedding, or renouncing of one's selfishness and the progressive participation in the pure, *a priori* functioning of life itself which, again, is there in and from the beginning. The functioning of "life itself" is *fully present* in all stages of development, encumbered, perhaps, but not stained by the body, by the flesh, by the corpse it animates, and the progress of development is a sequential "renunciation" of such encumbrances. Maturing thus has vaguely salvational overtones and, as such, it taints our understanding of that *from which* we are being saved: the unstable, easily disequilibrated, animal body of the child in which the *a priori* is present but immaturely housed.

Hidden within Jean Piaget's idea that each child, in each interaction with the world, has within them the universal and necessary functional *a priori* which must, over the course of maturing, lead to the development of structures which are proper and fitting to this *a priori*, is a shadow image of a Universal, caught in the ways of the flesh and struggling to free itself from such encumbrances and become what it essentially is (akin to a believer becoming who they essentially are only "in Christ").

Underwriting development and all the multifarious changes one undergoes in becoming an adult, is thus the "absolute continuity" (Piaget 1971b, p. 140) of the functioning of "life itself," the "One." The pristine principle of identity in mathematics (A=A), which is a perfect (Piaget 1973, p. 7) adaptation to this functioning of life itself, becomes entwined with God's self-affirmation of the "I AM" (see Chapter 2), and this through the same Cartesian affirmation regarding the core indubitable verity of our human "I am." It is not just that the functional *a priori* "saves" at each stage by being present in and from the beginning of development, however much encumbered by the flesh. The functional *a priori* serves a *missionary function*. It directs and orients development itself (Piaget 1952, p. 3), drawing the savage embodiment of life itself up into its pure, salvational self-sufficiency.

The willfulness of the infant in diapers, therefore, is not to be eradicated or broken but simply encouraged to develop an increasingly purified understanding of what it *is* and in fact has been from the beginning. Salvation and the shedding of the encumbrances of the flesh take time (even though "the good" is present in and from the beginning). How humans function in the world (providing that functioning cleaves to it's *a priori* necessity and universality) is thus how we are imaginable as being made in God's image. We are constructors of a world rendered universal and necessary by our cleaving to the *a priori* even though we, ourselves, are created beings. Piaget's work thus contains hints of the deeply held hopes of the late nineteenth and early twentieth century regarding science and progress. Thus, too, all of the pedagogies emerging from Piagetian developmentalism are premised, in small or large part, on salvational impulses.

This doesn't exactly directly repudiate childhood, but it does make childhood of interest only as, so to speak, the developmental *means* to human salvation:

> *Evans*: You stated that you were most fundamentally interested in the matter of how primitive man began to think, how knowledge evolves and that you became interested in cognitive development in children because this was the only way available of looking at the whole historical development of cognitive processes in man in general. Is this still your fundamental interest?
>
> *Piaget:* Yes. Of course that is quite right. My problem is the development of knowledge in general. Unfortunately, this history is very incomplete--especially at its primitive beginnings. So I am doing what biologists do when they cannot constitute a phylogenetic series, they study ontogenesis. (Piaget and Evans 1973, 48).
>
> The most fruitful, most obvious field of study would be reconstituting human history—the history of human thinking since prehistoric man. Unfortunately, we are not very well informed about the psychology of Neanderthal man. Since this field is not available to us, we shall do as biologists do [and such as Ernest Haeckel suggested] and turn to ontogenesis. Nothing could be more accessible to study than the ontogenesis of these notions. There are children all around us. (Piaget 1971a, p. 13)

Given the monotheistic core of Piaget's work—given this universal, necessary, and singular *a priori* functioning of life itself that is albeit variously housed in the sequential encumbrances of the flesh—it is little wonder that, in the end, Piaget declares that "a single truth alone is acceptable when we are dealing with knowledge in the strictest sense" (Piaget 1965, p. 216–17). Despite his often lovely and sensitive descriptions of children and their ways, the multifarious structural housings of the *a priori* throughout development are only egocentric encumbrances up until they are perfected in logico-mathematical knowledge. Thus, he is only interested in how those multifarious structural housings form stages on the path to their being developmentally overcome. Multifariousness is overcome as humanity matures and cleaves more and more to the Idea: to "processes common to all subjects" (Piaget 1965, p. 108). Thus, again, the retroactive taint: children's understandings of the world become visible as (albeit developmentally necessary) "deformations" of the truth (Piaget 1974, p. 50), that children often become "duped" (Piaget 1972, p. 141) by their ways of constructing the world, "victims of illusion" (p. 141), where the understanding and meaning they construct become "traps into which [they] consistently fall" (Piaget 1974, p. 73). In this light, established science becomes understandable as showing the true life of things, as a way to avoid being duped, avoiding illusion, no longer being trapped. Because there is a single truth when we are dealing with knowledge in the strict sense, it is little wonder (and, yet, still a bit of a surprise) that Piaget would say that, "the whole perspective of childhood is falsified" (Piaget 1972, p. 197).

Speculation, then: just as "war . . . makes cultures more alike" (Illich 1992, p. 19), just as goes the presumption that "modernity is a single condition, everywhere the same and always benign. As societies become more modern [more 'developed,' one might say], so they become more alike. At the same time, they become better" (Gray 2003, p. 1), so, too, with the developmental of knowledge itself. Embodied, convivial multifariousness will be overcome.

Moreover, in its leading to "processes common to all subjects" (Piaget 1965, p. 108), development is implicitly pictured as warlike (since it leads to individuals becoming more alike), and the savage childhood of the human race is overcome and salvation is had only and solely through taking on what becomes of us under such besiegement.

Savage childhood is overcome with war.

CHAPTER FOUR

"Sickness is now 'out there'"

DAVID W. JARDINE

I

I find today that patients are more sensitive than the worlds they live in. Rather than patients not being able to perceive and adapt "realistically," it is the reality of the world's phenomena that seems unable to adapt to the sensitivity of the patients. I am astounded by the life and beauty in the patients *vis-à-vis* the dead and ugly world they inhabit. The heightened awareness of subjective realities, that soul sophistication resulting from one hundred years of psychoanalysis, has become incommensurable with the retarded state of external reality, which moved during the same one hundred years towards brutal uniformity and degradation of quality.

. . . .

Ecology movements, futurism, feminism, urbanism, protest and disarmament, personal individuation cannot alone save the world from the catastrophe inherent in our very idea of the world.

. . . .

> To place neurosis and psychopathology solely in personal reality is a delusional repression of what is actually, realistically, being experienced.
>
> . . . .
>
> Sickness is now "out there." (Hillman 2006a, p. 28, 47, 28, and 30).

In these passages from James Hillman's "*Anima Mundi*: Returning of Soul to The World," I believe there is a cluster of insights that are key to the well-being of education itself and which give a clear voice to what seems, sometimes, to be a systemic blindness in our profession. If we leave "our very idea of world" fragmented, degraded, and brutalized, knowledge of that world becomes fragmented, degraded, and brutalized. If this happens, then our understanding of the disciplines of knowledge themselves becomes fragmented, degraded, and brutalized. And thus the world *into which* we are educating new teachers and into which they, in turn, are educating their students, will be degraded, retarded, and brutal. In one last awful turn, if I become educated in such a world, I, too, must become degraded, retarded, and brutal in order to live and survive in such a world. Either that or I must retract and retreat into subjective realities more sensitive and beautiful than the world that surrounds me. In such sadly understandable retraction and retreat, the well-being of the world is abandoned; its degradation thus deepens which, in turn, deepens our cause for retreat.

I am reminded, in passing, of Wendell Berry's (1986, p. 51) disturbing reminder of this terrible intimacy between the world in which we nestle and what becomes of us in such nestling:

> It is impossible to divorce the question of what we do from the question of where we are—or, rather, where we think we are. That no sane creature befouls its own nest is accepted as generally true. What we conceive to be our nest, and where we think it is, are therefore questions of the greatest importance.

No matter how abundantly, rapidly, and twitterly "connected" are our inner lives, it is *where we think we are* that has become unnestled. As the etymology of the word "nest" betrays, in the confines of schools, there is nowhere left in the world(s) of knowledge entrusted to teachers and students, to *sit down* together and nestle in the comfort of such world(s) and learn to inhabit them, care for them, and become someone *worldly* in the process. In the dimwitted confines of one more boring mathematics worksheet-fragment, *the living world of mathematics itself* has fallen ill. It has become uninhabitable, inhospitable, uninviting.

First thesis, following Hillman: there is a catastrophe inherent in our very idea of the world and *this* is what needs our love and devotion and attention. This is where the root of our sickness is held and the Way to our sanity lies. Even though we feel it intimately, sickness and its remedy are outside of our *selves*.

Sickness is now "out there." Inward meditations on our grief, melancholy, and insanity will no longer suffice.

Second thesis: our turn "inward" to beautiful subjective realities, understandable as a refuge from a befouled world, has had an unintended hand in perpetrating, perpetuating, codifying, and confirming the reality of the very befouled world from which it has retreated.

II

> Meditation is working with our speed, our restlessness, our constant busyness. Meditation provides space or ground in which restlessness might function. Meditation practice is not a matter of trying to produce a hypnotic state of mind or create a sense of restfulness. Trying to achieve a restful state of mind reflects a mentality of poverty. Seeking a restful state of mind, one is on guard against restlessness. There is a constant state of paranoia and limitation. We feel we need to be on guard. This guarding process limits the scope of the mind by not accepting whatever comes.
>
> Instead, meditation should reflect a mentality of richness in the sense of using everything that occurs in the state of mind. Thus, if we provide enough room for restlessness so that it might function within the space, then the energy ceases to be restless because it can trust itself fundamentally. Meditation is giving a huge, luscious meadow to a restless cow. The cow might be restless for a while in its huge meadow, but at some stage, because there is so much space, the restlessness becomes irrelevant. (Trungpa 2003, p. 218–19)

David G. Smith showed me this passage from Chogyam Trungpa's *The Myth of Freedom* years ago now, and it has served well ever since as abundantly full of images for pedagogy and its prospects, for what happens when it goes right and what happens when it goes wrong.

When it goes right, pedagogy is akin to a meditative practice which, *when practiced*, can come to provide enough imaginative and intellectually vigorous and compelling "room" for students and teachers alike. Pedagogy can provide huge and luscious meadows, where each seemingly isolated topic mandated by the curriculum becomes a living *topica* (like the roots of the term topography, or topology, the logos of a "place" and its inscriptions; see Gadamer 1989, p. 21) ripe for the cultivation of memory and character (see Gadamer 1989, p. 21; Jardine 2006d) and the ameliorating of restlessness. In a beautiful, diverse, and abundant field, restlessness can become adventurousness, love, affection, exploration, creation. When it goes right, we can begin to catch sight of those who have worked in this field before our arrival: ancestral bloodlines, ancestral workings of this field, traces of *works* handed down to us, each a "transformation into structure" (Gadamer 1989, p. 110 ff.) of *Spiels* played out in this living field. This, with all its gaps and occlusions and contestations, is our nest.

Pedagogy is thus conceivable as an intergenerational, ecological act, since "only in the multifariousness of voices does [any living 'field'] exist" (Gadamer 1989, p. 284). Coming to know takes on the character of cultivating a

> . . . sense of "nativeness," of belonging to the place. Some people are beginning to try to understand where they are, and what it would means to live carefully and wisely, delicately in a place, in such a way that you can live there adequately and comfortably. Also, your children and grandchildren and generations a thousand years in the future will still be able to live there. That's thinking as though you were a native. Thinking in terms of the whole fabric of living and life. (Snyder 1980, p. 86)

Pedagogy becomes understandable and practicable as the ongoing cultivation of the ability to care for that in which we nestle, that which houses (Latin *ecos*) not only us but all beings, all images and ideas, all bloods, and ancestries in nets of dependent co-arising. Every seemingly separate self-existence is "*always already everywhere inhabited* by the Other in the context of the fully real" (Smith 2006c, p. xxiv). This slowly evaporating water ring left on the table from the summer ice water houses the measures of Black-Capped Chickadee swoops from tree to feeder and back. It houses this weird Latinate inheritance, *Parus atricapillus*, come down to us through Linnaeus and back, from him, through all the efforts of categorization, all the talk of Kingdoms and Species and Genera, of tribes and their characteristics, of who belongs with whom, of insiders and outsiders, of where the fences should be wrought and why:

> All things in the world are linked together, one way or the other. Not a single thing comes into being without some relationship to every other thing. (Nishitani 1982, p. 149).
>
> Even the tiniest thing, to the extent that it "is," displays in its act of being the whole web of circuminsessional interpenetration that links all things together. (p. 150)

Black-capped Chickadees can suddenly and unexpectedly become an occasion to hear, off at an allegorical distance, echoes of talk of multiculturalism and its sustainability and life.

Even those sequences of arching, undulating Chickadee waves of flight, even the over-mappings of these waves with Cartesian coordinates. Thus, the great urge to formulate these coordinated swoops that can be experienced first-hand and immediately into something adequate to them, something *aequus*, some quadratic equation—all this is our nest. And in this mix, too is the variegated ways in which each of us enters these territories as "I myself," not some abstract subjectivity but this person, having lived this life and traversed, knowingly and unknowingly, some of these territories. Lifting up that sweating water glass and hearing, instead of the usual *chick-a-dee-dee*, this, *dee-dee* (two descending notes—to illustrate, from an A down to an F#)—this shift to a mating call is a sign of springtime in the Rocky Mountain foothills. It is a sign, too, of me feeling the thus-far slow ebb of my life's measure. The passing of these seasons is my own passing and, most telling, *it has always been thus* "over and above [my] wanting and doing" (Gadamer 1989, p. xxviii). This Chickadee swoop thus no longer has

> the character of an object that stands over and against us. We are no longer able to approach this like an object of knowledge,

> grasping, measuring and controlling. Rather than meeting us in our world, it is much more a world into which we ourselves are drawn. [It] possesses its own worldliness and, thus, the center of its own Being so long as it is not placed into the object-world of producing and marketing. The Being of this thing cannot be accessed by objectively measuring and estimating; rather, *the totality of a lived context has entered into and is present in the thing*. And we belong to it as well. Our orientation to it is always something like our orientation to an inheritance that this thing belongs to, be it from a stranger's life or from our own. (Gadamer 1994, p. 191–2, my emphasis)

The restlessness that then arises has been invited outside of itself. It has a place to work itself out and settle itself down into the comfort of this place, this Dharma field that embraces the kinship of this passing Chickadee, caught, over and above my wanting and doing, in the glance of a passing life.

"Within each dust mote is vast abundance" (Hongzhi 1991, p. 14). When it goes right, then, Trungpa's words bespeak enfielding the restless narrows of schooling in the abundance of the world (see Jardine, Clifford and Friesen 2006). In such enfielding, I myself have the opportunity (Latin *porta*, "gate,"—note that Hermes was understood, among other characteristics to be the god of gates, of moments thus liminal and "between": "*the true locus of hermeneutics is this in-between*" [Gadamer 1989, p. 295]) to become "roomier" (Augustine, cited in Carruthers 2005, p. 199). I become drawn out into a world, "summoned" (Gadamer 1989, p. 458) out of the confines of my restless self and my "experiences" (*Erlebenisse*) into a venture (*Erfahrung*) in and through the nestles of things, nestles which include the traces of those who have ventured here before (*Vorfahren*, the German term for "ancestors"; *Vorfahrung* means "move foward"). "Meet all beings as your ancestors" (Hongzhi 1991, p. 33).

This text by Hongzhi Zhengjue's (1091–1157) is entitled *Cultivating an Empty Field*. When it goes right, what is won is the experience (*Erfahrung*) of each and every "topic" entrusted to teachers and students in schools as being empty (Sanskrit *shunya*) of self-existence (Sanskrit *svabhava*). Things, ideas, images, selves, *are* dependently co-arising (Sanskrit *pratitya-samutpada*) in fields of assembly and are thus impermanent, entailed, interdependent, and ecologically held in their being. Thus, not only do things exist in a fashion that empties them outward into their fields. I, too, along with my students, experience *myself* as drawn out into a world in which my "self" itself empties of its own restless containedness.

The sort of experience that is won, here, is only won by a certain labor (see Ross and Jardine 2009). "Understanding *begins* when something addresses us" (Gadamer 1989, p. 299), but it only *begins* there. This pedagogical experience of abundance is thus a practical matter *that must be practiced* in order for this experience to take root and grow. It must be cultivated, protected, shared, returned to, loved.

III

> My theories of neurosis and categories of psychopathology must be radically extended if they are not to foster the very pathologies which my job is to ameliorate. (Hillman 2006a, p. 28)

And, make no mistake, what is won, here, in the practice of meditative interpretation, is also a deepening experience of the horrors that have been wrought and the sicknesses that have been produced "out there" in the narrowing hallways of some schools, some classrooms, some students' and teachers' lives. Chögyam Trungpa's words help sketch out what happens *when things go wrong*. The experience of abundance requires a form of practice and thinking that is not especially indigenous to schooling and its efficiency-driven (see Boyle 2006; Callahan 1964; Gatto 2006; Kanigel 2005; Friesen and Jardine 2009 and especially Taylor 1903, 1915), "anti-intellectual" (Callahan 1964, p. 8), surveillance and management structures. Such talk of abundance too often ends up being experienced as nothing more than a threat to the efficiencies and surveillance regimes that many schools have worked so hard to establish.

In too many classrooms, especially in these last hundred years (as James Hillman [2006a, p. 28] noted, during which "external reality . . . moved . . . towards brutal uniformity and degradation of quality"), the opposite of this expansive movement is commonly done in the face of restlessness. We narrow to fix and become thus narrowly fixated, terms that mix together images of repair with those of fastening, securing, pinning down and being increasingly uniform and unwavering.

What very often happens in schools when students become restless and encounter difficulties with the work they face is that teachers (and sometimes assessors, testers, curriculum developers, and remediators) zoom in on that trouble, narrowing attention, making the "meadow," the "field of relations," available to that restless student, less huge, luscious, rich and spacious (this defines, of course, precisely what can happen to a restless teacher in a school as well). As Trungpa notes, paranoia and limitation *increase* in response to restlessness. In a tragic but terribly understandable turn, restlessness begins to be blamed on the fact that the field is *too* big, *too* luscious, alluring, and distracting. Abundance, lusciousness, variegation, and multifariousness become transformed into threats set on breaching the narrowing security fences. This is similar to the ecological argument that Wendell Berry (1986) makes regarding how greenhouse walls transform that which is outside of those walls into a threat to what is inside the walls rather that *in relation to which* and *in the midst of which* and *in concert with which* life is made vigorous and health and whole.

Abundance is thus replaced with scarcity and paucity, lusciousness with thin gruel, variegation and multifariousness with uniformity, in order to fix on the source of restlessness.

Inside such narrows, the locale of restlessness, the reason we had to "clamp down" in the first place, becomes more and more clearly targeted: *It's the cow*. What can be witnessed here is "what [Enrique] Dussel (1995) called the 'gigantic *inversion*' [where] 'the innocent victim becomes culpable and the culpable victimizer becomes innocent'" (Smith 2006f, p. 76). And in a horrifyingly familiar fell swoop we glimpse the logic of abuse: "She made me do it." "I warned her." "It is for her own good."

This abusiveness takes on great specificity in some classrooms. Tasks facing a restless student become stupider, more menial and demeaning, more degrading to be part of, less interesting, less alluring, and all of this *because of the student and their restlessness*. Thus, in the early twentieth century, schooling was ripe for the arrival of the efficiency movement as proposed by Fredrick Winslow Taylor (1903, 1911), whose images of industrial assembly took educational reform by storm (see Raymond Callahan's now-classic [1964] detailing of this [still ongoing] storm in *America*,

Education and the Cult of Efficiency; see Ayres 1909, 1915; Boyle 2006; Braverman 1998; Cubberley 1922; Dufour and Eaker 1998; Gatto 2006; Friesen and Jardine 2009; Kanigel 2005; Wrege and Greenwood 1991). As with the worker on Taylor's assembly line (here cited from one of his lectures from June 4, 1906), ideally one is aiming for a situation in which "we do not ask for the initiative of our men. We do not want any initiative. All we want of them is to obey the orders we give them, do what we say, and do it quickly" (cited in Kanigel 2005, p. 169). The worldly correlate to such obedience and, so to speak, "disinitiative," is to require of the worker the doing of an increasingly narrow and meager task, one that *does not require* initiative but obedience, not only to what is to be done but to precisely how, when and for how long it is to be done. "What [Taylor] really wanted working men to be [is] focused [to use the language of education, 'task oriented'], uncomplicated and compliant" (Boyle 2006); parallel to this, the world inhabited by the worker at the same time becomes degraded, retarded, ugly, and demeaning.

There are only disconnected, unrelated bits and pieces and their disinterested, obedient, standardized, time-clocked assembly. Ideally, here, any worker on the line is *replaceable*. Inversely put, things are designed in such a way that it makes no difference that *this* person is here, since the conditions under which those doing the work might have some effect on what occurs has been deliberately and systematically eradicated in the name of efficiency. Just as the life is drained out of mathematics in the efficiency-oriented classroom, so, too, the initiative is drained out of those assembling it out of such lifeless bits. We "approach [mathematics] like an object of knowledge, grasping, measuring and controlling." It is no longer experienced as "a world into which we ourselves are drawn" but as something now "placed into the object-world of producing and marketing" (Gadamer 1994, p. 191–2). We "teach to the test" that is now organized around the testing of assembly efficiency and the "accountability" of teachers is measured by cleaving to this logic.

Thus, when this shadow falls over schools, even if initiative and interest might accidentally rear up in the midst of the endless line of worksheets (each sequenced and dated and timed, with exact[ing] criteria of "how to do it" ["the *critica* of Cartesianism" (Gadamer 1989, p. 21]) there is, so to speak, nowhere (no "where," no "field," no sense of "the old *topica*" [p. 21]) in the world of such a classroom that might warrant or reward such rearing, that might embrace it, challenge it, shape and care for it, nurture it, feed it, *teach* it. In fact, the opposite becomes true. A world of bits and pieces under managerial surveillance *rejects* and *rebukes* rearing up. Initiative becomes a *detriment* to efficiency. The rearing up of initiative and interest become subjectivized into a *property of the restless student*. Such rearing only meets reprimand for its interrupting of the uniform movement of "the line." Or, alternatively, such rearing is coded as "gifted" (and then the gifted student gets bullied in order to help him or her get "back in line"), which is simply another way of ejecting interruption from the "normal" line of the "ordinary" classroom. Questions consequently become experienced as problems that must be fixed in order to prevent further questions, further interruptions. This is all confirmed if we look at two of the inventions of Taylor's efficiency movement in large industries. First is the suggestion box, where workers could deflect their uprisings into suggestions ("we want to hear from you"—the great new noble lie). But recall that only those suggestions are implemented in such a logic that *increase* efficiency and therefore *decrease* the need for further suggestions. Second, the staff psychologist whose job it is to help workers "cope" with (as many teachers call the ravages of schooling) "the real world."

And so it continues like a wheel turning. The *more* trouble a student has, the *smaller* and *simpler* and *less interesting* the "bit" doled out to them.

And the more restless they become.

And the more our paranoia and need for limitedness increases.

In this catastrophic logic, *time itself changes* (see Chapter 9, Ross 2004; Ross and Jardine 2009). As things fragment, time accelerates because there is nothing to slow it down since no one of these isolated bits or pieces requires any prolonged attention. Thus, any ancestral tethers or memories or tales are only invoked in classrooms as *means* of getting across the requisite bits. Moreover, the future constantly becomes experienced as larger, more looming, more high-stakes, increasingly imminent, *ever-sooner*.

We get increasingly restless. Therefore, the future *into which* the line of unfielded bits accelerates becomes increasingly experienced as a potential threat that requires its own fences, its own preemptive, targeted "outcomes" or already-mapped-out developmental sequences which run ahead of students and lay out in advance any possible future they might have. Thus, David G. Smith's (2006a, p. 25) horrifying insight about "frozen futurism": "there *is* no future because the future *already* is." Hence, the end-times logic of Francis Fukyama (2006) and much of neo-conservativism (see Smith 2006, 2008) dovetails with the concern for what happens "at the end of the line" in Taylorism and how his "one best way" preemptively determines the end in advance as well as the means of achieving it. Part of this efficiency means is all too familiar to teachers and students in schools: induce in workers the low-level concern that "time is always running out" (Berry 1983, p. 76) in just the right measure that student workers as well as their teachers remain focused and "on task" at all times.

Time is always running out and I can always be replaced.

Once school tasks no longer need initiative and interest, they are not only rejected and repelled but are subjectivized and privatized, and such "urges" are, in a terrible gesture of "delusional repression" (Hillman 2006a, p. 28), cast back into the one who is restless. In such repression, the skittering of attention cannot excuse itself by pointing to the fact that nothing in our surroundings *needs* prolongedness. Instead, the sickness out there is left in place and students who continue to be restless become in need of specialized intervention (an assembly "sub-line" like a "special needs" classroom or an Individualized Program Plan [IPP]) where fragmented tasks are designer-made to suit the particular pathology of restlessness—note, since each child is preciously believed to be "an individual," such designer-made-ness is now being bandied about as good for every student. Deeper: every student, in this repression, *deserves* an IPP.

Every student will get what they deserve. This is not a threat. We're here to help.

Otherwise restless students become portends of utter, unutterable Chaos. As I've witnessed in many High Schools, there is the unuttered belief that if you let go for a minute of the narrowed and fenced regimes of management and control, quite literally, *all Hell will break lose*. That this hallucinatory vision of the threatening Hellishness portended by restlessness is, in some part and however unintentionally, *produced by* the very narrowing set up to protect us from such a threat—this becomes too horrible to contemplate. This is the Great Knot of delusional repression in which much contemporary schooling still has so much unutterable stake. This perhaps accounts, in part, for the profoundly disproportionate heat, fear, accusation, and anger that can arise when one attempts to name this knot, to understand its binding character, and to look for the possible means of its untying.

To hark back to Chogyam Trungpa's words, in the process of such narrowing, restlessness does not become irrelevant. It becomes *paramount*. The restlessness now no longer has places ("fields") that are patient, forgiving, variegated, rich, and rigorous enough so that our troubledness might be able to work itself *out*.

It can now only be worked *on*.

Poor restless cow has a problem.

IV

> I resolved to assume that everything that ever entered my mind was no more true than the illusions of my dreams. But immediately afterwards I noticed that whilst I thus wished to think all things false, it was absolutely essential that the "I" who thought this should *be* somewhat, and remarking that this truth, "*I think therefore I am*" was so certain and assured that all the most extravagant suppositions brought forward by the skeptics were incapable of shaking it. And then, examining attentively that which I was, I saw that I could conceive that I had no body, and that there was no world nor place where I might be; but yet that I could not for all that conceive that I was not. I do not yet know with sufficient clearness *what I am*, though assured *that I am*. (Descartes 1955, p. 90)

There is a terrible and familiar beauty to this binding logic, its movement and its delusional repression. This narrow logic is a recapitulation of movement of doubt in Cartesianism, which methodically narrowed the field of that which can be relied on (our "nest"—recall Wendell Berry's admonishment, *not necessarily* "where we *are*" but "where we *think* we are") until all that was left over was a clear and distinct "I am" which deems any and all fields of emergence—lusciousness, spaciousness, and hugeness—as contaminations of its own, now-cleaned and clarified ("the unclear is the unclean" [Turner 1987, p. 7]) self-existence.

Cartesian doubt thus provides a convoluted allegorical twist on the tale of Eden: in order to outrun the grief of the expulsion from the luscious meadow, we, in the full hubris of Euro-Enlightenment, take on the task of *preemptively self-expelling*. In such a movement, we take charge of that within us that recapitulates God's image in us: the "that I am" (*Exodus* 3:13–3:14) of God's utterance becomes the *sum* of the *cogito ergo sum*. And just as God banished humanity from Eden, so, now, Descartes, through methodical doubt, *banishes himself* to his own "I am" bereft of any worldly fields of traverse or comfort or inhabitation. My "self," under the threat of doubt, has no home in this world. Therefore, I most indubitably *am* without the world, completely, utterly, and absolutely "fenced off." I become inalienably indivisible, *individuus*, an "individual" in a sense ripely new to the world where modern science was burgeoning, while, at the same time, feeling old and familiar, this "I am" now sent out to clarify the world in its own image.

At work here amidst a myriad cluster of echoes and ancestries is a catastrophic ontological idea of how things, in their deepest substantive reality, *exist*. Things *exist* only insofar as they are no longer divisible: "A substance is that which requires nothing except itself in order to exist." So goes Rene Descartes (1955, p. 255) recapitulation of an old Aristotelian truism that echoes through the Abrahamic bloodlines in God's assertion "that I am." The "I am" becomes exemplary of this "is-what-it-is-independently-of-everything-else" substantiveness, purged, through doubt, of all its fieldings and all its dubious, roomy relations. This isolated, unnested, unworldly subjectivity then projects this hard-won exemplar on the world: if the truth of the "I am" is that I exist independently of everything else, then the truth of every thing, every word, every gesture, every idea, must live up to this (catastrophic) idea of self-existence. Every thing must, through doubt, be *rendered* clear and distinct and self-identical and separate in order for it to participate in the truth of the "I am," in order, that is, for it to truly *be* what *it* is. Every thing must be cleaved until it throws itself back against such division and can be cleaved no further. It must become an *object* (literally, from the Latin, something thrown [*jacere*] against [*ob-*]). Every thing is what it is independently of every other thing (thus recapitulating the core adage of mathematics and formal logic, the principle of identity, where A=A, and where this can be affirmed universally and for every possible A). "The essence of truth," so this old story goes, "is identity" (Heidegger 1978, p. 39).

We must, therefore, on behalf of the truth of things bespoken by this substance/identity-logic, break things apart until they will break no further (until A is just A with no other tethers or attachments or surroundings). This effort becomes akin to a purification ritual bent on burning or washing away any contamination, anything accidental or despoiling of the separate self-existence of the self or anything in the world. Relatedness, interdependency, familialness, kind-ness, resemblance, ancestry, ecological placedness, allegorical similitudes, reminderliness, memorality, expansiveness, invocation—all forms of "dependent co-arising" (Sk. *pratitya-samutpada*)—are all secondary, accidental, "revocable and provisional" (Gray 1998, p. 36). Things *are* fenced off and separate. Any relationship with any other thing or any surrounding field is ontologically *post hoc*.

Thus bodes a catastrophic idea inherent in our very idea of the world. In this ontological light, *everything* starts to "unfield." Everything starts to fragment, disconnected, untether. We hear in this the future prospects of F. W. Taylor's efficiency movement which codified this fragmenting logic into both the substance (separate bits and pieces) and the standardized method or means of industrial assembly (F. W. Taylor sought "one best way" [see Kanigel 2005] of any assembly, and required its identical application by any worker), which then was adopted, almost holus bolus, by educators at the beginning of the twentieth century. Education then starts to take on the character of industrial assembly. Ellwood P. Cubberley, Dean of the School of Education at Stanford, in his book *Public School Administration*, originally published in 1916 (cited here from Callahan 1964, p. 97) says:

> Our schools are, in a sense, factories in which the raw products (children) are to be shaped and fashioned into products to meet the various demands of life. The specifications for manufacturing come from the demands of twentieth-century civilization, and it is the business of the school to build its pupils according to the specifications laid down. This demands good tools, specialized machinery, continuous measurement of production to see if it is according to specifications, [and] the elimination of waste in manufacture.

Thus, Gadamer (1989, p. 336) speaks of "the ideal of knowledge familiar from natural science [especially, not coincidentally, from the version of natural science taking hold right at the time of Taylor's work in industrial assembly], whereby we understand a process only when we can bring it about artificially." And thus we get a description of such an ideal that is perfectly in line (pun intended) with Taylor's imagines of industrial assembly:

> The object is disassembled, the rules of its functioning are ascertained, and then it is reconstructed according to those rules; so, also, knowledge is analyzed, its rules are determined, and finally it is redeployed as method. The purpose of both remedies is to prevent [preempt, one might say] unanticipated future breakdowns by means of breaking down even further the flawed entity and then synthesizing it artificially. (Weinsheimer 1987, p. 6)

It is only half a step, then, to the work of Franklin Bobbitt (1918, 1924) and Werrett Charters (1923); one hop from there to Ralph Tyler (1949), and one more to the underpinnings of No Child Left Behind.

V

> The unnoticeable law of the Earth preserves the Earth in the sufficiency of the emerging and perishing of all things in the allotted sphere of the possible which everything follows and yet nothing knows. The birch tree never oversteps its possibility. It is [human] will which drives the Earth beyond the sphere of its possibility into such things that are no longer a possibility and are thus the impossible. It is one thing to just use the Earth, another to receive the blessing of the Earth and to become at home in the law of this reception in order to shepherd the mystery and watch over the inviolability of the possible. (Heidegger 1987, p. 109)

It is often the case that a dominant discourse displays the depth of its dominance in its ability to define and shape the nature and limits of any resistance to that dominance. Stepping away from this catastrophic idea inherent in our very idea of the world has, in some educational quarters, assumed the very thing for which it meant to provide an alternative.

Here is what has happened with one of contemporary education's most recently popular and lusty love affairs.

Education noticed that the dispelling of initiative and interest would no longer do. However, this noticing took place within the atmosphere of a catastrophic idea. Once living fields become understood and treated as something artificial, their "life" is experienced as issuing from our assembling artifice, from our "wanting and doing." The field-nature of the world (which surrounds us and which we inhabit) becomes imagined to be a sort of ego-issuance.

Education thus began to resist this industrial assembly-line image of education by touting the activity and initiative and "doings" of the individual student. In an understandable but vainglorious effort to recover our lost initiative (r)ejected from the industrial assembly-line image of knowledge and its teaching and learning, we *leave the catastrophic, inanimate "world" of bits and pieces in place* and become *constructivists* who are involved in *making up a world*, "imposing cosmos on the chaos of experience" (Piaget 1971a, p. xii):

> Accordingly, the spontaneity of understanding becomes the formative principle of receptive matter, and in one stroke we have the old mythology of an intellect which glues and rigs together the world's matter with its own forms. (Heidegger 1985, 70)

And here is the next step in this nightmare.

Now that our old faiths in logic, mathematics, and the natural sciences have crumbled, now that the singular confidence voice of the white male European "I am" has been replaced by a "multifariousness of voices" (Gadamer 1989, p. 295), now that "one best way" has been deeply interrupted in multiple ways and with multiple intelligences, our constructions become a sort of democratized Cartesianism, where each of us is our own "I am" and the nature and limits of our constructing becomes a sign of our "individuality" which we are then free to impose on an infinitely malleable "world."

A sort of opening up and broadening of the fences seems to have occurred around each restless cow, but there is no longer any field there, just bits to be assembled as we will (or, with social constructivism, bits to be assembled with others).

Lusciousness and spaciousness themselves, once vaguely understood as the source of our sustenance, have become subjectivized and "personalized." Inhabitation has become a choice.

Now that the array of unearthed modernist confidences are fading from view, all that has changed from Fredrick Winslow Taylor's assembly line in the post-modern flurry that then ensues is that each of us is now "left to [our] own devices" (Arendt 1969, p. 196) in a retarded and degraded world.

After all that, Cartesian nightmares rear up anew.

What we now each make is irrelevant. It is our willful making that is key. *Willful grasping itself* is what is most real. Restlessness as truth and anything that interrupts its furtive pursuit of its own satisfaction is rendered secondary to this truth.

Thus, Friedrich Nietzsche (1975, p. 346) unveiled *the will* underlying every claim, and the pure affirmation of the will and its power over that which is now its "wanting and doing," becomes the most real. It is in its own affirmation and the felt resistance to that affirmation that the will feels its power (its lost "initiative," we might say):

> The will to power can manifest itself only against resistances; therefore it seeks that which resists it. Appropriation and assimilation are above all a desire to overwhelm, a forming, shaping and reshaping, until at length that which has been overwhelmed has entirely gone over into the power domain of the aggressor and has increased the same.

Thus arrives the boding of the will's triumph. That very fearful and restless, doubting and grasping Ego that precipitated the unfielding of the world into bits and pieces becomes the key to its (re)making as an act of war, of violence, of domination. We begin to take recourse in the *feeling* of power found in that very inwardness that then oversteps its earthly possibility (a possibility which is now just a distant Edenic dream dreamt by ecologists and their ilk) and is thus impossible, yet *there it is*.

That there is an ecological disaster portended here becomes like a peripheral penumbra of dread, unnameable, like something vital that has been somehow forgotten and that wisps away like a dream when we try to glimpse it.

There is no way out of this nightmare except to simply stop.

CHAPTER FIVE

"A hitherto concealed experience that transcends thinking from the position of subjectivity"

DAVID W. JARDINE

Now the question arises as to how we can legitimate this hermeneutical conditionedness of our being in the face of modern science. We will certainly not accomplish this legitimation by making prescriptions for science and recommending that it toe the line—quite aside from the fact that such pronouncements always have something comical about them. Science will not do us this favor. It will continue along its own path with an inner necessity beyond its control and it will produce more and more breathtaking knowledge and controlling power. It can be no other way.

— (Gadamer 1977, p. 10)

If the application of science were simply the problem of how, with the help of science, we might do everything we can do, then it is certainly not such application that we need as humans who are responsible for the future. For science as such will never prevent us from doing anything we are able to do. The future of humanity, however, demands that we do not simply do everything we can. (p. 196–7).

The hermeneutic phenomenon is basically not a problem of method at all. It is not concerned primarily with amassing verified knowledge, such as would satisfy the methodological ideal of science–yet it, too, is concerned with knowledge and with truth. But what kind of knowledge and what kind of truth?

— (Gadamer 1989, p. xxii)

I

There is something of Immanuel Kant's 1784 Enlightenment declaration in the character of hermeneutics: "*Sapere Aude!*: 'Have courage to use your own understanding!' – that is the motto of the Enlightenment" (1983, p. 41). Hermeneutics, too, is about growing up and becoming experienced and knowledgeable in and about the world, and learning to take responsibility for the way you make through that life and that world. But, as Gadamer asks, what kind of knowledge and what kind of truth, if not amassing verified knowledge? What kind of knowledge and what kind of truth, if we ceased being wrapped up in increasingly breathtaking controlling power?

Hermeneutics is interested in our "hermeneutic conditionedness," that is, in the convivial lives we live, the life everything in the world lives, full of all its multifariousness, casualness, ambiguity, interdependency, and doubt. It resists the grandiose exaggerations and simplifications that often pass as knowledge, and resists, too, the in-the-end unfounded belief that we can definitively secure ourselves against our interdependent *being* in the world. We can, of course, do what is needed, make ourselves safe within the limits of time and space, and it is often precisely right to do so. However, despite all of its real and feigned controlling power, modern science and its breathtaking accomplishments, along with political assurances and their regimes of surveillance and terror alerts, along with the numbness of ill-founded opinion, still leave us in a finite world with finite lives, still, each of us, responsible for the future in which it may not be right to do everything we can do simply because it is possible to do so. We're left still having to understand what is going on and what do to in this difficult convivial world of ours that inhabits us as much as we inhabit it.

Hermeneutics is thus also about raising ourselves up out of thoughtlessness and the stifling confines of an unexamined life and learning to experience and understand what we can of this interdependent being *without* putting ourselves in the place of Kant's judge who *demands* that life simply follow orders (as goes the implicit image of constructivism [see Chapter 3]). Learning to experience and understand this interdependent being doesn't involve a conservative maintenance of the traditions that, in part, shape everyday life at its most routine and thoughtless, but something more difficult. It involves seeking out those moments when traditions are opened up by the arrival of the young, the new, "the fecundity of the individual case" (Gadamer 1989, p. 37), and are called to account by such arrivals. This, hermeneutics suggests, is where the convivial *life* of *living* traditions and *living* disciplines of knowledge *lives*. In these moments, what might have passed for a finished, secured, and self-enclosed identity (of ourselves and of the things we experience) can, even momentarily, "waver and tremble" (Caputo 1987, p. 7) and, in such movement, start to show forth and remake its flourishing interdependencies and worldliness, and revive, perhaps, its "hospitality for what is to come [*avenir*]" (Derrida and Ferraris 2001, p. 31).

Hannah Arendt (1969, p. 192–3) encapsulates the situation that is of deep hermeneutic interest in education:

> We are always educating for a world that is or is becoming out of joint, for this is the basic human situation, in which the world is created by mortal hands to serve mortals for a limited time as home. Because the world is made by mortals it wears out; and because it continuously changes its inhabitants it runs the risk of becoming as mortal as they. To preserve the world against the mortality of its creators and inhabitants it must be constantly set right anew. The problem is simply to educate in such a way that a setting-right remains actually possible, even though it can, of course, never be assured. Our hope always hangs on the new which every generation brings; but precisely because we can base our hope only on this, we destroy everything if we so try to control the new that we, the old, can dictate how it will look. Exactly for the sake of what is new and revolutionary in every child, education must be conservative; it must preserve this newness and introduce it as a new thing into the old world.

In the midst of these realities, overcoming immaturity, hermeneutically conceived, is not had through "the repudiation of childhood" that Susan Bordo (1987, p. 98) locates at the heart of the Cartesian project (and which likely underwrites Immanuel Kant's Enlightenment call for "maturity" [see Chapter 3]). In understanding the convivial world and our hermeneutic conditionedness in it, always at the heart of such conditions are the multifarious, delicate, and difficult relationships between the old and the young, the new and the established, the revolutionary and the conservative, traditions and their transformations. At its heart, hermeneutics is interested in these moments of setting right anew, cultivating, caring for and becoming experienced in this possibility, although it can, of course, never be assured. This is why Hans-Georg Gadamer (1977, p. 51), in describing hermeneutics, easily links up "the new, the different, [and] the true," and why it is to this that our attention must turn to understand what hermeneutics offers. Also, this describes in short order why there is something deeply pedagogical about hermeneutics and its understanding of our convivial knowledge of the world. The young and the old, the established and the new, the student and the teacher, are already present in how the convivial life of that world is lived. How we might approach that living that occurs between the old and the young, without the old simply reprimanding the young for its immaturity, hints at how hermeneutics hints at a pedagogy left in peace.

Even failing such hospitality—even under conditions of threat and retrenchment, when possibilities of setting right are shut down, when the new and the different becomes suspicious—ancestral traces of the traditions that have foreclosed around us can be *understood*, not just suffered. The binding threads can sometimes be loosened, made visible, utterable, and thus *possibly* made more forgiving and susceptible to transformation. And as cannot be denied, sometimes such moments can be met with increased violence, vigilance, and closure. There is no universal hope here (here is one spot where hermeneutics steps out of line with Immanuel Kant's Enlightenment motto), simple plan or path, no ensuring methodology, and there is certainly nothing inevitable about becoming experienced in the ways of the world and what such experience might bring. Coming to understand these matters as a matter of profound delicacy and contingency, always in need of being revived and renewed, is at the heart of hermeneutic work, and key, here, is the presumption, now a bit more distantly akin to the Enlightenment call, that understanding our suffering just might help ameliorate it. It might help us flourish. It is here, again, that hermeneutics bears a kinship to the contingent hopes of pedagogy. Its fragile hope lies in the good of becoming experienced in the ways of the world and becoming someone in the process.

There are, of course, many other shadows to such Enlightenment-like hopes and promises. I've worked with teachers who, once they begin to be able to experience the tightly bound threads that wind around the hallways and classrooms of their own schools, their own students, their own practices—all of which so often silently passes as "the real world," or "just the way things are"—find these experiences unbearable. Some find themselves sometimes looked at askance and with suspicion when they try to articulate that which heretofore had gone without saying, as if articulation of this life living under the surface is itself some sort of threat to the feigned calmness of "the real world" of schooling. My own depression, distraction, hopelessness, and pain attest, as well, to the weight that experience sometimes brings, even with its sometimes joyous promise. Nevertheless, and (to accord Derrida his due [see Gadamer and Derrida 1989]) with the presumption of good will:

> The hermeneutic imagination works from a commitment to generativity and rejuvenation and to the question of how we can go on together in the midst of constraints and difficulties that constantly threaten to foreclose on the future. The aim of interpretation, it could be said, is not just another interpretation but human freedom, which finds its light, identity and dignity in those few brief moments when one's lived burdens can be shown to have their source in too limited a view of things. (Smith 1999c, p. 29)

Hermeneutics is, therefore, about becoming educated, becoming experienced, and this freedom of which David Smith speaks is not had through cutting ourselves off from this difficult, convivial life, and becoming some autonomous fantasy-self, some abstract "I am" (see Chapter 2), but finding ways to open up and understand that very life, my very life, with all its lived entanglements that I knowingly or unknowingly inhabit:

> Some wishes cannot succeed; some victories cannot be won; some loneliness is incorrigible. But there is relief and freedom in knowing what is real; these givens [what Gadamer calls our "hermeneutic conditionedness] come to us out of the perennial reality of the world, like the terrain we live on. One does not care for this ground to make it a different place, or to make it perfect, but to make it inhabitable and to make it better. To flee from its realities is only to arrive at them unprepared. (Berry 1983, p. 92)

There is thus a pedagogy to hermeneutics, the cultivation and work it requires, and freedom it portends, and it is not for the faint of heart. This is not the freedom of an abstract, autonomous, worldless, self-determining individuality, but frail, vulnerable, *human* freedom.

Hermeneutics wants to ground understanding back into an experiential conviviality of the world, the very life-world seemingly fragmented and re-built under logico-mathematical surveillance by the Cartesian threats and doubts. It wants to understand the world's dependent co-arising out from under the shadow of threat. This is part of the phenomenological origins of contemporary hermeneutics, that it includes a desire to undo our forgetfulness of our interdependent being, and to let things be (see Heidegger 1962) what they convivially *are*, fully "contaminated," unrendered, and unpurged by the demand for clarity and distinctness.

This is why, in educational research, hermeneutic work always includes efforts, again and again, and in the circumstances of the topic being discussed, to break the spell of those threats and doubts, to open up anew to their worldly interrelatedness the remnants of fragmentation and isolation found scattered in the world. In the world of education, such shards are found everywhere—in schools, in curriculum guides, in assessment procedures, in institutional structures and the fetishes of method and surveillance, in the worries of student-teachers who've been schooled for years, in the ancestral legacies of current educational presumptions, and so on. This is a difficult hermeneutic truth, that the fragmentation, security regimes, and surveillance that come under threat becomes codified in the very images and ideas, hopes, and desires that students and teachers bear with them in such settings. They become codified in such a way that they are experienced simply as "the way things are." Requisite of such ordinariness, it seems, is a profound sort of amnesia, where we can no longer quite remember how things became like this, or why, or whether anything was ever any different. Thus, hermeneutics, in part, involves a cultivation of memory (see Chapter Eight). This is one thread of the kind of truth it seeks (more on this below).

Even knowledge itself bears these scars in the fragmented bits and pieces often found in curriculum guides and their requisite schooled assessment procedures (see Chapter 4). Attempts, in hermeneutics, at interrupting this codification and opening it up, and attempts to revive the threads of interdependence and co-inhabitation, therefore, are often experienced as themselves the *source of threat* (see Chapter 1), rather than as attempts to ameliorate threat and its codified consequences by referring back to the life heretofore cast in a zone of deep shadow.

Under threat, things, so to speak, contract, and their rich, difficult relatedness is foregone and forgotten (as if these connections were "revocable and provisional" [Gray 2001, p. 35–6]), in favor of the simplified, the efficient, the universally standardizable and manageable, the certain, the clear, the tried and true. Left in peace, things can flourish, and their convivial conditionedness can become admitted, experienced, and understood. Left in peace, we can allow ourselves to experience this truth: "we are *always already everywhere inhabited* by the Other in the context of the fully real" (Smith 2006c, p. xxiv). Glimpsed, here, is that, *even under threat*, everything and everyone, every image and every idea we encounter in this full reality is abundantly and irrevocably inhabited, always, already and everywhere. Convivial connections and relationships are everywhere and start to slowly become experienceable and understandable once the "hardened identity" (Huntington 2003, p. 266) induced by doubt and demands for secured clarity and distinctness is cracked. Even the retractions and hardening that threat induces no longer bespeak just "the way things are" but hint allegorically at old and familiar war stories. This, too, is part of the co-inhabited lives we have lived, this story of entrenchment and protection and security, these descriptions of high schools as "the trenches," and the one about the old, battle-scarred teacher who is always ready to tell fresh-faced and newly arriving teachers of their inevitable fate, and that he or she, too, was once hopeful and full of enthusiasm.

Hermeneutics can begin to open up a way for students and teachers to experience the abundant flourishing of relatedness that is afoot in the world, for good or ill. But—and this point needs constant reiteration—pursuing these explorations also can make it more difficult, more painful, to witness the flattening and deadening of such matters in far too many school settings.

Once the world becomes interpretable and its mutual co-inhabitations and interdependencies become visible and experienceable, one can, ironically, begin to feel more isolated.

II

Given its interest in our interdependent conditionedness, hermeneutics cannot begin by attempting to secure an independent, unconditioned, purified, self-identical subjectivity as a platform for launching inquiry into this world and our lives in it. Hans-Georg Gadamer (1989, p. 276) bluntly states, "subjectivity is a distorting mirror" in the endeavor to inquire into the convivial, multifarious, co-inhabited lives we actually live. The image of subjectivity that we have inherited (even into the project of education, where conviviality is key) comes, in part, as a consequence of the Cartesian project of threatening the convivial world with doubt and purging it of anything not clear and distinct. This purging has two correlates: I am purged of my being someone and become an abstract, self-identical, "I am" who wields the methods of logico-mathematical knowledge (see Chapter 3), and the world becomes subjected to this self-purged subject's demand that the world itself be purged of anything not clear and distinct. The convivial world thus becomes the world only insofar as it is rendered beyond doubt, that is, only insofar as it is, so to speak, "logico-mathematizable" (the core idea of which is the principle of identity, A=A). And, as the wielding of state-based standardized examinations proves, such purging has become the developmental goal of education itself, to produce "subjects" (students) who, *only* when subjected to objectively standardized assessment procedures (themselves purge of the convivial knowledge and ways of the living disciplines whose knowledge is supposedly being tested) can then be judged to be or not to be "educated." (See Chapter 2; see also Chapter 4, for more on how the efficiency movement and images of industrial assembly helped underwrite early twentieth-century educational reforms that are still in effect today.)

Up against this long and convoluted inheritance, Gadamer states that "the idea that self-consciousness possesses the unquestioned primacy that modern thinking has accorded it may now quite justifiably be doubted" (Gadamer 2007d, p. 272), thus pushing aside the long-standing, presumed starting point for inquiry within the self-clarified security-perimeters of the "I am." Such a starting point—the platform of the controlling power of modern science—belies and occludes the lived realities of the always already everywhere, of conviviality, of mutually inhabited and inhabiting co-existence. This is not a matter of suggesting that modern science "toe the line" (Gadamer 1977, p. 10) in these matters. Modern science, in light of the Cartesian inheritance, is quite clear that this is *precisely* where it begins. Hermeneutics is not interested in arguing *this* point, that perhaps modern science should do something else. It is not antiscience. There is not a so-called paradigm war here over the same ground. What hermeneutics is interested in unmasking is how the *dominance* of this way of thinking has occluded and cast into deep shadow our convivial lives and the knowledge and truth of those lives—the very convivial world that modern science cannot know, given its demands to purge this very world of what it deems its convivial contaminations.

"A substance is that which requires nothing except itself in order to exist" (Descartes 1640/1955, p. 255). Regarding this founding presumption, Gadamer (1989, p. 242) states, "the concept of substance [and its formal-logical consort, the principle of pure, uncontaminated identity, A=A] is . . . inadequate for historical being and knowledge. [There is a] radical challenge to thought implicit in this inadequacy." It is this radical challenge—setting down the threat-induced fixations with subjectivity, self-consciousness, and substance—that is posed by Gadamer's understanding of the hermeneutic enterprise: "I have retained the term 'hermeneutics' . . . not in the sense of a methodology but as a theory of the real experience that thinking is" (Gadamer 1989, p. xxxvi) once it gives up the threat-contraction mechanism of Cartesian substance/identity as inadequate to the matters at hand.

What is at stake in hermeneutics is "a hitherto concealed experience that transcends thinking from the position of subjectivity" (Gadamer 1989, p. 100). And it is this experience—hermeneutic experience—that forms the core prospect of a pedagogy left in peace.

III

Where do we find this experience? At first blush, it seems that it might be rare and rarified, but in fact, it is quite ordinary. It is something commonly recognizable, but not commonly recognized for what it *is*.

To recover something of this experience and help us recognize what kind of knowledge and what kind of truth it portends, *Truth and Method* (1989) begins with a discussion of *aesthetic experience*, and how our understanding of what this experience *is* has been depotentiated, in fact *falsified*, under the shadow of Cartesianism. Gadamer believes that aesthetic experience offers a clue to the experience of the conviviality of the world, although this character of aesthetics has been hidden from view because of the dominance and pervasiveness of modern science and its understanding of knowledge and truth.

Key to Gadamer's long and often convoluted exploration (1989, p. 42–100) is an interest in an immediate phenomenological reality: in our everyday experience of the world, simple things sometimes strike us, catch our fancy, address us, speak to us, call for a response, elicit or provoke something in us, ask something of us, hit us, bowl us over, stop us in our tracks, make us catch our breath. "Over and above our wanting and doing," things sometimes "*happen to us*" (Gadamer 1989, p. xxviii, emphasis added) and calls us to account:

> The word for perception or sensation in Greek was *aesthesis*, which means at root a breathing in or taking in of the world, the gasp, "aha," the "uh" of the breath in wonder, shock, amazement, and aesthetic response. (Hillman 2006a, p. 36)

Rich and memorable events and experiences happen to us, catch our attention and ask things of us. As such, the venture of coming to understand such things is characterizable as "more a passion than an action" (Gadamer1989, p. 366)—we often experience ourselves drawn out of ourselves and into the charm of unsecured things, drawn into thinking, questioning, admiring, exploring, participating, far beyond the limits of methodological self-security, far beyond, often, the limits where we had heretofore comfortably come to rest. These interruptions of subjectivity can be large or small, profound and life-changing, or simply quizzical turns of attention. Aesthetic experience is thus the experience of being drawn out of our subjectivity, summoned, one might say, out of any foreclosed or "hardened" (Huntington 2003, p. 266) identity, and into a teeming world of relations that lives "over and above our wanting and doing."

We don't experience the thing summoning us thus as simply an object sitting in front of us from which we are indifferently gleaning data. The thing experienced thus is, so to speak, experienced as witnessing us, *facing us*:

> Things speak; they show the shape they are in. They announce themselves, bear witness to their presence: "Look, here we are." They regard us beyond how we may regard them, our perspectives, what we intend with them, and how we dispose of them. (Hillman 2006a, p. 33)

The object of aesthetic experience is experienced as *addressing us*. *We* are caught in *its* regard and not just vice versa. Every teacher understands this experience that one's students are not just there in front of us but are thinking about us as much as we are thinking about them. And the book we are reading or the mathematical equation we are pondering sometimes tells us something about ourselves and our thinking as much as we are attempting to tell each other about it. Sometimes we can experience a student's geometric musings as holding an insight we need to catch up to, and sometimes we're not fleet enough, and the track trails away beyond our ken. All this, again, is phenomenologically and pedagogically commonplace.

The object, thus aesthetically experienced, "would not deserve the interest we take in it if it did not have something to teach us that we could not know by ourselves" (Gadamer 1989, p. xxxv). *It* has something to teach *us* because it speaks out of a cluster of occluded, perhaps unnoticed relations and dependencies we are already living within, that are *already at work* "before you know it," that is, before the deliberate deployment of methods aimed at controlling and managing its arrival. This sense of binding threads of obligation, commitment, implication, responsibility, and so on, is how the convivial world is experienced. We *belong to it* "beyond our wanting and doing," and aesthetic experiences make the living character and limits of such belonging experienceable, thinkable, utterable, and perhaps transformable. They make experienceable, thinkable, utterable, and perhaps transformable who we understand this "we" and what we understand this "belonging" to be, and how we may have unwittingly limited or falsely presumed things about this "we" and this "belonging."

What is *striking* in such experiences is the realization that these convivial co-inhabitations have already always and everywhere been going on and that I have already always and everywhere been living in their midst, however unaware I may have been of their formative and constitutive effects (Gadamer [1989, p. 341–80] calls this phenomenon "historically effected consciousness"). Again, this is why self-consciousness is not an adequate starting point for understanding such experiences. Such experiences are often accompanied by a weird, almost embarrassing bemusement, even humiliation, regarding that unawareness: "*Where have I been?*" (Jardine 2008c, p. 161)

In another context, Gadamer (2007a, p. 131) beautifully alludes to Rilke's poem "On the Archaic Torso of Apollo" (see Palmer 2007, p. 124), when he describes this same experience in light of the work of art:

> The intimacy with which the work of art touches us is at the same time, in enigmatic fashion, a shattering and demolishing of the familiar. It is not only the impact of "This means you!" ["*Das bist du!*"] that is disclosed in a joyous and frightening shock; it also says to us: "You must change your life!"

Aesthetic experience, writ large or small, is thus a reverse of the movement of the inward contraction necessitated by the "requires nothing but itself" logic of substance. Once you become practiced in allowing such experiences to "expand to their full breadth of illuminative meaning" (Norris-Clarke 1976, p. 188), something very disorienting begins to occur:

> *Every word* breaks forth as if from a center and is related to a whole, through which alone it is a word. *Every word* causes the whole of the language to which it belongs to resonate and the whole world that underlies it to appear. (Gadamer 1989, p. 458, emphasis added)

This is a central characteristic of this concealed experience of thinking exemplified, but not limited to, aesthetic experience. To be a word, a thing, a person, entails this outward movement, a "responding [to] and summoning [of]" (p. 458) multiple and multifarious worlds. Gadamer characterizes this ecstatic outward movement—a "dimension of multiplication" (p. 458)—as an *ontological* matter that "breaks open the *being* of the object" (p. 362). It breaks open not only *what* we understand something to be, but also *how* we understand it, and our understanding of it, to *exist*. The ontology of the thing and the ontology of the one experiencing that thing undergo a shift away from the logic of substance, where a thing or a self is what it is independently of anything else. The thing experienced and the one undergoing such an experience are both released from the seeming security of self-containment out into convivial, difficult, and multifarious worlds, and we can begin to understand and experience the world and ourselves as such, as multiple, as making and being made, as unfinished and full of co-inhabitations that go far beyond my experience of them. In "enigmatic fashion," the once-familiar, routine, ordinary and taken-for-granted becomes strange and full of forgotten relations who have something to say to be about who I thought I was and who I might be becoming.

"A substance is that which requires nothing except itself in order to exist" (Descartes 1640/1955, p. 255) will not do, here. On the contrary, hermeneutically understood, "only in the multifariousness of voices does [any word, any thing, any 'self'] exist" (Gadamer, p. 284), even though we live, for the most part, in sleepy unawares of this ontological condition and the experiences that invoke, invite, and betray it.

There is, of course, an ecological echo here to this image of breaking forth wherein each seemingly isolated thing in reality *is* its constitutive ecological surroundings. Things *are* all of their convivial relations. We can *draw* boundaries around such matters, and such drawing is commonplace and often vitally necessary. But we can't *give* such matters a boundary (Wittgenstein 1968, p. 33). Even though, in the day-to-dayness of things, we can identify this tree, that bird, and so on, this familiarity and ordinariness can block our ability to experience and understand that somehow, that Pine Grosbeak at the feeder *is* these Rocky Mountain foothill surroundings, as it also somehow *is* the breath I intake when it suddenly appears, wakes me up and whispers, in a small a fleeting way, that I must change my life if I am to understand this ecological, pedagogical, and hermeneutic complicity and conditionedness.

The sort of knowledge and experience requisite of such a challenging ontological insight is tellingly characterized by Gadamer (1989, p. 260) in a way that itself has ecological echoes. It is "knowing one's way around."

IV

This is the radical challenge that comes from letting go of the ontology of substance (see Chapter 11). Any word, any thing, any "self" requires *everything else* in order to exist. Differently put, any word, thing or self only properly *is* in the whole world. Experienced or understood out of relation to the whole, a word, thing, or self is no longer understandable as *what it is*, but only *as rendered* by our wanting and doing. And even as thus rendered, our rendering is *itself* part of this whole. It is one of the things we can do, sometimes to breathtaking effect. If we forget this, and project the (again, often warrantable and necessary and understandable) *outcome* of our isolating rendering as the reality of the world, we commit a grave error, mistaking our willful drawing of boundaries for an ontological reality that antedates the convivial life in which such drawing occurs as a sometimes-warranted way to proceed.

This inversion is what hermeneutics wishes to critique in its critique of sciences' dominance and forgetfulness. It is not that it should "toe the line" and do something different within the domain of its doings, but that it, in its dominating power, has occluded *its own living origins*. The convivial life-world, that very world which hides under the will to dominate and control, is the world *within which* dominating and controlling are often vital and worthwhile ways to proceed *and not the other way around*. The world under threat does not capture "the way the world really is" but describes, rather, one of the things that we, *in* this convivial, ongoingly negotiated and multifarious world, can and sometimes must do, often with breathtaking results. The clarity and distinctness of threat-induced and hardened identities (A=A) that result "does not change in the least the fact that these are human formations, essentially related to human actualities and potentialities and thus belong to . . . the life-world" (Husserl 1970, p. 130). By reversing this situation and claiming objectivity for itself and subjectivity for all others, logico-mathematical knowledge erases from memory its own living basis, the very basis that makes it a *living* discipline. Once we take the *results* of threat to be the "reality" that was there all along, hidden underneath what then becomes understood as the convivial "surface" (underneath, one might say, the "veil" of conviviality—see Chapter 1), everyday life becomes imagined to be a sort of opinion-filled, perspective-filled, "these are my experiences"-filled, post-hoc, revocable and provisional, subjective froth with no knowledge or truth value attached.

It is thus not the objective sciences' *understanding of the world* that is at issue for hermeneutics. It is the objective sciences' *understanding of themselves* that has gone amiss, especially within the confines of schooling. For example, the life of mathematics as a living, convivial, traditional and contemporary, debatable and settled, set of practices, forms of evidence, ways of speaking and arguing, ways of demonstrating and debating, is replaced with the amassed and to-be-memorized information demanded by standardized examinations. Teachers start "teaching to the test" by teaching, not the practice of mathematics, for example, but only its rote and repeatable rules and their efficient application. One loses track of the living fields out of which such rules emerge and within which such rules might find the proper measure of their application. Students and teachers alike thus get cut off from the very life-world of that living discipline as something actually practicable in the world.

This systematic and deliberate erasure, in schools, of the convivial experiences of the living practice of a living discipline of, say, mathematics, and instead teaching to the test that requires only filled-in blanks on standardized examinations that can be marked by a machine, even fails at its own goal. Even though many teachers protest that, with high-stakes examinations coming, there is no time for the "frills" of convivial exploration, such seeming "frills" prove to be vital to those teachers' professed interests, the interests of their students, and the well-being of the living disciplines of knowledge that are entrusted to them in schools. In a study of 12,800 students from 26 elementary and secondary schools, those who worked in classrooms that engaged mathematics as a living discipline saw a statistically significant increase in their performances on standardized provincial examinations, as high as 1.5 standard deviations in some classes. Those who were in classrooms that maintained the status quo and continued to "teach to the test" saw no statistically significant change in such measures of student performance (Friesen 2010).

V

"The sciences are self-sufficient and alone guarantee their own reflection" (Piaget 1965, p. 225). This captures in quick turn the dilemma hermeneutics faces when attempting to step outside of the logic of self-enclosure, and how hermeneutics must constantly have an ear cocked to how this logic has become deeply encoded in the convivial world and our attempts to understand it. The promise to be self-sufficient and self-guaranteeing that comes from threat-based enclosure in fact occludes its own ability to understand itself and its origins in the convivial world.

Even that most obvious and commonplace of things, "experience," is entangled in these shadows and dropped threads. This is why, in *Truth and Method,* a great deal of attention is given to the difference between the two German terms for "experience": *Erlebnis* (Gadamer 1989, p. 60–80) and *Erfahrung* (p. 346–61). *Erlebenis* is etymologically linked to the intimacies of one's personal and inner life (*Leben*, to live). *Erfahrung* contains the roots both of a journey (*Fahren*) and of ancestry (*Vorfahren*, those who have journeyed [*Fahren*] before [*Vor-*]). Hermeneutically understood, therefore, in these aesthetic moments, we are drawn out of ourselves, our constructions, our methods and our "our"-centeredness, and invited into something of a worldly sojourn, an *experience* (*Erfahrung*) that does not issue from "myself."

Of course, there is something of *Erlebnis* in such moments of being drawn out of ourselves—"This means you!" (Gadamer 2007a, p. 131); "from it no one can be exempt" (1989, p. 356), it is "not something anyone can be spared" (p. 356) or undergo on someone else's behalf (see Arthos 2000). Moreover:

> Everything that is experienced is experienced by oneself, and thus contains an unmistakable and irreplaceable relations to the whole of this one life. Its meaning remains fused with the whole movement of life and constantly accompanies it. One is never finished with it. (Gadamer 1989, p. 67)

And this is because, as with my students and them with theirs, I am never finished with living the life *in which* a particular experience has occurred and in which it is constantly being re-sorted, re-evaluated, remembered, forgotten, highlighted, or ignored. However, *what* I am summoned to experience (*Erfahrung*) transcends the limits of my experience (*Erlebenis*) and is not available in a simple reflection upon an inner inventory of my perspectives, beliefs, or opinions. "The whole of this one life" is not lived inside a "cabinet of consciousness" (Heidegger 1962, p. 89) and interacting with the world only within the limits of my own wanting and doing. This is why hermeneutics does not remain within the confines of phenomenology and its interest in reflecting on the immanent confines of what is *given* in lived-experiences (*Erlebenisse*). My convivial life in and through the world is not laid out in front of me as a given open to simple self-conscious reflection, nor is it laid out as something whose shape and future is wholly within the purview of my wanting and doing. My life and my experiences are experienced, not as a given but as "a task that is never entirely finished" (Gadamer 1989, p. 301), and, despite its lived intimacy as my life and no one else's, it is experienced as a task which is akin to Bronwen Wallace's (1987, p. 47–8) wonderful insight about anthropological artifacts: "The shards of pottery, carefully labeled and carried up through layered villages flesh out more hands than the two that made them." That pottery shard itself carries this convivial ontology with it, fleshing out villages and hands, summoning worlds, breaking forth "*as if* from a center" (Gadamer 1989 p. 458, emphasis added), and *Erfahrung*, "experience," bears a kinship here to this convivial ontology. It is something undergone in the world, with others, and within the not-at-all revocable and provisional limits of that multifarious co-inhabitation. My own life, in all its lived, experiential immediacy (summoned by the term *Erlebenisse*) fleshes out more lives and is full of more "experiences" (*Erfahrung*) than this confine of "myself."

Differently put and just like this pottery shard, *I am* only in the whole of the world which I will not outlive or outrun. Unlike this pottery shard, I also must learn to *live with this insight* and suffer it. This whole, convivial world does not belong to me as my conscious and cabinet possession. I belong to it. This is the great movement of part and whole that Gadamer explores far beyond the confines of textual interpretation. It is important to note that it also hints at how this hitherto concealed experience is full of a penumbra of *mortality* that is at the heart of the pedagogical prospect of setting things right anew. "What has to [be] learn[ed] . . . is not this or that particular thing, but insight into the limitations of humanity. This experience is the experience of human finitude. The truly experienced person is one who has taken this to heart" (Gadamer 1989, p. 357). I can only speculate that perhaps it is *this insight* that is most deeply concealed and most deeply and silently serves as the hidden impetus for our often-frantic and often-accelerating efforts to secure ourselves against the conviviality of the world and ourselves within it. To the extent that our very impermanence and mortality itself is experienced as a threat against which we can secure ourselves, we find ourselves in "a state of permanent war"

(Wood 2006, p. 16) and the convivial world, and our insight into its mortal life and our mortal lives within it, becomes once again occluded.

VI

This sort of knowledge and truth that hermeneutics seeks—one might call it "becoming *worldly*"—bodes not just for the displacement and decentering of self-consciousness but also for its humiliation. What comes along with cultivating this hermeneutic experience of the convivial world is the inevitable insight: "*The center is everywhere.* Each and every thing becomes the center of all things. This is the absolute uniqueness of things, their reality" (Nishitani 1982, p. 146):

> *Kai enthautha*, "even there," at the stove, in that ordinary place where every thing and every condition, each deed and thought is intimate and commonplace, that is, familiar, "even there," in the sphere of the familiar, *einai theous*, "the gods themselves are present." (Heidegger 1977a, p. 234)

"Something awakens our interest–that is really what comes first!" (Gadamer 2001, p. 50). "Something is going on, (*im Spiele ist*), something is happening (*sich abspielt*)" (Gadamer 1989, p. 104; we can see in the German terms here the reason for Gadamer's [1989, p. 101ff.] exploration of "play" [Spiel] as providing a clue to the ontology of such matters). Something is *always already everywhere* going on, something has *always already everywhere* happened and this happenstance of the aesthetic experience of such already-realities always arrives too late for a consciousness bent on asserting is dominance over such matters.

This is the *aesthesis*, the intake of breath—the "hale" in its suggestion of wholeness—when something happens that hits home and calls for our attention. "Understanding begins . . . when something addresses us. This is the first condition of hermeneutics" (Gadamer 1989, p. 299) and in such address, we experience ourselves as *called upon* to make something of the world(s) that thus open up and surround the life we thought we knew. This is the breaking of the hubris of self-consciousness that imagines itself to be first and foundational. This is the "hitherto concealed experience" (Gadamer 1989, p. 100), often cast in a zone of deep shadow (Illich 1992, p. 19).

When we are struck and drawn out into the convivial world, what we encounter no longer has

> the character of an object that stands over and against us. We are no longer able to approach this like an object of knowledge, grasping, measuring and controlling. Rather than meeting us in our world, it is much more a world into which we ourselves are drawn. [It] possesses its own worldliness and, thus, the center of its own Being so long as it is not placed into the object-world of producing and marketing. The Being of this thing cannot be accessed by objectively measuring and estimating; rather, the totality of a lived context has entered into and is present in the thing. And we belong to it as well. Our orientation to it is always something like our orientation to an inheritance that this thing belongs to, be it from a stranger's life or from our own. (Gadamer 1994, p. 191–2)

This hermeneutic insight into the convivial interdependence of things weighs a bit heavy at first, but it does portend a pedagogy left in peace that is simple, pleasurable, and intellectually venturous and immediate.

Pursuing such a pedagogy has a strange but familiar effect. An inheritance—wherein every thing we encounter (the hesitations of commas, this hypotenuse, that characterization of democracy in Social Studies, in fact, *every single curriculum mandate*) has within it the totality of multiple lived contexts—is never experienced as just indifferently lying there but has been, deliberately or otherwise, *handed to us* as something we are always already everywhere multifariously and variously *in the midst of*. We find *ourselves* living there, multifariously and variously, here, and there, aware or unawares. It is never an object we are dealing with but always an entrustment, and our already always everywhere "interest" (Latin, from *inter* ["in the middle of"] *esse* ["things"]) in such matters is what teachers wish to cultivate in their students and in themselves. It is as if we are being handed back ourselves in being handed such matters. Finding these threads of interest is finding the hermeneutic experience at the heart of pedagogy.

VII

> The knowledge, skills, and attitudes listed in the curriculum guides are not fixed and final and given and meant simply to be delivered. Rather, such matters are, by their very nature, susceptible to a future (new questions, concerns, evidence, applications, transformations, additions, re-interpretations, explorations, occlusions, discoveries, happenstances and so on) that is *still arriving*. *That* is what it means to call mathematics or poetry or biology or writing a *living* discipline. It doesn't simply mean that there are lots of old books, old ancestors, and fixed cannons of wisdom that students must simply accept as given and finished and final. It means that this still-arriving, yet-to-be-decided future will have something to say about what we have understood these old books, these canons, these wisdoms and ancestors to mean, [more strongly put, what we have understood them to *be*]. In such a light [each moment of convivial work] *adds itself* to that ongoing, living conversation. In understanding a contour of, for example, the living discipline of mathematics, we take part in something which abounds beyond the bounds of our own efforts and, in such partaking, we keep such matters open to question, susceptible to the future. That, we suggest, is what good teachers spontaneously do–they keep the world(s) open to the arrival of the young, and they teach the young the ways of such worlds. And, to spin this again, we learn from the young what might become of this world, because they always bring with them the questions that we could have not asked without their arrival. Simple, in its own way. To experience such abundance–to experience, paradoxically, how a curriculum topic goes beyond my experience of it–is an experience of its truth. (Jardine, Clifford and Friesen 2006, p. 211–12)

Those very mundane topics listed so dully in the curriculum guide thus undergo an "increase in being" Gadamer (1989, p. 40), if we treat them properly. If we treat them properly, as living features of a convivial world, nothing is quite yet what it will be. Those topics undergo such an increase because they "are not" yet fully themselves because they *are* open to a future that has yet to arrive where they will be taken up anew, beyond our wanting and doing. "A" is thus never quite equal to itself. This defines their *living* character. Thus, even though, to use Jean Piaget's term, we find that our living shapes itself into plateaus of equilibrium (but see Chapter 3), or, to use Hans-Georg Gadamer's terms, that the Spiels of our living transform themselves, with our work and attention, into "structures" and "works", this transformation is not into something impervious and self-identical. These structures and works and plateaus remain vulnerable and susceptible, they remain interpretable. Treating them as if they are not, trying to harden them so that they become invulnerable to the threat of becoming, changes their nature.

So, "even there, in that ordinary place," in my Elementary School Curriculum Inquiry class a few years ago, something familiar and commonplace comes up, a structure that has seemingly lost its Spiel. Many of the students had practicum placements in classrooms where, routinely, every morning, day after day, children and teachers gathered to "do calendar." Many of my students complained that this had become a time of rote repetition, of a rather mind-numbing slowness. A sense of heavy familiarity surrounded these classroom practices.

An envelope with the names of the days of the week, another with the names of the months of the year, another with the numbers 1 through 31, plastic slots where the words "Yesterday was . . . " "Today is . . . " and "Tomorrow will be . . . " were carefully printed out, and where, each day, the names of the days of the week could be re-slotted. Each morning, yesterday's yesterday-name gets put back in the day-names envelope, and yesterday's today-name gets move to the "Yesterday was . . . " slot. Yesterday's tomorrow-name gets moved into the "Today is . . . " slot, and a new name is fished out of the names-envelope to fill the now-vacant "Tomorrow will be . . . " slot. Often the numbers of the days already past that month are read through in unison, and the next number is found and clipped on to the display. And, as for the numbers 1–31, during October, they were printed on orange pumpkins in an effort to liven up things a bit with Halloween approaching, and everyone in my class, now coming up to mid-January, already knew that there were numbers on red hearts coming in February, and 31 neatly numbered green construction paper Christmas trees were already stored away 'til next December.

And, of course, each day, a Popsicle stick was put in a cup marked "ones" tacked to the wall underneath the calendar. And each day, the number of sticks was counted. And every 10 days, these "ones" were bundled up with an elastic band and put in another cup marked "tens," and those bundles themselves were re-counted on each arrival of a new bundle.

As one practicum student said, "My kids 'get it' already. They're bored. Enough!" Things had deadened, flattened out, and this morning ritual had become full of hardened, mindless repetitions. Everyone in my class knew about the (admittedly limited and unspectacular) value of learning the days of the week, learning about past, present, and future tenses, about place value, and so on and on. But this time was no longer a convivial morning gathering and settling, no longer educative or informative, no longer interesting. As the old Latin etymology indicates, teachers and students alike no longer experienced this as being in the middle (*inter*) of something (*esse*) to which we variegatedly belong. Nothing, it seems, is going on. Little is happening. Despite the joyous perseverance with which this classroom routine may have begun at the beginning of the school year, it now "speaks out of a story which was once full of enthusiasm, but now shows itself incapable of a surprise ending. [We have] heard enough" (Smith 1999d, p. 135).

So the question came up: "Should we do calendar in our classrooms?"

"Young people [my students, and those students in their practicum and future classrooms] want to know if, under the cool and calm of efficient teaching and excellent time-on-task ratios, life itself has a chance, or whether the surface is all there is" (Smith 1999d, p. 139). We began a discussion in our curriculum class about whether the surface is all there is in these days of the week, and this odd parade of names that circle by our students, and us, over and over again. Why do we repeat these over and over again? Is there life here, or just routine thoughtlessness and memorization, stuff students simply "need to know"? Is there some experience to be had here, some memory to be revived, some story to be told, here, under the hardened, flattened, familiar surface?

> A teacher who remembers well teaches curriculum as a story, not just as a collection of trivia which seems to have no connection with anything but itself and which must be remembered in an unhealthy was, that is, crammed, to pass an exam. (Smith 1999d, p. 135)

Despite the immediacy of the arrival aesthetic experiences and their draw, at first, when we come upon something heretofore unexamined and unconsidered, some cultivation is often necessary, some work is needed to prepare ourselves, to break up the hard ground, to invite arrival. It often takes whiling and gathering and returning—work and persistence—to become able to experience being addressed. We all, after all, have been well-schooled out of such matters and such practice. As we slowly began our curriculum class discussion, variously and multifariously, different students knew something of these days and their names, had thought or heard of it once, or had never heard of it before and thought it was just a bunch of names, and on and on. Laptops opened. Brief searches. Scrawls on whiteboards.

"Look at this!" and a few students gather around a screen, one search leads to another, one thread gets caught in the weave of another.

Things, slowly, started to *stir*. And at first, these matters are precisely that: slow, timid, chaotic, and we don't yet understand if we would even recognize whether or not something was telling in what we found.

Sunday, Monday, Tuesday, Wednesday, Thursday, Friday, and Saturday.

This old Biblical round of seven. Even just saying this much causes inhalations of breath, a recognition that not only have we spotted something about these matters but also we have been spotted by something that knew us before we knew it. It becomes a bit more understandable why, if this is perceived as a threat, we might try to close such things down and prevent them from ever happening again. Here, in the comfort (etymologically linked to common strength or fortitude) of our class, we are left in peace and thankful for the leisure, time, and opportunity that such thinking requires. Not all of my student-teachers are so blessed in their practicum placements, nor will they necessarily be offered teaching positions in schools where such thinking is cultivated and condoned. This, too, is part of our hermeneutic conditionedness and a frequent topic in our classes.

The names that light day and night, a cluster of old Norse and German gods, and One old Roman name for one of the wanderers, one of the planets (itself from the Greek *planan*, "wanderer").

Moments of *aesthesis*, "brought up short and alerted to possible differences" (Gadamer 1989, p. 268). "What?" "Really?" Plus, of course, a low-level anxiety as something heretofore seemingly fixed, finished, and solid starts, just slightly, to *quicken*.

One brief text we read together more than once in this class is a passage from Clarissa Pinkola-Estes' *Women Who Run with the Wolves* (1996, p. 27–8). It reads like an allegory to the experiences we are undergoing in searching for the life in the often dull, dry bones we've inherited:

> The sole work of La Loba is the collecting of bones. She is known to collect and preserve especially that which is in danger of being lost to the world. Her specialty is said to be wolves.
>
> She creeps and crawls and sifts through the *montanas* . . . and *arroyos* . . . looking for wolf bones, and when she has assembled an entire skeleton, when the last bone is in place and the beautiful white sculpture of the creature is laid out before her, she sits by the fire and thinks about what song she will sing.
>
> And when she is sure, she stands over the *critura*, raises her arms and sings out. That is when the rib bones and leg bones of the wolf begin to flesh out and the creature becomes furred. La Loba sings some more, and more of the creature comes into being; its tail curls upward, shaggy and strong.
>
> And La Loba sings more and the wolf creature begins to breathe.
>
> And La Loba sings so deeply that the floor of the desert shakes, and as she sings, the wolf opens its eyes, leaps up, and runs away down the canyon.
>
> Somewhere in its running, whether by the speed of its running, or by splashing its way into the river, or by way of a ray of sunlight, or moonlight hitting it right in the side, the wolf is suddenly transformed into a laughing woman who runs free toward the horizon. (Estes 1992, p. 23–4)

My students had already expressed how this routine of calendar had become like dry bones, and we've started to collect more and more at-first skeletal pieces until, as we start to sing over these bones, they begin to flesh out, to take on a life of their own, a life we are able to experience as a living world into which we are drawn.

And that last few lines about *La Loba*, that, by some happenstance of sunlight, moonlight, splashing, or running, the wolf becomes the one who has been singing, now laughing. As happens so often in this class, once the dry bones get sung over properly, the life they take on proves to be the life in the midst of which I have already been living without quite knowing it.

This "doing calendar" business is not an arms-length object we're exploring, but—as paradoxical as it might seem—it is something of our own living we've been singing over. We, too, have quickened.

Breathe. This quickening is not a threat but a sign of life, and again, hermeneutics claims this experience as an immediate phenomenological reality, one that happens over and over again in classrooms dedicated to a pedagogy left in peace. It is not some sort of poetic trick (even though Hermes, along with the wolf's cousin, Coyote [see Jardine, Clifford and Friesen 2008e], were most certainly tricksters). It is experientially available, cultivatable, repeatable, and, over time, we can become experienced in such "singing."

This quickening is a sign, like a track that has been found that portends something as yet unseen, a clue to an always already everywhere world of living relations we didn't quite know we had.

Tracks. Latin: *vestigia*, like the root of the word "investigation."

So, the Sun, the Moon, Tiw, Odin, Thor, Frieia, and Saturnus.

Day, Night, Law/War/Heroism, Wisdom/Magic/Poetry/Leadership, Thunder, Love/Beauty, and Agriculture (but also slowness and melancholy).

"Every experience worthy of the name thwarts an expectation. Insight is more than the knowledge of this or that situation. It always involves an escape from something that had deceived us and held us captive" (Gadamer 1989, p. 356). This captures another thread of the German term *Erfahrung*—it means suffering something in the sense of undergoing something, being affected by or subjected to something. The old familiar belief that these names of days were just names is shown to be deceptive and to have been holding us captive, and letting go of that familiarity and its cold comforts lends credence to the idea, explored by Gadamer (1989 p. 356), of "'learning through suffering' (*pathei mathos*)." The trick, of course, is to not retract from such learning as if it were a threat to myself. It is, rather, formative of my self, my becoming who I am (*Bildung*), and without it, I simply, as Wendell Berry (1983, p. 92) put it, arrive at the world unprepared. *This* is what is involved in the hermeneutic version of the Enlightenment call "*Sapere Aude!*" Thinking for oneself about and in the midst of this convivial world in which we live must be won and re-won over the course of one's life. "This experience is always to be acquired, and from it no one can be exempt" (Gadamer 1989, p. 356), and, as my student-teachers slowly learned, every time a new topic, a new curriculum mandate, a new routine, a new student, arrives, one must venture *all over again*.

Make no mistake, "understanding is an adventure and, like any adventure, it always involves some risk" (Gadamer 1983, p. 141). (An "adventure is 'undergone,' like a test or a trial from which one emerges enriched and more mature" [Gadamer 1989, p. 69]—this is why, in schools, there is a great conversation to be had about having *good* tests). The thing that takes courage and resolve is to experience how venturing out into these surroundings is not a threat to my*self*. It *is* "myself" in its full countenance. What is put at risk is only that false sense of permanence and self-containment and that false security-belief in the permanence and containability of the things we teach and learn.

So, perhaps, with "doing calendar," what has become routine is in reality a ritual, festive, weekly return, a whiling and recurring time, perhaps, to remember something that is easily forgotten. Instead of just being a way to memorize the days' names (like a curriculum requirement to be "covered"), perhaps this passage of names and days also can be taken up as a way to make these matters alive and *memorable*, even *memorial* (Jardine 2006d; see Jardine, Bastock, George and Martin 2008b).

Our classroom conversations then began to roil. Students began experiencing that these threads were no longer simply a vast pile of anonymously amassed knowledge but rather sketches of a convivial life we were *already living*, around which we had already been convivially gathering, day after day, without quite knowing it.

"What about, every Monday, reading an old story about the moon?"

"The Hubble has new pictures. I saw them this morning on the news."

Already it seems like we memorially remember and invoke the night and its light, the Moon, every seven days. Nocturnalness is part of who we are in a myriad of ways (cascade—night-time animals, what the city does at night, darkness and light, and on and on).

> A new idea is never only a wind-fall, an apple to be eaten. It takes hold of us as much as we take hold of it. The hunch that

> breaks in pulls one into an identification with it. We feel gifted, inspired, upset, because the message is also a messenger that makes demands, calling us to quite a present position and fly out. (Hillman 2005a, p. 99)

Monday on the calendar (from the Latin *calendarium*, "the account book") becomes an opportunity, an opening, into old and multifarious tales about the world, one seemingly being now told *to* us, faint whispers at first.

"Perhaps something about storms on Thursday?"

"We need to talk about that hail we had, and this climate change thing."

Or some old mythological tales of Odin and his Northern European wanderings? Perhaps any old tale of journeys, then, might befit something of Wednesday and its convivial undertow. Perhaps even Max's journey to and from *Where the Wild Things Are* (Sendak 1988) might be worth reading here, read differently than we had perhaps first imagined, read as a distant kin to those journeys of Odysseus delved deeply into years and years ago with Grade Two students (Jardine, Clifford and Friesen 2008d). Wednesday—the day we celebrate journeys—might become *interesting* and its repeated return might become of *festive* celebration and returning and gathering:

> In each of these diverging stories all the others are reflected, all brush by us like folds of the same cloth. If, out of some perversity of history, only one version [A=A] of some mythical event has come down to us, it is like a body without a shadow, and we must do our best to trace out that invisible shadow. (Calasso 1993, 147–8)

As we slowly worked our way, in our class, to trace out these invisible shadows, what slowly developed was

> a polyphonic text, none of whose participants would have the final word in the form of a framing story or encompassing synthesis. It might just be the dialogue itself, or possibly a series of juxtaposed paratactic tellings of a shared circumstance, or perhaps only a sequence of separate tellings in search of a common theme, or even a contrapuntal interweaving of tellings, or of a theme and variations. (Tyler 1986, p. 126)

Slowly, our own festive returning and reweaving of this once-routine and untelling list of names and days became an allegory for how these student-teachers might begin weaving their way through these tales in their own classrooms.

VIII

Then, in that University class and its interweaving and crisscrossing roil of days and names and stories, two sudden events.

One student mentioned French day-names, *Lundi*, Luna, and the old tales of madness, lunacy. Another feature of *aesthesis*: laughter, where the Moon and Luna and lunacy suddenly reveal themselves as having always been enjoined and the insight hits home.

Another, German, Thursday, Thor's day, *Donnerstag*. "*Donner* is the word for thunder in German, like Thor and his hammer."

Another student called out "Donner and Blitzen, yeah, thunder and lightning" and that *aesthesis* moment that James Hillman spoke about, the "uh" of halted breath that indicates the truth of such experiences, occurred in spots around the class.

One student, in hearing what was for him the long-since familiar, Christmassy names of Donner and Blitzen, and experiencing them breaking open right before his eyes, smiled, yet muttered "Oh no." Something is going on, always, already, everywhere, "even there ... in that ordinary place where every thing and every condition, each deed and thought is intimate and commonplace" (Heidegger 1977a, 234). We are "always already affected" (Gadamer 1989, p. 300). Spotted!

But there is always a sting here in this "oh no." One might believe that we are just playing with possibilities, here, brainstorming, seeing opportunities everywhere. However:

> [o]pportunities are not plain, clean gifts; they trail dark and chaotic attachments to their unknown backgrounds, luring us further. One insight leads to another; one invention suggests another variation. More and more seems to press through the hole, and more and more we find ourselves drawn out into a chaos of possibilities. (Hillman 2005a, p. 99)

We can easily get caught up in flightiness and, "before we have taken thought, we have been seduced into enterprises beyond our resources" (p. 99). Or, as Gadamer (1989, p. 106) describes, the onrushing *Spiel* of these matters can "outplay" us. This is why, after a long section on play as a clue to an ontological explanation of this eruptive, convivial ontology, Gadamer has a section in *Truth and Method* (1989, p. 110–20) rather ominously called "Transformation into Structure and Total Mediation." It is easy to let these storming experiences simply unravel, overwhelm, and exhaust us. Hermeneutics is not a chance for us, inquiring into these lives of ours, to simply become the flighty *puer*-spirit that runs off in all directions and in haste. In not repudiating childhood but embracing its vivifying potentialities, hermeneutics does not then want to be left "stand helpless before the child" (Arendt 1969, p. 181) and simply overrun with enthusiasm, breathlessness, haste, difference, newness, and flight. Key to hermeneutic work is the need, in the face of and in thanks to these flighty gifts, to compose ourselves in the middle of all this tumultuousness, to become experienced in these matters, not to be simply unraveled into an interdependent, co-arising world.

Herewith is named the great ambivalence of a pedagogy left in peace. It neither repudiates the flight of the new while sternly holding traditions closed against its arrival, nor the opposite:

> In education [we] assume responsibility for both the life and development of the child and for the continuance of the world. These two responsibilities do not by any means coincide; they may indeed come into conflict with each other. The responsibility for the development of the child turns in a certain sense against the world: the child requires special protection and care so that nothing destructive may happen to him from the world. But the world, too, needs protection to keep it from being overrun and destroyed by the onslaught of the new that burst upon it with each new generation. (Arendt 1969, p. 185–6)
>
> The old unilateral options of *gericentrism* (appealing to the authority of age, convention, tradition, nostalgia) and *pedocentrism* (child-centered pedagogy) only produce monstrous states of siege which are irresponsible to the matters at hand, that is, to the question of how life is mediated through relations between old and young. (Smith 1999b, p. 140)

A pedagogy left in peace, therefore, requires "living in the belly of a paradox wherein a genuine life together is made possible only in the context of an ongoing conversation which never ends yet which must be sustained for life together to go on at all" (p. 138).

> Ambivalence, rather than being overcome . . . is a way in itself. *Ambivalence is an adequate reaction...* to these whole truths. Thus, going by way of ambivalence circumvents *coniunctio* efforts of the ego, because by bearing ambivalence one is in the *coniunctio* itself. This way works at wholeness not in halves but through wholeness from the start. The way is slower, action is hindered, and one fumbles foolishly in the half-light. The way finds echoes in many familiar phrases from Lao Tzu, but especially: "Soften the light, become one with the dusty world."(Hillman 2005b, p. 41)
>
> *The true locus of hermeneutics is this in-between.* (Gadamer 1989, p. 295)

IX

What kind of truth is there in such hermeneutic experiences, if they are so full of ambivalence, paradox, fumbling, hindrances, and unfinishedness? It cannot be the sort of truth that pertains to knowledge that has amassed, where statements that are true of "X" are statements that properly correspond, within prescribed methodological and evidential limits, to objective states of affairs. In hermeneutics, we are no longer talking about statements matching up to objective states of affairs, but an experience of the breaking forth and opening up of the world in which we *already live* and in relation to which we are not the commanding, clarifying, and demanding center of that life. When we find that the names of the days of the week are cascading with possibilities, multiple, hidden lives and possible ventures, the truth of this finding does not precisely have an "object" to correspond to. We experience how what once seemed to be just amassed ("all this information is on the Internet, so why do we need to go over this?") is actually living threads that have long since been pulling on our lives and the lives of our teachers and students, shaping and defining us, beyond our wanting and doing. Opening up our ability to experience these ways of the world is opening ourselves up to its truth and ours. We have, it seems, been living a life which knows us without our quite knowing it.

That is why Martin Heidegger (1977b) reverts to a pre-Socratic term to describe this experience of truth: *aletheia*. This term has multiple connotations. It entails

- opening up and revealing what was concealed or closed
- enlivening that which seemed routine, deadened, and lethal and
- remembering that which was forgotten (in the passage over the river Lethe, to the Greek underworld [see Jardine 2006c]).

This is how the truth of convivial life is experienced (in contemporary Greek usage, *aletheia* is translated into English as "*really*?").

My knowledge of the convivial life of the world and my convivial life in it is never simply experienced as a given but rather as a task that I continually face, "a task that is never entirely finished" (Gadamer 1989, p. 301). I experience myself, these University students and this small inheritance under consideration as "being situated within an event [an "opening," if you will] of tradition [all these names, these gods, these forgotten memories, these wild things, that old Odyssey, and the jingling of reindeer, uncover, open and start to enliven those heretofore closed off and deadened routines, and all my hitherto concealed complicities and locatedness in such matters], a process of handing down" (p. 309). "Doing calendar" is thus a process of "handing down," and the truth to be had here is one of opening up what was closed, enlivening that which has become sedimented and dead, and struggling to remember what has been forgotten in this thing handed to us and handed down in schools. The terrible moral quandary here—the quandary about what the right thing to do might be—is that even the deadly and boring routine that many of those student-teachers experienced in their practicum placement is *itself* a "handing down." Either way, the truth to be had is *about this thing in the world*, *about those with whom I engage* in thinking about this thing, and, of course, it is *about me and the convivial life I've been living* beyond my wanting and doing.

Here is another feature of our hermeneutic conditionedness. A quick and cursory look around the hallways and classrooms of many schools quickly proves that there is nothing necessary or unavoidable about taking up the task of learning to experience the abundance of the world:

> The Gadamerian dystopia is not unlike others. In his version, to be glib, little requires human application, so little cultivates it. Long alienated from abiding in inquiry as a form of life and way of being, a restless humanity defers to models, systems, operations, procedures, the ready-made strategic plan, and first and last to reified concepts, long impervious to deconstruction. (Ross 2004)

The nature, culture, language, history, and institutional encoding of this type of "levelling down" (Heidegger 1962, p. 165) inherent in everyday life, and how to learn to live out from under its shadow, is part of the difficult and treacherous venture of becoming a teacher (see Ross and Jardine 2009). The flatness and self-enclosedness of things is thus a product not simply of a sort of war consciousness bent on threat and doubting demands but is also in the very nature of convivial life itself. This convivial life can fall into a zone of deep shadow with equal easy under the numbness of familiarity and routine. Ironically, leaving things thus numbed gets identified with leaving things in peace, and disturbing the peace on behalf of our convivial life becomes experienced as a threat.

X

"*Understanding proves to be an event*" (Gadamer 1989, p. 308), a moment of the fluttering open of the meticulous co-arisings that repose around anything. A second small event in our University class discussion demonstrates anew what Gadamer (1989, p. 38) called this "fecundity of the individual case" and its centrality to the cultivation of our convivial experience of the world.

The previous week, one student had mentioned that two newly arrived Afghani children, brother and sister, had joined their Grade Two class. Both knew a bit of English, but their first language was Pashto. Suddenly, now that our discussion had cracked the dull surface of the routine, "doing calendar" became disorientingly alive. It was no longer especially warrantable to simply say that these two new children would pose special problems in learning the names of the days of the week. These new arrivals were not a *problem*.

The living knowledge of days and their names is not just held by "us" nor is it held anonymously on-line. It is convivially held, in lives, in places, in languages, in traditions, as a living topic in the world. It, so to speak, faces us and addresses us while, at the same time, also faces elsewhere and speaks in languages and tones that are beyond us. And this occurs such that this thus-far presumed "us" rebounds back, such that not only calendar but also "us" starts to break open as if from a center, witnessed, not just witnessing, known, not just knowing. This is its life and ours and theirs and now ours anew as this "us" shifts, and brushes by us again, folds of the same cloth, these children, here, asking after the names of days in English, asking parents for Pashto names and their origins, helping open anew the now-very-strange Northern Europeanness of our ongoing discussions.

"What *are* the days of the week called in Afghanistan?"

Silence.

No one in our University class knew, but everyone experienced, in different ways, how the world itself unraveled and unrolled ahead in great, almost unbearably rich, abundance. We settled down a bit (one mild version of "transformation into structure" out of the cascading *Spiel* of things are those moments in a class when we gather together and gather up what we've done, what we've found) and talked, too briefly, about how the arrival of these two new students in the Grade Two class potentially made what was originally the dull routine of "doing calendar" even *more* convivially alive than it would have been without their arrival. If we begin exploring these threads, they do not just add themselves to knowledge already amassed. What we find will, inevitably, rattle through what we've come to already know and experience, reopening, re-enlivening, and remembering (both in the sense of the cultivation of memory and in the sense of adding new members to this "we," new folds to this cloth, this weave, this text). Knowledge convivially held in the life world is, *of ontological necessity*, vulnerable to being taken up anew in the midst of the ongoing exigencies of everyday life. This vulnerability is in its nature, and securing it against such vulnerability changes its nature.

The wonderful and difficult pedagogical news here is that the more we come to know about this matter and therefore about these worldly selves that we seem to have lost track of, the *greater* is that sense of being drawn. As happens in becoming familiar with learning to love a work of art, so, too, with these old names of days: "[the world] compels over and over, and the better one knows it, the *more* compelling it is. This is not a matter of mastering an area of study" (Gadamer 2007c, p. 115).

XI

> Why did he tell us to practice and find out for ourselves? Some people really worry about this. "If the Buddha really knew," they say, "he would have told us. Why should he keep anything hidden?" This sort of thinking is wrong. We can't see the truth in that way. We must practice, we must cultivate, in order to see. (Chah 2005a, p. 111)

"Why don't you just tell us?" This is a common and understandable complaint. If the knowledge in question is already amassed on the internet, why do we need to have these discussions? Can't I just have my class look it up if they are interested?

Gadamer (2007e) says that hermeneutics is, in the end, a practical philosophy that needs to be practiced. These students' complaints are always *almost* correct. There *is* something hidden from view. However, the demand to be just "told" has a hand in *keeping it hidden*. The error is in believing that someone "has" what is hidden and amassed somewhere and could just tell it if they wanted to. This hidden thing *is* available, but I, for myself, must cultivate my ability to invite, experience, articulate, remember, and care for its appearance, as must these students asking to be just told. This is a form of knowledge, but it is knowledge only cultivated and gained through *practice*. Each of these student-teachers, now having opened up a bit about "doing calendar," must, each in their own ways, find out how they might make their way with these openings and opportunities in their classrooms and in theirs and their students' lives, and they know that their students, each year, even each turn of day, will have something to say about how this unfolds and remains practicable. Their knowledge of these convivial threads of the world must be thus "ke[pt] open for the future" (Gadamer 1989, p. 340) where the prospect of setting right anew, with new students, and new circumstances, will always be at hand.

This is why learning to teach matters such as calendar cannot involve teachers simply "downloading" everything they have found onto their students. But neither can students be simply "left to their own devices" (Arendt 1969, p. 196). You cannot practice this knowledge by yourself and alone and only within the confines of the devices you have already mastered, because this *is not how this knowledge is held in the world*. Conversing, debating, investigating, reading, exploring, studying, composing, changing your mind, illustrating, performing, demonstrating what you know and giving a public account of that knowledge, letting others read back to you what they understand your understanding to be—these are not just effective pedagogical techniques, means, or vehicles for "getting across" amassed knowledge that could have just be *told*. These are not *means* but are rather *constitutive conditions of the life of this knowledge*. They are *how* this knowledge lives and is held and is cultivated in the world, and practice in these practices is becoming knowledgeable, becoming "educated." If my student-teachers want their future students to understand how this knowledge actually lives in the world and what must be engaged for such living to be cared for, they must invite their own students into the living practicability of these days and their names, and this is a one-way street. Thus, practical knowledge "demands of the person learning it the same indissoluble relationship to practice that it does of the one teaching it" (Gadamer 2007e, p. 232).

Over time, becoming more experienced in such pursuits makes you more able and willing to let this process unfold anew and more able to feel less threatened by such ventures and the transformations, small and large, that they ask of us. One learns, slowly, and left in peace, to trust, more and more, how we might "entrust ourselves to what we are investigating to guide us safely in the quest" (Gadamer 1989, p. 378). The more I practice experiencing the world this way, the more practiced I become. And the more practiced I become, the more experienced I become in being able to experience the world this way:

> The truth of [hermeneutic] experience always implies an orientation to new experience. "Being experienced" does not consist in the fact that someone already knows everything and knows better than anyone else. Rather, the experienced person

> proves to be, on the contrary, someone who . . . because of the many experiences he has had and the knowledge he has drawn from them, is particularly well equipped to have new experiences and to learn from them. Experience has its proper fulfillment not in definitive [amassed] knowledge but in the openness to experience that is made possible by experience itself. (Gadamer 1989, p. 355)

It was, after all, *because of* our opening up of calendar to Norse gods and reindeer that the absent names of days in Afghanistan hit so hard and true to the life of these matters. Our expanding experiences not only made the object under consideration more compelling the more we experienced. It made us more able to experience the compelling, re-invigorating, setting-right anew truth (*aletheia*) of this new arrival. Unpracticed, the arrival of these new children would have been simply one more thing to fit into an already established routine.

New knowledge is thus created in becoming experienced, but this new knowledge does not amass but rather, so to speak, always accrues to *someone*. It is always *someone* who is becoming experienced, and no one can become experienced on someone else's behalf. This is in the nature of our convivial knowledge of the convivial world, that it is a knowledge we have learned to live with, and we are not replaceable with each other in this learning. As such, each of us has an irreplaceable part in this convivial whole. To re-cite, "each and every thing becomes the center of all things. This is the absolute uniqueness of things, their reality" (Nishitani 1982, p. 146). Or, differently put, if those Afghani children were *not* in that student-teacher's classroom, if that speculation about their language and its names for days did not arise, *everything* would shift. Each of us thus takes on an *irreplaceable role* in the community of conversation that ongoingly constitutes this knowledge and its cultivation. For this type of knowledge, "just tell me" is inadequate.

Thus, even though this hidden thread of our convivial life *is* available, it is never fully available, all out in the open and once and for all. This hints at another feature regarding what kind of truth hermeneutics cultivates:

> Truth has in itself an inner tension and ambiguity. Being contains something like a hostility to its own presentations. The existing

> thing does not simply offer us a recognizable and familiar surface contour; it also has an inner depth of self-sufficiency that Heidegger calls "standing-in-itself." The complete unhiddenness of all beings, their total objectification (by means of a representation that conceives things in their perfect state) would negate this standing-in-itself of beings and lead to a total leveling of them. A complete objectification of this kind would no longer represent beings that stand in their own being. Rather, it would represent nothing more than our opportunity for using beings, and what would be manifest would be the will that seizes upon and dominates things. [In becoming experienced] we experience an absolute opposition to this will-to-control, not in the sense of a rigid resistance to the presumption of our will, which is bent on utilizing things, but in the sense of the superior and intrusive power of a being reposing in itself. (Gadamer 1977, p. 226–7)

Becoming experienced in some topic and practiced in its ways, therefore, has a strange effect, requiring a strange formulation: "beings hold themselves back by coming forward into the openness" (Gadamer 1977, p. 227). It is not only that the more experienced I become, the more compelling does that topic become. The more experienced I become, the more I experience how my experience is incommensurate with the living reality of the thing. What emerges, then, does not simply "exhaust itself in momentary transport" (Gadamer 1989, p. 127). Even this small Elementary School topic of calendar—the more I explore it, the more it starts to "stand there," "reposing in itself" over and above my wanting and doing. The more experienced I become, the more able I become to leave this reposing thing in peace in my understanding and experience of it. To become educated, then, means to learn to let things stand *there*, not here under the shadow of my wanting and doing.

Practice helps cultivate a sense of the abundant array of possibilities that are housed there, in the thing under consideration, and to experience them *as* possibilities that surround and house our lives, always already and everywhere. This is "not merely mastery of . . . expertise, whose task is set by an outside authority or by the purpose to be served by what is being produced" (Gadamer 2007a, p. 232). Neither is it "a question of a mere subjective variety of conceptions, but of the [topic's] own possibilities of being that emerge as the [topic] explicates itself, as it were, in the variety of *its* aspects" (Gadamer 1989, p. 118, emphasis added). Thus, part of what we are becoming experienced in is the knowledge that new students will arrive, and these old matters in which we've been living will be called to account in ways that are unforeseeable. We "must accept the fact that future generations will understand differently" (Gadamer 1989, p. 340), not because of our failure to gain command over these things, but because we succeed in understanding that the things under consideration stand there beyond any attempts to stop them from being "set right anew" (Arendt1969, p. 192) by the interdependent conditionedness and occassionality of the convivial world.

There is thus something deeply temporal in hermeneutic work, and we can catch a quick glimpse of how profound was Martin Heidegger's linking up of *Being and Time*. "Understanding and interpretation are not constructions based on principles, but the furthering of an event that goes far back" (Gadamer 1989, p. xxiv). Thing do not *exist* as objects that simply are what they are. Things *are*, in their lived, convivial reality, inherited from the past that has already shaped us, and, at the same time "open for [a] future" (Gadamer 1989, p. 340) that has yet to arrive and that will reshape what we have understood that shaping to have been. Even that which seems over and done with will turn out to be different than it was. (After all, who would have imagined that speaking in particular of the arrival of Afghani children would have the portend it has come to have? This is as much beyond our wanting and doing as is what might come of this in the future.) The full reality of things is thus always experienced as "standing in a horizon of . . . still undecided future possibilities" (Gadamer 1989, p. 112). This is why David G. Smith's (2006e) explorations of "frozen futurism" are so important to the prospect of hermeneutic pedagogy left in peace, as is a consideration of the developmentally sequenced futurism of developmental theory in education (see Chapter 3).

Knowledge of such matters, then, always involves getting in on the always already everywhere ongoing conversation, "the conversation that we ourselves *are*" (Gadamer 1989, p. 378). Such conversations "keep the object, in all its possibilities, fluid" (p. 330) as per their convivial life. As such, the economic, political, linguistic, institutional, cultural, and other forces that set up regimes aimed at excluding voices, closing off possibilities, and shutting down such conversations are the perennial target of hermeneutic critique and hermeneutic labor.

XII

> An aesthetic response to particulars would radically slow us down. To notice each event would limit our appetite for events, and this very slowing down of consumption would affect inflations, hyper-growth, the manic defenses and expansionism of civilization. Perhaps events speed up into proportion to their not being appreciated; perhaps events grow to cataclysmic size and intensity in proportion to their not being noticed. (Hillman 2006a, p. 41)
>
> We are . . . active participants in the communality of our experience of the world. Discussion bears fruit. The participants part from one another as changed beings. The individual perspectives with which they entered upon the discussion have been transformed, and so they have been transformed themselves. This, then, is a kind of progress—not the progress proper to research but rather a progress that always must be renewed in the effort of our living. (Gadamer 2007e, p. 244)

There is a pedagogy here, and it is, in its own way, hard work to maintain ourselves in this spot. I've had the luck and great fortune to spend time in dozens of classrooms with dozens of teachers and hundreds of students who understand things about these matters and their living practice, even in the shadows of troubled schools and troubled students. This way of teaching can, in small ways, begin to ameliorate suffering, and heal something of lost relations.

This spot of being left in peace so that things might break forth in all their relations and where we might then become educated and experienced in these ways of the world—this is not a spot of quietude and laxity, and it is also a bit of a rare gift, fragile, fleeting, finite. It is much easier to lose than it is to win, and is often embattled, given the embattlements that have shaped modern schooling (see Chapter 4; Friesen and Jardine 2009).

This pedagogy left in peace bespeaks a type of knowledge and a type of truth about our existence, that we and the things of this living world are always becoming what they we, and we are never finished, and this is not a problem that needs fixing or one that the promise of an ever-accelerating amassing of knowledge might ever outrun:

> One has to ask oneself whether the dynamic law of human life can be conceived adequately in terms of progress, of a continual advance from the unknown into the known, and whether the course of human culture is actually a linear progression from mythology to enlightenment. One should entertain a completely different notion: whether the movement of human existence does not issue in a relentless inner tension between illumination and concealment. Might it not just be a prejudice of modern times that the notion of progress that is in fact constitutive for the spirit of scientific research should be transferable to the whole of human living and human culture? One has to ask whether progress, as it is at home in the special field of scientific research, is at all consonant with the conditions of human existence in general. Is the notion of an ever-mounting and self-perfecting enlightenment [a notion that finds its Ideal in the self-contained ness of the "I am" and its objective correlate, A=A] finally ambiguous? (Gadamer 1983, p. 104–5)

CHAPTER SIX

"Figures in Hell"

DAVID W. JARDINE

So how do we love the world anyway? Is there a way to bless it and be blest by it, to use the language of Yeats? Despite all my revulsions over its ugliness and injustice, and my bitterness over defeat at its hands, the world remains loveable anyway. But anyway *also means any which way, any way at all, implying that there are many different openings out of self-enclosure and towards love of the world.*

—(Hillman 2006b, p. 128)

Where is our comfort but in the free, uninvolved and finally mysterious beauty and grace of this world that we did not make, that has no price, that is not our work? Where is our sanity but here? Where is our pleasure but in working and resting kindly in the presence of this world?

—(Berry 1989, p. 21)

I

A pedagogy left in peace is no tranquil and passive spot. It is the peace had in being who we *are*, the peace had in letting things and words and topics and ourselves show themselves as they are (Martin Heidegger's [1962] definition of phenomenology as *Gelassenheit*, "leaving" [see Pezze 2006] or "letting be"). Things as they are, left in peace and not retracted under the illusion of self-containment produced of threat, *are* "breaking forth as if from a center" (Gadamer's [1989, p. 458] ontological disposition of things and selves and words). They are, unthreatened, out in the open. *Even under threat they are thus*. Such is the grasping for, in the end, illusory permanence.

This points to the ecological being of things always already everywhere nested in locales that themselves have impermanence as their being. It points to the being of knowledge itself, where every topic entrusted to teachers and students in schools is always already everywhere never an isolated thing but always an opening into a living *topography*. It points to how traditions and ancestries are not simply a dead weight that pushes down on us, but living surroundings, full of voices and ghosts that always already everywhere inhabit us beyond our conscious concessions.

It, too, is the occasion of an ecological self, where "I *am*" deeply fraught and full of earthly vulnerability, even in those rare occasions of being left in peace. Out from under the cover of threat, my self is not now impervious and unchallenged but precisely not this. This is the greatest grief that comes from threat, that we imagine, falsely, that if the threat is lifted and we are left in peace, that our suffering and the suffering of things is over. On the contrary, out from under threat, a "hitherto concealed experience" (Gadamer 1989, p. 100) of the suffering of things and our selves comes forward. Out from under the shadow of threat, I can experience the permeability of my own life and experience.

I can walk, this morning, amidst the turning Fall in the Rocky Mountain Foothills and experience the bewildering, heartbreaking relief that slowly comes from knowing that these matters, and their swirls of yellowed aspens rattling in that aching blue arc and cold wind, will be open here before me on assuredly and unavoidably fewer and fewer occasions. I can experience myself being inevitably outlasted. Until I can experience myself as outlasted by these matters, I can't properly experience them as "standing there" and reposing in their own being (Gadamer 1977, p. 226–7; see Chapters 5 and 9). Of course, I sometimes experience this as a threat to myself and retract. But when I'm blessed again with the occasion of returning, cultivating, and practicing the arrival of this peace, these matters are right where I left them, patient, forgiving, waiting.

This is difficult knowledge to bear and, at the very same time, it is deeply ecstatic, generative, abundant, sensuous, and a great exhaling relief at the sudden inhaling *aesthesis* (Hillman 2006a, p. 36, see Chapter 5), because this fragile self can be experienced, in such moments, as momentarily held up in the common strength, the comfort of the world.

This is a self (of myself and of things in the convivial world) that is empty of self-existence, impermanent. We don't win real peace by desperately grasping for permanence in the face of this fact. Threat aggravates this grasping and therefore deepens this illusion of permanence. Once it gets ontologically codified into the ontology of substance—that a thing is what it is independently of its surrounds—the suffering that comes from such grasping and its inevitable disillusion (one might equally say "dissolution") becomes the ontologizing of war consciousness into hardened identities that, in reality, are "always already everywhere" (Smith 2006c, p. xxiv) co-inhabited, "fluid" (Gadamer 1989, p. 330), and passing. Under threat, we might imagine that being left in peace means each thing and each self being "left to their own devices" (Arendt 1969, p. 196), thus projecting the *outcome* of our own embattlement as the underlying ontological reality we might sometime in the future experience when left in peace.

Getting glimpses of this impermanence and experiencing ourselves and the world this way need not lead to despair or to a sort of existentialist radicalization of subjectivism (Gadamer 1989, p. 99–100) that seemingly blocks my self into its self. "The . . . question involved here is directed precisely at this subjectivism itself" (p. 99):

> *Geneson*: So when Sartre . . . goes to the tree, touches the tree trunk and says, "I feel in an absurd position. I cannot break through my skin to get in touch with this bark, which is outside me," the Japanese poet would say. . .?

> *Snyder*: Sartre is confessing the sickness of the West. At least he is honest. The [poet] will say, "But there are ways to do it, my friend. It's no big deal." It's no big deal, especially if you get attuned to that possibility from early in life. (Snyder 1980, p. 67)

It is noticeable, here and in much of his work, how Gary Snyder invokes a possibility of experiencing ourselves and the world to which one can become attuned "early in life." He also invokes (Snyder 1980, p. 86) images of living and working in a place in such a way that it remains possible to set the place right anew with our living, generation after generation:

> Some people are beginning to try to understand where they are, and what it would mean to live carefully and wisely, delicately in a place, in such a way that you can live there adequately and comfortably. Also, your children and grandchildren and generations a thousand years in the future would still be able to live there. That's living in terms of the whole fabric of living and life.

This echoes Hannah Arendt's invocation of a mortal world, which must be able to be set right anew, generation after generation: "the problem is simply to educate in such a way that a setting-right remains actually possible, even though it can, of course, never be assured" (1969, p. 192; see Chapter 5).

Both these threads from Snyder and Arendt invoke a pedagogy (see the Introduction and Chapter 11). And both form around something difficult and unspoken, that without the ontological reality of our living in an impermanent, convivial, interdependent world, pedagogy would not only be unnecessary. It would be impossible.

Inward contraction away from this difficult truth of interdependence and impermanence into a false and falsely comforting sense of "hardened identity" (Huntington 2003, p. 266) (either through the positing of a pure and eternal, fixed once and for all "I am," or through the radicalization of subjectivity found in the "blind commitment" and "nihilistic despair" of existentialism [Gadamer 1989, p. 100], where truth is simply the willful affirmation of one's despairing self [which, in our contemporary times in North America, has become little more than having an opinion that one has the "right" to loudly shout or madly type in 100 characters or less]) sets pedagogy on a path that leads, inevitably, to a state of perpetual war (Postel and Drury 2003). And this state of war, of course, sets the conditions for the continuance of such hardening.

II

Getting glimpses of this impermanence and experiencing ourselves and the world this way can lead to a cultivatable, practicable ability (see Chapters 5 and 11) to experience and love things in a "hitherto concealed" way "that transcends thinking from the position of subjectivity" (Gadamer 1989, p. 100). Think back to that strange grief of Sartre's hand trying to touch the bark of the tree. There is relief to be had in finally allowing ourselves to let go of the absurdity that comes from grasping for permanence, and experiencing, instead, the *ekstasis* (Greek, literally, out of *stasis* into movement—"break[ing] forth," recall, "*as if* from a center" [Gadamer 1989, p. 458]) of myself, a "standing outside of myself" in which I am experienced as *being* "outside":

> The self is here at the home-ground of all things. It is itself a home-ground where everything becomes manifest as what it is, where all things are assembled together into a "world." This must be a standpoint where one sees one's own self in all things, in living things, in hills and rivers, towns and hamlets, tiles and stones, and loves these things "as oneself." (Nishitani 1982, p. 280–1)

But again, to understand "the self in [this] original countenance" (Nishitani 1982, p. 162), we must also understand that, at the very same time, "*the center is everywhere.* Each and every thing becomes the center of all things. This is the absolute uniqueness of things, their reality" (Nishitani 1982, p. 146). This self, like all things, convivially co-arises and is therefore "not" its (self-contained) "self" in being itself:

> To say *that a thing is not itself* means that, while continuing to be itself, it is in the home-ground of everything else. Figuratively

> speaking, its roots reach across into the ground of all other things and help to hold them up and keep them standing. It serves as a constitutive element of their being. *That a thing is itself* means that all other things, while continuing to be themselves, are in the home-ground of that thing; that precisely when a thing is on its own home-ground, everything else is there too; that the roots of everything spread across into its home-ground. This way that everything has of being on the home-ground of everything else, without ceasing to be on its own home-ground, means that the being of each thing is held up, kept standing, and made to be what it is by means of the being of all other things; or, put the other way around, that each thing holds up the being of every other thing, keeps it standing, and makes it what it is. (Nishitani 1982, p. 149)

Every word breaks forth *as if* from a center, and that center is empty of self-existence. That "center" *is* its fielding irradiance. Every topic taken up in schools, in reality, is full of threads and reflections, of surroundings, of lives leading out into the open or into shadows left undisturbed. Things *are* empty of self-existence, which is at once to say, they are all their relations.

A pedagogy left in peace is thus a matter of, as Hongzhi Zhengjue (1091–1157) put it, cultivating an empty field (Hongzhi 1991).

III

> Within each dust mote is vast abundance. (Hongzhi 1991, p. 4)

If it is up out of the world that I, so to speak, "come to" and come to compose this impermanent self, if the self becomes itself only in relation to the company it keeps—if this is the "self in its original countenance"—what of those odd things we often surround teachers and student with in schools? Fragmented bits and pieces of once-living knowledge, shards now seemingly self-enclosed, isolated, and put under the threat of surveillance? Objects that have been deliberately stripped of any sense of ancestry, place, and topography?

If we accept this ecological and pedagogical reality, that we compose ourselves in the keeps of our surroundings (see Chapter 7), what happens to us when we surround ourselves, not with rich worldly surroundings and topics (which require the risks of venture and suffering if they are to show themselves in their being what they are), but with seemingly self-contained and isolated things?

Let's consider an ecological analogy to these isolated, deliberately unsurrounded, worldless, school activities (with the re-affirmed caveat from Ludwig Wittgenstein [1968, p. 33], that we can draw boundaries, here, but we cannot *give* these matters such isolated boundedness). Consider this Styrofoam cup I'm just about to throw away. Any relations of it or to it cannot be cultivated, chosen, cared for, remembered, enjoyed, either by us or anything else that surrounds it. I cannot easily become composed around such a thing and it does not ask this of me. There will be no mourning at its loss or destruction. It is not something to be saved or savored. It does not show its having-arrived-here and we have no need to try to remember such an arrival. All the traces of relations and endurance are seemingly gone. It appears, and then disappears, and its appearance is geared to not being noticed.

This Styrofoam cup does not *endure*. It does not age and become becoming in such aging. It breaks.

It does not reflect back to us the becoming of things, their fragile, impermanent composition and it is unbecoming to be around. It flashes on, then off. It cannot learn from its surroundings and show the wear of such learning on its aging face. And therefore, in its presence, the prospect of pedagogy is turned away.

In fact, it is produced *deliberately* in order to *not* last, *not* hold attention, *not* take on character, and *not* arouse any sense or possibility of care or concern. *It is deliberately produced in order to not be remembered.*

It is deliberately produced of forgetting. It is *Lethe*. It is lethal (see Chapter 5, for the connection here to the hermeneutic notion of truth as *aletheia*).

It is what we use so that our ability to remember the care and suffering that constitutes the interdependencies of the Earth (and therewith the possibility of remembering our own suffering) is not visible and seems to be not necessary. It very presence (which seems absent in its easy usage and disposability) de-worlds us. *It "is" in such a way that care, cultivation, and practice and the becomings (of things and of ourselves) that come with these things—all this is not even possible.* It is impossible.

And, to the extent that our lived, convivial, human life, along with the life of every word, every thing, every gesture, every culture, and tongue is, in its deepest full reality, constituted by the convivial, dependent co-arisings of all its relations, to that extent, this Styrofoam cup appears to be *impossible*, even though *there it is*.

So the problem with such things—and therefore the problem with surrounding ourselves and our children with such things—is their ecological and pedagogical impossibility. The problem with the effortless disposability of this cup is thus not simply the products or by-products of its manufacture or the nonbiodegradability of what remains of it after its use (this is ecologically consciousness at its most literal minded). The deep ecological and pedagogical problem with it is that it is unable to be cared for and living in its presence therefore weakens, undermines, or occludes our ability to see how our lives and this Earth are constituted by such convivial suffering.

This Styrofoam cup thus becomes a perfect example of a Cartesian Substance: something that is seemingly bereft of any relations, something that seems to require "nothing except itself in order to exist" (Descartes 1955, p. 255). This Styrofoam cup thus stands there in the world "by itself," as an object produced of such bereaving, and the only relief to be had around it is found precisely in its disposability. But it also promises to help us get over our sense of loss through a relentless, ever accelerating stream of consumptiveness: one faceless, bodiless, placeless, careless cup after the other all bent to the cause of never once interrupting our "wanting and doing" (Gadamer 1989, p. xxviii). It flits by fast and asks nothing of us.

We can, of course, become arousedly taken up with the conditions of its production, and with other ecological concerns, but these concerns cannot well adhere to this thing that so quickly slips away and falls from memory, this thing that is deliberately designed to do so. Remembering cannot well penetrate its slick surface. Thinking cannot easily save it from its deliberately produced isolation, because thinking has precisely been rendered unthinkable.

It's just a cup, after all, just one of billions flittering by daily.

In the summer of 1998, I taught a graduate course on hermeneutics at the University of Victoria, and we spent our last class considering James Hillman's "*Anima Mundi*: Returning the Soul to the World" (republished in 2006a). There is a certain point in this essay where the image of an object cut off from all its relations is brought up.

We had been thinking through these ideas of ecological fields of relations as a way to imagine how classrooms might be experienced. Van Gogh is not what he is without Theo (see Chapter 7), or the surroundings of the cold muds of the northern potato eaters, or the bright palettes of Arles (and how it was van Gogh that taught us to see this), or Gauguin, or the whole weird arc of European art-ancestry, its ecstatic openings and oppressive traditional weights.

The days of the week are never just names even though we try to draw such boundaries and make "calendar" simply a routine (see Chapter 5).

The rules for dropping perpendicular lines are live in their rulings (see Friesen and Jardine 2009).

So, too, with the seemingly isolated operations of one-digit addition on this Grade One classroom worksheet (see Jardine, Clifford and Friesen 2008c). These teachers in this summer class talked of how, even if this mathematics worksheet is perfectly purged of any connection to its surrounding fields of relations, those surrounding fields still surround it as its *future*. Place value and the mysteries of carrying and borrowing (to name just two relatives in the fields surrounding an isolated, one-digit-addition worksheet) will arrive, but this worksheet has cut off our access to them, and any sense that they might be our relations. This worksheet has *seemingly* cut off not only its relations to its surroundings but also its relation *to its own future*. Just like F.W. Taylor's assembly line, the surroundings and the future are not part of "what does this person," this teacher who handed out this bereft sheet, "want me to do right now?" (Taylor, cited in Boyle 2006).

The cost of this purging and sequencing of one worksheet after another, each one purged of all its relations, is that, as Wendell Berry (1983, p. 92) put it, each time a new sheet arrives, we always seem to be arriving at it unprepared. Each sheet is one more thing to do, added on to the growing, accelerating list of one piece after the other. There is nothing indigenous to any one sheet that might slow down our attention over it. Each one, like that Styrofoam cup, is designed to go by and be done with and replaced with what is next.

In that summer class, we talked about how, without the co-presence of all of its relations, something is not what it actually *is*, that is, a "relative" in a field of "relations," dependently co-arising with and in that field, exquisitely necessary to it and irreplaceably particular in its irreplaceability. It becomes rendered into an object which simply is what it is independently of anything else, that old Cartesian definition of substance (and, I've since discovered, that old F. W. Taylor condition of efficient assembly [see Chapter 4]). The difficulty in trying to invert this logic, and the common plaint that the idea of fields of relations seems too fuzzy, too large, and impracticable in an actual classroom:

> This is one of the secrets of ecological mindfulness. To understand what is right in front of us in an ecologically sane, integrated way is to somehow see this particular thing *in place*, located in a patterned nest of interdependencies without which it would not be what it is. Differently put, "understanding 'the whole'" involves paying attention to *this* "in its wholeness." This rootedness in the particular is what helps prevent ecology from becoming woozy and amorphous – a disembodied idea that misses the particularities in the flit of *this* ruby-crowned kinglet pair in the lower pine branches and how this movement is so fitting here, in the coming arch of spring in the Rocky Mountain foothills. (Jardine 2008b, p. 143)

We also considered how the idea of isolating something from its living field of relations constitutes a type of *illness*. We considered Wendell Berry's injunction: "the concept of health is rooted in the concept of wholeness. To be healthy is to be whole. The word *health* belongs to a family of words: *heal, whole, wholesome, hale, hallow, holy*" (Berry 1986, p. 103; I'm tempted, but I'll leave for now the connections between hale, the Latin *halitus*, "breath," and James Hillman's invocation of the breath of *aesthesis* and its centrality to hermeneutic work [see Chapter 5], as well as the centrality of a meditation on the breath to Buddhist considerations of the dependent co-arising of things, and how they and the "self" considering them, are empty of self-existence).

But there is something worse than mere illness afoot here.

IV

> Please, let me insist: by aesthetic response [that *aesthesis* outward breath where the breaking-forth emptiness of things and selves is experienced; see Chapters 4, 5, and 11] I do not

> mean beautifying. I do not mean planting sidewalk trees and going to the galleries. I do not mean gentility, soft background music, clipped hedges—that sanitized, deodorized use of the world "aesthetic" that has deprived it of its teeth and tongue and fingers. What I do mean by aesthetic response is closer to animal sense of the world—a nose for the displayed intelligibility of things, their sound, smell, shape, speaking to and through our heart's reactions, responding to the looks and language, tones and gestures of the things we move among. Thing-consciousness could extend the notion of self-consciousness from the constrictions of subjectivism. (Hillman 2006a, p. 40)

In that University of Victoria graduate class where we were studying James Hillman's "*Anima Mundi*: Returning the Soul to the World" (republished in 2006a), I offered up the image of a fragment of that Styrofoam cup buried 10 feet underground in some long-forgotten dumpsite. Darkwormyness. The roiling relief of decays, where all things begin, as Hillman coined it, to return to the surroundings that made them, let go of their momentary, in reality *illusory* containments, and begin to empty out into all their relations, all they relations that they *already are* (just like "every word breaks forth as if from a centre" [Gadamer 1989, p. 458] if we become practiced in hermeneutic experience [see Chapters 5 and 11]).

And then, suddenly, we arrive unprepared. Right in the midst of these rich sufferings, this dry bright-lit bright-white self-contained, "clear and distinct" (Descartes 1640/1955), fully present piece of an old coffee cup, strange to call it old, because it is freshly new in front of us, unable to let go of its self, unable to find or betray or evoke its lost relations. To use an old Heideggarianism (1962), it arrives fully present and unable to *world*. No future, no past, no relations. Bereft. It "cannot weather or age. [Its] existence is hurried by the push of obsolescence as one generation succeeds the next within a few months. [Its] suffering is written on [its] face" (Hillman 2006a, p. 39). This is no longer the gentle, heartbreaking suffering of being left in peace to impermanently become composed in the embrace of the world. It is a deeper suffering produced of illusion, one that conceals this difficult, convivial peace that comes with the experience of impermanence.

Hillman (p. 39) says that this image of an object that has "no way back to the Gods" is precisely an image of a "figure in Hell."

A sealed off, closed, purged identity (A=A), intended so often in the ancestries of Abraham and Greece as an image of a purified, heavenly figure freed of everything presumed, in light of such purity, to be "revocable and provisional" (Gray 2001, p. 36), is, ecologically and pedagogically understood, an image of a hellish figure cut off from what ought to be there for it *to be* its convivial, earthly self.

This is something worse than mere illness.

"Evil is the absence of what ought to be there." (Hardon 1985, p. 136)

CHAPTER SEVEN

Filling this empty chair

DAVID W. JARDINE &
JENNIFER BATYCKY

I

I [Jennifer] listened to many classes about hermeneutics, and after each class I seemed to be filled with the same feeling of confusion. It was not so much a confusion about what hermeneutics was, but more a perplexed feeling about how this style of inquiry was going to impact my life as a teacher. From what I initially gathered, in some sort of "magical" way, something remarkable from the life world of the classroom would simply present itself to me. It seemed that my role would be to take up this particular event and care for its message, so that the beauty of its dailiness was gently uncovered and honored. Well, I certainly had no intention of holding my breath and waiting for the hand of the curriculum god to tap me on the shoulder, delivering a profound message! As a teacher, I felt so tangled up in the everydayness of the classroom, I wondered if I could ever step far enough out of the situation to see and hear the possibilities that presented themselves daily. By the middle of October, I had resigned myself to the fact that everyone in my graduate course had received a special message from Mercury, except for me.

Wednesday, October 28, 1998. My plan for the morning was to provide the children with an opportunity to apply their imagination and skills to a descriptive writing passage. Rather than simply "teaching" all about what descriptive writing entails, I decided to select an art reproduction and share my own writing about it. My intention was to draw upon our collective background experience with art and use that as a springboard to create beautiful writing. Since the beginning of the year, the walls of the classroom had been filled with reproductions of the works of van Gogh, Gauguin, Monet, Manet, Matisse, and several others. Available, too, was a large pile of smaller, 8″ × 10″ reproductions that children could take to their work areas and ponder. Daily, we would sit in front of large reproductions and talk about them, how they made us feel, made us think, and we learned of the lives of these artists, their troubles and successes. As I read my own paragraph based on van Gogh's painting of a bedroom, I could instantly sense a connection between myself and the children. I remember thinking "This is going to be a great lesson."

One of the first student books I picked up to read was Nathan's. He had written two pages on the image of van Gogh's chair:

> The sad and lonely chair sits alone in a cold and empty room. The only warmth is a little smokeless pipe. So as the chair sits alone with still only a little warmth, the chair waits for something. But what is it? It still waits for the moment, that moment that the chair thinks will never come. The brick floor gives a chill in the air. The chair still sits by the door, waiting for the moment. But the door doesn't budge. Days pass, but everything is still. Still as a rock. So everything goes like this day after day after day. This goes on and nobody sits on the chair. Nobody even notices the chair and that's how it will stay.

When I read Nathan's passage, I felt a chill up my spine, knowing that the chair was waiting for van Gogh to return from the field in which he shot himself. During the weeks that followed, I shared Nathan's writing with colleagues both at my own school and in the system. I also shared it with friends and family members because I didn't want this event to simply be held under an awful educational gaze. Each time I shared his writing, I was met with a stunned look, followed by always well-meant comments which always seemed to dismiss this gift Nathan had given us.

"Nathan is so thoughtful. He always says the most amazing things." "What grade did you say you teach?" "You are so lucky. I could never do that with the children in my class. They just aren't capable." "Nathan is really gifted. He really ought to be tested." "Well, how are you going to extend this child's learning now? Perhaps he should have an opportunity to take his own writing and create his own picture."

How should I extend Nathan's learning? How absurd! The real question that Nathan's writing presented me with was about *my own* learning being extended. For days I carried his book and picture around with me; to my home, to meetings, around the school . . . just wondering what to do next. I found myself tempted to sit Nathan down and drill him about why he wrote what he did about van Gogh's work and what it meant. Thank goodness I refrained. Because, upon reflection, I realized that asking Nathan about his own work in this way was not going to give me what I was looking for.

In almost all of the responses to Nathan's writing no one could find a way to speak of *the work* he produced: what does this writing tell us about this painting and what we ourselves may have failed to see, to feel, to understand? About the loneliness and sadness and isolation and emptiness that van Gogh often hid under such colorful images?

What also became troublesome were questions like these: would Nathan's writing have been this rich if he had no images to build from, to rely on, if we had not pursued and practiced, with the whole class, how to respond to such works with care and thoughtfulness, if we had not read passages of Vincent's letters to Theo, or watched parts of Sister Wendy's affectionate history of art (see http://www.pbs.org/wgbh/sisterwendy/), if we had not deeply explored the worlds that these painters evoked and how they offered us a new vision of our own world, if we had not listened to what each other said about the paintings we were looking at? What does it really mean to call Nathan's work **his**? Yes, of course, it is, but what is this "of course."

When David [Jardine] came into the class later that week, I asked Nathan to read his work to him.

They went out into a quiet spot in the hall, and after reading his work to David, Nathan said "He's buried next to his brother, you know."

II

> Empty chairs had been a feature of van Gogh's thinking since childhood. The memories that crowd behind this single image are connected with deep mournfulness, with thoughts of the omnipresence of death. His own chair, simple and none too comfortable, with his dearly-loved pipe lying on it, stands for the artist himself. We may well be tempted to recall the pictorial tradition that provided van Gogh with his earliest artistic impressions. Dutch Calvinism sternly insisted on an iconographic ban that prohibited all images of the Holy Family except symbolic ones: the danger that the faithful might be distracted by the beauty of the human form had to be avoided at all costs. Thus Christ could be represented by a "vacant throne." (Walther and Metzger 1997, p. 8)

Thus, too, for van Gogh himself. He, too, can be represented by his vacant room, by the place he has inhabited—the pipe, the chair, the modesty of the surroundings, the colors that speak of Arles. This is so unlike the dark muddiness of his *The Potato Eaters* (1885), which these Grade One students also explored and discussed—and whose colors they practiced with chalks and inks and paints—which places its inhabitants so differently, in hues and colors that seem to place them right into the ground out of which their meal has come. But here, too, the surroundings are, in their own way, a portrait of those they surround. These paintings, these discussions and writing and illustrating now surround these young children and are themselves becoming, in variegated ways, part of a portrait of the children they are coming to surround. This is part of this mysterious "of course" regarding Nathan's work and what that possessive case entails.

Jennifer had her Grade One students doing "self-portraits" the same year as Nathan arrived, not by literally drawing pictures of themselves, but by drawing pictures of their rooms, the spaces they live within. She also introduced me to a wonderful, disorienting book called *Room Behaviour* (1997) by Rob Kovitz. From the back cover:

> *Room Behaviour* is a book about rooms. Composed of texts and images from the most varied sources, including crime novels, decorating manuals anthropological studies, performance art, crime scene photos, literature and the Bible, Kovitz shapes the material . . . to create an original, fascinating and darkly funny rumination about the behaviour of rooms and the people they keep.

Those room portraits that the children did, like van Gogh's painting, were akin to portraits of "vacant thrones"—portraits of spaces that a nonportrayed "subject" (for lack of a better term) inhabits. But this is not quite correct—"the subject" *is* portrayed, but the portrait is of a particular *sort* of subject. These are not portraits of an isolated, autonomous, "I myself" that somehow sits at the center of any inhabitation, but of a "self" that issues up out of and leaves traces within an inhabitation, a "keep." This "self" that these Grade One "room-portraits" (like van Gogh's painting) portray is both an ecological and a pedagogical self. It is ecological in the sense that it is empty of self-existence, and rather issues up out of and in to a world of voices and relations and ancestries and kin, of colors and palettes and hues, images and tales, up out of places, memories, and topographies and even up out of the most ordinary, everyday objects that we find ourselves surrounded by. It is pedagogical in that it is the self that is never simply itself but is always becoming itself through its worldly sojourns.

This thread is, of course, *not at all* in line with the Dutch Calvinist idea of "the vacant throne." On the contrary, what we are pointing to here is a way of loving the world and its places and loving our own straggly, convivial emergence into being who we are. These Grade One room portraits thus provide a simple critique of Cartesianism and its belief in the logical and ontological precedence of an abstract, empty, worldless "I am" in favor, instead, of an inhabitation that is the Earthly self's keep and an "I" that grows up out of and in to its sojourns in the world. It is up out of the world that I, so to speak, "come to" and come to compose "myself."

"Myself" doesn't simply disappear in ventures into such alluring, difficult places, only its sense of enclosure. This "myself" is experienced as issuing up out of the course of the experiences, not that I *have* (*Erlebnisse* [see Gadamer 1989, p. 60–70]) but that I *undergo* (*Erfahrung* [see Gadamer 1989, p. 240–62]) in and through the world. This world in which I undergo or suffer experiences, is not just inhabited and formed and fashioned by myself and by and within by own(ed) experiences, but is "always already everywhere" (Smith 2006c, p. xxiv) co-inhabited. It has always and already been formed and fashioned by shared and contested inheritances, voices and ancestries, up out of which I must slowly and continually "find" myself becoming who I am. I am surrounded by a "multifariousness of voices" (Gadamer 1989, p. 295)—and not just those issuing up out of the human inheritance, but out of all Earthly calls and keeps.

Even these late autumn birds locate, form, and fashion this worldly "I am" (Jardine 2000) in ways far "over and above our wanting and doing" [Gadamer 1989, p. xxviii])—here, spotted by these Pine Grosbeaks "before I know it" and whether I have a "lived experience" of it or not (differently put, this is a way to distinguish between phenomenology and hermeneutics [see Chapter 5, 8, and 9]).

This frail, contingent, finite, emergent, dependent "self," then, slowly finds and forms itself in and through its inhabitations, through the "rooms" that are this self's keep. But here, the possessive case is still misleading because each individual self (whatever this exactly now means) does not simply possess its keeps but is also kept by them. The character (*Bildung* [see Gadamer 1989, p. 9 and following) of this emerging self is dependent, at least in part, at least to some terrible extent, upon the company it keeps.

III

Consider, then, another take on something oddly both akin to, and radically different than, "the vacant throne." Jacques Derrida (Derrida and Ferraris 2001, p. 30–1) is speaking to the question of the difficulty of his own writing and an image arrives:

> [O]ne does not always write with a desire to be understood–that there is a paradoxical desire not to be understood. It's not simple, but there is a certain "I hope that not everyone understands

> everything about this text", because if such a transparency of intelligibility were ensured it would destroy the text, it would show that the text has no future [*avenir*], that it does not overflow the present, that it is consumed immediately. Thus there is the desire, which may appear a bit perverse, to write things that not everyone will be able to appropriate through immediate understanding. There is a demand in my writing for this excess . . . a sort of opening, play, indetermination be left, signifying hospitality for what is to come [*avenir*]. As the Bible puts it–the place left vacant for who is to come [*pour qui va venir*].

Here, the place left vacant with bread and wine at the Seder table, waiting for Elijah to arrive, does not be speak someone who has *left* but someone who is *coming*. As with "the vacant throne," it represents someone who is not here, who is not a given, not present. But this absence is no longer like the vacant throne, pointing to a once-present and now vacated Self which is now Risen, now elsewhere and still governing, perfectly akin to some Cartesian "I am" or some Husserlian "transcendental subjectivity," which experiences itself as "above this world" (Husserl 1970, p. 50). This empty chair now stands for *a future which has yet to come* (*avenir*). The futurity represented by the empty chair is not a given, not "frozen" (Smith 2000; Loy 1999), not "foreclosed" (Smith 1999d) but full of "still undecided future possibilities" (Gadamer 1989, p. 112). What will become of me, what will become of this work I am producing—all this is still coming, is not yet settled, and no amount of hurry or anxiety or effort will outrun this convivial and difficult eventuality.

In this light, the empty chair, like the Grade One room portraits, portray an inhabitant who *has a future*, who is always yet-to-be-itself, yet to fully and finally arrive. So even Nathan's lamentations over van Gogh's empty chair and the impending sense of loss and death it portends points to the fact that here we are—again, who would have thought?—over a century later and half a world away, experiencing van Gogh's suicide and the work signs he left of his life, and the room-portrait trace of his leaving. Here we are, still living out the Spiels of work he left. Not unlike Nathan himself, what van Gogh's work will turn out to be is still yet-to-be-decided and it is being decided anew right here, right now, in this Grade One classroom, and here, again, in trying to write, trying to read this convoluted chapter on this topic.

Just to complicate matters further, not just this "self" but these "keeps" are *themselves* not frozen or foreclosed or finished. They are not givens but are "open for the future" (Gadamer 1989, p. 340). The places we venture with (or without) children in (and out of) school—spelling, reading, mathematics, poetry, art, biology, chemistry, philosophy, Dutch Calvinism, Impressionism, writing, hermeneutics, ecology, and so on—are continuously becoming constituted and understood and inhabited differently. They are, so to speak, *living* places or spaces or rooms, (or, if you will, "living disciplines") that form part of our living Earthly inheritance, and as such—as *living*, that is, as susceptible to the future— we "must accept the fact that future generations will understand differently" (Gadamer 1989, p. 340). When Jennifer surrounded her classroom with prints of van Gogh, Monet, Matisse, Picasso, she was providing her class with a "roomy," generous topic/topography (see Gadamer 1989, p. 32) whose full meaning is, in its very temporal, finite, contingent nature, still being decided. To paraphrase a phrase of Derrida's (in Derrida and Ferraris 2001, p. 32), this topic and that one still has an empty chair at its table of contents, and the task of a pedagogy left in peace is to keep this chair available for arrival, and not try to fill it, secure it, or nail it down (to use another old Biblical image of attempts to, shall we say, nail down the Word once and for all and prevent it from rising up anew, with the herald of the young child by the rock rolled away from the burial Tomb) under threat of a looming future.

After all, in originally writing this chapter in 1998–9, who could have imagined that threads of Dutch Calvinism, which "sternly insisted on an iconographic ban that prohibited all images of the Holy Family" (Walther and Metzger 1997, p. 8) would have come to dovetail as it has with furor over images of Mohammed by a Danish cartoonist?

IV

The Austrian art historian Hans Sedlmayr gives the title "The vacant throne" to the final chapter of his essay in cultural criticism, *The Loss of the Centre [Verlust der Mitte]*. Sedlmayr

> writes: "In the 19th century there was an altogether new type of suffering artist: the lonely, lost, despairing artist on the brink of insanity." Van Gogh's chairs constitute a metaphor of the crisis of the entire century. (Walther and Metzger 1997, p. 9)

Here we have the late-nineteenth-century equation of the "loss of the center" with unworldly madness and despair. This line of argument is also followed in Gadamer's (1989) concern over the image of the artist as a mad or tortured genius who has no place in the world and whose works thus became like "vacant thrones" with an off-stage genius as their absent occupant. Under such an image:

> Whenever one "comes upon" something that cannot be found through learning and methodical work alone–i.e., whenever there is *inventio* where something is due to inspiration and not methodical calculation–the important thing [or so it is presumed,] is *ingenium*, genius. (Gadamer 1989, p. 54)

Under such a logic—what Gadamer (1989, p. 42–81) broadly called the "subjectivization of aesthetics"—we don't look to the works and what they have to say to us, but to the creator, the one who has generated this work, its "genius" and what the work has to say about this creator-genius ("Nathan is really gifted. He ought to be tested"). Either this, or we look to the author to tell us the "real meaning" of the text. We look for the "origin of the work of art" (Heidegger 1971, 1972) in a subjectivity, some great, off-stage "I am" that has uttered the work into existence, sometimes seemingly *ex nihilo*. Worldly works are therefore understood as "creations" which are comprehensible only insofar as we unearth or recreate the "creator" of the work. This was, according to Gadamer (1989, p. 187 and following) a central desire of Schliermacher's (1768–1834) version of hermeneutics, where understanding the work of a creator-genius, in fact, understanding any living inheritance, becomes a matter of not conviviality but "congeniality"—a matter, one might say, of "like-*mindedness*."

In Nathan's case, rather than approaching his work and the worlds it opens up and thus encountering him becoming himself *in the midst of* and *in the keep of* and *in relation to* these worlds which we, too, inhabit in our own ways, we pursue a type of subjective, psychologistic attribution of talents, backgrounds, skills, proclivities, likes, dislikes, or gifts. We want to fill the empty chair by metaphysically positing a genius/generative "I am" from whom the work gets its original/originating, authoritative/authorial meaning, its *mens auctoris*. Thus, under what could be called "the metaphysics of genius," we call out to the author to save us from the task of interpreting the questions that the work itself places *us* under.

Under the metaphysics of genius, to understand the work, then, is, to some extent, to *turn away from the work itself* toward its creator. This, of course, recapitulates a much older metaphysic (see Chapter 2): that the world itself, in all its rich array, is understandable, venerable, worthy of our attention, only insofar as it is understood as a sign of God's creative beneficence. All things are only *ens creata*, and, under this gaze, becoming enamored of any worldly thing in and for itself or in terms of its mundane, Earthly inhabitations is a form of fallenness and a source of potential deceit, deception, seduction, or betrayal. Hence an old argument that the Church has long since had with the advent of modern science: figuring out the worldly causes of worldly things is a vacuous, dangerous, and pretentious enterprise. Why? Because, in their deepest reality, all worldly things *are* "vacant thrones" pointing to the One great off-stage Creator (which becomes recapitulated in the Enlightenment's capitalization of Reason). And, to the extent that humanity is made in God's image, we, too, although in much more contingent and mundane ways, are both the Crown of the *ens creata* ("created things") *and* are ourselves, in God's image, creators of works, *ingenia*—all of which, again, becomes recapitulated in the Enlightenment's vision of Reason (see Chapter 3).

Even though it appears that we have arrived in a place that is quite arcane, traces of this phenomenon are rampant in education. To understand this gift that Nathan has handed us requires *handing it back to him*. It's *his*. Doing anything else, under the metaphysics of genius, would simply involve imposing our own views on his, robbing him of his voice and replacing his *ingenium* with ours.

We can't believe, perhaps, in reading his words that this empty, inviting, chair has been left empty *for* us.

It is my own inhabitance that is beckoned here.

You must change your life! (Gadamer 2007a, p. 131)

V

> [Martin] Heidegger shows that the work of art [and, in his later work, Earthly things and even words themselves] [are] not merely the product of an ingenious creative process, but that [they can be] *works* that [have their] own brightness in [themselves]; [they are] there [*da*], "so true, so fully existing." (Gadamer 1994, p. 23–4)

Having been through the twists and turns of this chapter, I now experience how both van Gogh's painting and Nathan's writing (and with them, all the tangle of convivial threads that weave themselves around these topics) have each become much more fulsome, troublesome, provocative, and substantial than they initially were. Each of them has become, so to speak, "stronger" and more robust than either would have been without the appearance of the other (this is a version of what Gadamer [1989, p. 367] calls the "art of strengthening"). When I imaginally venture how, at the moment of his death, Christ, the Word, called out to his father, his Author, and felt forsaken, and thread this around how the word must stand without the author to save it from interpretation, from "ongoingness," from a yet-to-be-decided future, I feel both strengthened and more vulnerable, all at once.

In fact, unexpectedly venturing into this world of Impressionist painting once again in this Grade One classroom, and ventured back into the cleaves of scholarship that surround it, having been in this place many times before and from many directions, facing Nathan's words and the reappearance of van Gogh and this cascade of empty chairs and vacant thrones and dreams of rooms and habitations, I'm struck again by how increasingly incommensurate to this Earthly place is my knowledge and experience of it. In fact, the more I experience of this place, the more often I find my way around it, the more threads of referentiality and ancestry and dependence and kin that I can muster, the more incommensurate my knowledge and experience become.

Put the other way around, the more often I venture to this place, the more experiences I have of it, the better *it* gets. If we are blessed enough to be left in peace to cultivate this way of experiencing the world, "[the world] compels over and over, and the better one knows it, the *more* compelling it is. This is not a matter of mastering an area of study" (Gadamer 2007c, p. 115).

This is, in fact, a rather ordinary thing: the more we learn and experience about a particular artist or composer, or about a painting or piece of music, the more often we return to a piece of wilderness in all its various seasons, the more we pay attention to the cycles of Pine Grosbeaks and their tethers to Weather and Sun, the more often we arc together circle-segment cross-hatches in the bisecting of angles (see Friesen and Jardine 2009), the more deeply do we experience the fact that these things have lives of their own, "beyond my wanting and doing" (Gadamer 1989, p. xxviii), beyond my "rigging and gluing" (Heidegger 1985, p. 70), beyond "the will that seizes upon and dominates things" (Gadamer 1977, p. 227). "Peace is that condition under which each culture [each word, each topic, each self] flourishes in its own incomparable way" (Illich with Cayley 1992, p. 17). And a pedagogy left in peace is the cultivation of the ability to experience and come to know this incomparability and for each of us to experience our own frail incomparability in such knowing.

Therefore, as my experience-of-this-place grows, I come to realize more and more deeply a profound ecological point: *this place is not just here for me.* It does not just "face this way," so to speak. It "stands-in-itself" (Gadamer 1977, p. 226) and has its own "repose" (p. 227). But by standing in itself, it stands not only as always already everywhere inhabited but also stands "empty," vulnerable to what might arrive, mortal and in need of being "set right anew" (Arendt 1969, p. 192) by these new inhabitants in whose care it will stand or fall.

There is thus a doubling here, where the thing experienced becomes increasingly in repose, and I, in cultivating this experience, compose myself (*Bildung*) in the light of this reposing inhabitation that shapes and forms that composition. This experience of repose is not simple, familiar, and easily had. Repose is not a surface feature that is simply lying there, somehow out in the open and immediate and obvious. Access is not freely had but only "won by a certain labor" (Ross and Jardine 2009). The appearance of the living repose of things *requires something of us.* There is some truth in Jennifer's colleagues saying that her own concerted work of coming to know her way around these Impressionist paintings and their tales is a condition of her openness to Nathan's words. But this doesn't mean that his words belong to her any more than to him. It does not mean that she is a genius ("I could never do that with my kids"), but that she became *practiced* and expected, encouraged, and protected the practice of her students. Both of them, and then me in arriving in that classroom, and now, here, in some small way, in this chapter—we've all been entrusted in multifarious ways to the life we were already living.

An experience of repose has to be *cultivated*, and it has to be cultivated each and every time we open up a new topic for investigation in the classroom. It always needs remaking because that is how both it and we *live* in the world. It takes time, work, love, and patience—all these features of a pedagogy left in peace—to come to experience this place in its convivial repose, as standing there in ways that no amount of my experience, no amount of my life, however ingenious, can fill.

CHAPTER EIGHT

"Youth need images for their imaginations and for the formation of their memory"

DAVID W. JARDINE

I

It is necessary that a man should dwell with solicitude on, and cleave with affection to, the things which he wishes to remember.

Thomas Aquinas, paraphrasing the *Ad Herennium* (cited in Yates 1974, p. 75)

I've recently been reading Mary Carruthers' work on the Medieval arts of memory (2002, 2003, 2005) as well as Francis Yates' wonderful work *The Art of Memory* (1974) and Brian Stock's (1983) work on eleventh- and twelfth-century images of written language. This study began on the advice of Michelle Bastock, a recent PhD graduate of the University of Calgary whose wonderful dissertation on the relation between word and image opened up for me this new area of exploration and intrigue (see Bastock 2005; Bastock and Jardine 2006).

I was especially interested in these matters for a couple of reasons. First, in my work in elementary schools, rarely do I hear teachers and students talking about memory except perhaps under the guise of rote memorization of spelling lists and the like. However, and in direct contradiction to this, some classrooms I've witnessed (intriguingly, very often the youngest of grades) are taking on the task of remembering in a different way. They are exploring ancestries, following ancestors who have travelled down this road before them, finding out where these old objects in their houses have come from, and whose hands handed them along, and so on. They are asking themselves the question of what is it that is important to remember, and whose story is this anyway, and how shall we proceed, given what we now know and cannot pretend to forget.

This gracious, difficult work (work, not of rote memorization, but of, somehow, cultivating the experience of something memorable) plays with an etymological twist hidden in Hans-Georg Gadamer's *Truth and Method* (1989, p. 240–62)—the German-rooted relatedness of experience (*Erfahrung*) and ancestors/ancestry (*Vorfahrung*). Experience, here, is imagined as a journey (*Fahrung*)—an undergoing, a "suffering" (p. 256–7)—linked to those who have journeyed before us (*Vor-*). Even the English word "experience" hints at this sense of traverse and surroundings. "Experience" is what you get "out of" (Latin *ex-*) having been around (Latin *peri*). As Gadamer (1989, p. 260) suggests, becoming experienced in something is akin to coming to know your way around.

The link, it seems, is, at least in part, memory. But this is not memory understood as simply the compiling of information for later recall. What is at work here is a deeply embodied, fleshy, intimate sense of memory and knowledge and their cultivation. These kids I've worked with nearby are each becoming someone because of what they have learned and remembered. And this most pedagogical of tasks—becoming someone—is linked somehow to places that are traversed, territories that are journeyed through. I'm tempted to push this one step further and suggest that these places or territories, properly understood and "taken up," are the topics that curriculum guides entrust to teachers and students in schools. More on this later.

This leads me to another pedagogical clue regarding memory that I had found years ago regarding education and learning and the young, a clue which, in part, provides a new spin the interpretive critique of Cartesianism that is commonplace in contemporary curriculum theorizing: "Education cannot tread the path of critical research. Youth demands images for its imagination and for forming its memory. Thus [Giambattista] Vico [b. 1668] supplements the *critica* of Cartesianism with the old *topica*" (Gadamer 1989, p. 21). Somehow, regarding the path that education must tread if the demands of youth (someone new to a place, someone who hasn't especially "been around," someone "inexperienced") are to be met, images, the process of cultivating memory, and topics somehow fit together, and the clear and distinct methodologism of Descartes (*critica*) needs productive, substantive, imaginal, story-laden, allegorical, bloody, bodily, Earthly, supplementation. Without such supplementation, method can come to act with no sense of place and proportion, impulsively, in ways that are profoundly "inexperienced."

In this passage about Vico, I recognized something that I had experienced elsewhere. When a graduate student asks me about how to do hermeneutics, my first impulse is always to ask "What is your topic?" Following Vico, Gadamer is suggesting that anyone new to something ("youth," so to speak—Vico's pedagogical point is not necessarily or solely a chronological one) cannot begin the task of coming to understand through being told what method to use (*critica*, from Rene Descartes' [b. 1596] *Discourse on Method* [1637]). A method has no face, no body, no memories, no stories, no blood, no images, no ancestors, no ghosts, no inhabitants, no habits, no habitats, no relations, no spirits, no monsters, no familiars. Method doesn't help us get our bearings and learn our way around, because, so to speak, there is no "place" to it. We don't become experienced through the application of a method because a method, properly taken up, must be taken up as if I could be anyone. Nothing accrues to the one wielding such a method, and nothing about the one wielding such a method must affect that method's enactment.

On the contrary, the formation of memory, Vico suggests, requires supplementing questions of "how to proceed" with more substantive questions regarding one's *topica*, one's "topic" and the images and forms and figures—the bodies, one might say—that haunt that place. Thus, answer to the question "Where am I?" holds part of the answer to the question of how to proceed. Differently put, how could I know how to properly proceed if I don't know where I am? I cannot warrantably devise a method and then simply subsequently aim it at some topic. Topics, hermeneutically conceived, productively supplement, correct, transform or "set right anew" (Arendt 1969, p. 192–3) our desire to proceed without heed to where we are. Topics hold our ways through them in place (but if and only if we allow ourselves to learn from the place and in place how to pay attention properly to the place). The place tells us something of what it needs from us if we are to "understand." This is what it means to "learn" about this place—to realize, to deeply experience how it is that this topic asks something of me beyond what I might ask of it. It means, in part and in short, to become able to learn from the place, from the topic. Hidden here are vaguely ecological images of places, topographies, territories, and a sense of bodily bearings. Hidden here, too, are images of education as involving someone coming to "inhabit" a topic and learn our way around from the topic itself. "We can entrust ourselves to what we are investigating to guide us safely in the quest" (Gadamer 1989, p. 378). An adage that is hermeneutic, pedagogical, and ecological.

Pedagogy thus requires the cultivation of topographical imagination, and, as with ecological consciousness, this involves places, relations, ancestors, faces, ways, stories, songs, generationality, intergenerationality, and the vigorous presence of life beyond the merely human. Only in such cultivation can pedagogy avoid the excesses wrought by setting individual students loose into a territory as if each one is "the 'god' of your own story" (Melnick 1997, p. 372; see Jardine, Friesen and Clifford 2006, p. 137–48); as if somehow we are each able to constructivistically make up the topic in a narcissistic pool of self-satisfied and self-confirming reflection (see Chapter 3; Johnson, Fawcett and Jardine 2006; Bowers 2005). Stripped of substantive memory (stripped of topographical Earthliness and surroundings that house, shape, resist, and transform our actions), *critica* can let us act as if we've got no relations and that all we need to proceed is procedural "know how."

An ecological disaster in waiting.

Gadamer's work does not take us in this particularly ecopedagogical direction. However, in its dispelling of the natural–scientific link between method and truth, it does house a recovery of a deep linkage between the cultivation of memory, the cultivation of a sense of place ("topica/topics, from Gk. *ta topika*, lit. 'matters concerning *topoi*,' from *topoi* 'commonplaces,' neut. pl. of *topikos* 'commonplace, of a place,' from *topos* 'place'" [OED]) through the cultivation of a topographical imagination, and the cultivation of character (*Bildung* – an idea inherited from von Humbolt [2000/1793–4]; see Pinar 2006). Put less haughtily, there is a link between what I remember, how I imagine and remember and know and experience my where abouts, and who I have become (see Jardine 2000, p. 133–40). Becoming experienced in the ways of a place, as ecology profoundly reminds us, means becoming someone. As Gadamer (1989, p. 16) insists, "it is time to rescue the phenomenon of memory from being regarding merely as a psychological faculty and to see it as an essential element of the finite historical being of man." That is, through the dialectic of remembering and forgetting, I become myself and no one else. Memory, in this sense induced by Vico, is always mine. Even in those vile cases where a person's memory has been defiled or distorted or replaced with that of another—even (and unfortunately and despicably) in these awful cases, remembering serves this formative function (see, e.g. Morris and Weaver 2002).

II

In Medieval times in Europe, it was commonplace for students to engage in specific practices aimed at the cultivation of memory (see Carruthers 2003, 2005). It would be wrong to assume that the reason for this was because of the lack of available books such that students had to retain knowledge in memory. In fact, the reverse is almost true: books were understood to be not merely repositories for knowledge but simply (yet, of course, not so simply) reminders. But, in the eleventh and twelfth century, this began to change in the burgeoning European imagination: "Men began to think of facts not as recorded by texts but as embodied in texts" (Stock 1983, p. 62). Once books became understood as repositories, a great shift occurred. "As fact and text moved closer together, 'searchability' shifted 'from memory to page layout'" (Stock 1983, p. 62). No longer was it necessary to cultivate in oneself a memory of, say, Aristotle or Biblical texts or Gadamer's *Truth and Method*. One could leave such matters "housed" in texts (or, now, "online") and simply search them out or refer to them when the occasion might warrant. Even the layout of texts shifted at this juncture. Reference works, which were heretofore organized topically (around memorable clusters of things that had memorial affinities, relations of kind, imaginal "family resemblances" [Wittgenstein 1968, p. 32]), began to be organized alphabetically, leading to what Illich and Sanders (1988) referred to as the alphabetization of the modern mind. Even references (like the reference to Stock 1983, p. 62 above, or Illich and Sanders 1988) were transformed. In this paper, they are inserted after a cited passage in order to document where the text was found and to allow readers to find their way to the text which is the repository of the citation. Prior to the twelfth century in Europe, references were given before the cited text. This was not a matter of "authorizing" the citation to follow but of allowing readers to call to memory the images and topographies of the work about to be cited, so that the reader might be ready to "hear" its reminders. References given prior to citations gave readers a chance to prepare themselves (Carruthers 2005, p. 100) properly and adequately for the words that followed.

The shift away from memory (which I carry with me and which defines who I am) to texts (which are housed outside of me) entailed that as I made my way in the world, that sojourn was no longer necessarily taken in the company of what I remember, in the company of those ancients the memory of whose voices might fill me up with experience and wisdom. Only on the basis of books becoming understood as repositories is it possible to conceive of "myself" as some sort of autonomous individuality. See Ivan Illich's (1993) commentary on Hugh of St. Victor's *Didascalion* for lovely wanderings on these ways, and how our image of ourselves as an interior subjectivity arose parallel to new images of the nature of texts. Illich (1993) further argues (supported by Carruthers [2003, 2005] and Stock [1993]) that, to use Gadamer's terms, only on this basis do I come to imagine myself as a subjectivity who has experiences which are possessed as "interior" (*Erlebenisse*) states, and no longer especially experienced sojournally (*Erfahrung*). As we know from Descartes' meditations, methodical doubt has severed our relations to the world and its ancestries (*Vorfahrung*). Knowledge is no longer rooted memorially and is no longer linked to character and its cultivation. It is rooted, now, only methodologically. Only once these pre-Cartesian moves are made regarding memory, texts, experience, and subjectivity/interiority, does it become possible for the *critica*-methodologisms of Descartes to take such easy and firm hold on the newly emerging sciences of his day and ever since (especially, as we all know, in the halls of schools and their renderings of the world into manageable test results). Once experience becomes imaginable as a subjective interiority, Cartesian methodology's promise to speak boldly and commandingly and masterfully about "the objective world" becomes a tempting promise. However, as so many critiques of Cartesianism have demonstrated, this objective world is no longer the memorial and topographical and imaginal and Earthly world understood by the invocation of "the old *topica*." This objective world is a world that has been rendered by methodology into that which can be controlled, predicted, and manipulated at the wont of human agency. "Places" are no longer first. Human agency is first and knowledge becomes, in the work of Immanuel Kant, a demand made upon things and no longer a heeding (see Chapter 3; Jardine 2005).

Unlike the sorts of anonymous rote memory touted in many schools (paradoxically, looked at from the twelfth century, often the rote memorization of "facts" housed in "texts"), memory in the more bodily, topographical sense and its careful cultivation, hinted at by Vico and visible in the Medieval arts of memory, are thereby connected deeply to how I carry myself in the world, how I call myself up in the face of what comes to meet me. It is no longer simply a matter of "giving students a prodigious memory for all they might be asked to repeat in an examination" (Carruthers 2003, p. 9). I'm reminded, here, of an old Zen adage:

> A Ch'an master once wrote that the wise enshrine the miraculous bones of the ancients within themselves; that is, they do not regard teachings of ways to enlightenment as an external body of knowledge or information to be processed as an acquisition

> or believed or revered as inflexible dogma, but rather apply it as far as possible to themselves and their situations, vivifying the way of enlightenment with their own bodies and lives, not just in their thoughts. (Cleary and Cleary 1992, p. xviii)

Or, as Gregory the Great suggested, "we ought to transform what we read into our very selves, so that when our mind is stirred by what it hears, our life may concur by practicing what has been heard" (cited in Carruthers 2005, p. 164). Or, from *Truth and Method* (Gadamer 1989, p. 340), "[we] belong to the text [we] are reading. The line of meaning that the text manifests . . . always and necessarily breaks off in an open indeterminacy. [We] can, indeed [we] must accept the fact that future generations will understand differently." Or, as Hugh of St. Victor proposed, "reading is ethical in its nature, or 'tropological' (turning the text onto and into one's self)" (Carruthers 2005, p. 164). "Understanding begins," so goes the hermeneutic adage, "when something addresses us" (Gadamer 1989, p. 299). To interpret and remember a text is to read and remember it as if it were addressed to me. "Perhaps no advice is as common in Medieval writing [on reading and memory], and yet so foreign, when one thinks about it, to the habits of modern scholarship, as this notion of 'making one's own' what one reads in someone else' work" (Carruthers 2005, p. 164).

III

> Thinking is not a disembodied "skill"; there is no thought without matters to think with. People can only think with the contents of their memories, their experiences. And human memories are stored as images in patterns of places (or "locations" or "topics"). (Carruthers 2003, p. 89)

The ancient arts of memory involved cultivating in oneself an ordered, cared for, storehouse, an "architecture" if you will, of names and faces and images and ideas and tales and voices and experiences. The precise schemes varied, everywhere from what was called a "memory theatre" (an image used by Giulio Camillo [see Yates 1974, p. 129ff.) to "the feathers on the six wings of a seraphic angel, a five-story, five-room section of a house, a columnar diagram, the stones in the wall of a turreted urban tower, the rungs of a ladder, the rows of seats in an amphitheater. Gardens were also popular, with orderly beds of medicinal plants and fruit trees separated by grass and surrounded by a wall" (Carruthers and Ziolkowski 2002, p. 5–6). Many of the medieval efforts to portray this process of cultivating memory utilize architectural images—rooms, recesses niches. Students were often trained to picture a great empty house with a memorable array of empty rooms as the "places" where images could be carefully and thoughtfully stored. This architectural urge is understandable since the rootedness here is one of creating and composing, but also of building, of formation (*die Bildung*). Students were then shown how to deliberately place significant clusters of images in each room, mindful all the while of the order and sequence of the rooms and their images. Each imaginal item to be remembered had to be digested, meditated upon, ruminated over, worried, cared for, situated, studied, and then placed. Images that were vivid and memorable (even grotesque and exaggerated) were especially encouraged since the impression that these made on memory were understood to leave a lasting impression (see Yates 1973, p. 9). Such vivid images were best able to be recalled when, asked to remember, one would move, so to speak, from place to place, room to room, and "see" the images in each *topos* and "read" them for what they remind one of. This is directly in parallel to how "medieval public memory, in pilgrimage and in liturgy, was conducted processionally, as a way among sites" (Carruthers 2003, p. 116; an interesting way to think of "field trips" in schools and their memorial ancestries).

Memory, therefore, is topographically composed and in composing memory, one is, so to speak, composing oneself, gaining composure in the face of the world—becoming educated, one might say, in the "ways" of places and their inhabitants. This is often linked to a metaphorical extension of the Latin word *silva*:

> Within his memorial "forest," [silva] a trained student, like a knowledgeable huntsman, can unerringly find the place (*loci*) where the rabbits and deer lie. Quintillian observes: "Just as all kinds of produce are not provided by every country, and as you will not succeed in finding a particular bird or beast if you are ignorant of the localities where it has its usual haunts or birthplace, as even the various kinds of fish flourish in different

> surroundings . . . so not every kind of argument comes from just any place and for the same reason is not to be sought out in scattered and random places." As the huntsman finds game and the fisherman fish, so the student finds his stored material–by knowing its habits. (Carruthers 2005, p. 62)

The bones of the ancients that we slowly come to enshrine are not just stored away in anticipation of rote retrieval. The work of enshrining is, as St. Bede suggested, a meditative, memorial activity, "a process of meditative composition or collocative reminiscence—'gathering,' *colligere*" (Carruthers 2003, p. 33). What is gathered in memory must be worried over, worked, revisited, re-read, mumbled, "murmured" (Carruthers 2005, 164), so that when an invitation to write a paper like this one comes up, those matters can be called up from the recesses of memory, not as "raw data" but as inhabitants of places. In speaking of Quintilian, Carruthers (2005, p. 297–8) insists that "composition is not an act of writing, it is rumination, cogitation, dictation, a listening, a dialogue, a 'gathering' (*collectio*) of voices from their several places in memory" (p. 3). "*Memoria* is most usefully thought of as a compositional art. The arts of memory are among the arts of thinking, especially involved with fostering the qualities we now revere as 'imagination' and 'creativity'" (Carruthers 2003, p. 9). Carruthers (p. 11) notes, too, that *invenio*, as the Latin root of inventiveness, is also the root of the term "inventory." Inventiveness and creativity are impossible if we have nothing to think with. Unlike God, we cannot think and create *ex nihilo*. To think and create, we must "follow the trail" (Carruthers 2005, p. 62–3) and its *vestigia* (p. 20), the Latin term for "tracks" or "footprints." This is what constitutes an investigation.

This ties, inevitably, to a very different view of what knowledge is. Carruther's (2005, p. 199), in citing Augustine, talks in near body-liquid terms:

> "Cogitation makes us expand, expansion stretches us out, and stretching makes us roomier." For Augustine, the pieces brought together in *cogitatio* make a sum greater than its parts. Knowledge extends understanding not by adding on more and more pieces, but because as we compose [a composition, recall, which is intimately linked to memory and its cultivation] our design becomes more capacious, it dilates.

The gatherings of voices in memory, then, and our cultivation of them and our care and devotion to this process of self-formation actually expands "myself" to include, now, this weird voice of Augustine talking about becoming "roomier" as a result of learning and its meditative-memorial practices. I become different in learning about this heretofore unheard of connection between the dissolution of the self-containedness of the Cartesian-*critica* "I am" (see Chapter 2) and the great body-function of dilation.

IV

One last reflection for now. Clearly, the matter at stake in the cultivation of memory in the Medieval period was salvation and an experience of God. This constitutes, so to speak, the *telos* of dilation:

> "New" knowledge, what has not been thought, results from this process, for dilation leads ultimately, even through the deepest *cavi* of memory, to God. Augustine characteristically speaks of this as a "going through" [*Erfahrung?*]. How shall I reach God? he asks. "I shall pass through [*transibo*] even this power of mine which is called memory; I shall pass through I to reach Thee, sweet Light." God is indeed beyond memory, but the only way there is through and by means of it, "*ascendens per animum meum ad te*." (Carruthers 2005, p. 199)

This, of course, goes too far, even for me as an ex-Anglican altar boy. But there is another place in which Carruthers (2005, p. 67) cites a beautiful passage from E. K. Rand's Aquinas Lecture of 1945 that helps illustrate the effects of this cultivation of memory in a way that is, for me, more palatable and more experientially available. This passage helps me understand something I experience a much more meager version of first hand:

> St. Thomas has learned from many men of wisdom, but on the present occasion they are summoned to court [to discuss, in this particular instance, the nature of temperance with a waiting audience], summoned from their chambers in his mind. I am not going to name them all, but they are hovering

> outside the courtroom in crowds, ancient Greeks and ancient Romans, members of all the philosophical schools, some of their poets . . . and Christian poets like Ambrose, doctors of the Roman church and of the Greek, Popes all down the line, saints and heretics-at least the mighty Origen-writers of the early Middle Ages from England, France and Spain, writers of the Renaissance of the twelfth century, writers of his own day, the Hebrew Rabbi Moses, or Maimonides, the Arabs with Averroes at their head, mystics, monastics, and metaphysicians, writers of law books and decretals, Church councils and liturgy, yes, Holy Scripture, Old Testament and New and the glosses thereon.

When St. Thomas, with his great memory and experience, shows up, a Great Council of Beings shows up, just like when the wanderer who experienced in the ways of a forest shows up, that place's ways can be experienced. "Only in the multifariousness of such voices" (Gadamer 1989, p. 284) does Aquinas' experience and knowledge exist.

We know full well that this Great Council that shows up surrounding Aquinas (or any one of us) is not Absolute, that it is surrounded (I would suggest, necessarily surrounded) by a dark and irremediable penumbra of absences. The pantheon of caveats regarding the exclusivities of the list cited by E. K. Rand is infinite because Aquinas is finite. Aquinas is someone, and his memory is his own. And yet, we can hear the memorial kinships at work when we read the descriptions of what occurs when Buddha comes to the Royal Palaces on Mount Grdhrakuta to deliver the *Sutra of Innumerable Meanings* (Kato, Tamura and Miyasaka 1987, p. 3). There were

> [g]reat assemblages of great bhikshus, in all twelve thousand. There were eighty thousand bodhisattva-mahasattvas. There were gods, dragons, yakshas, gandharvas, asuras, garudas, kimnaras, and mahoragas, beside all the bhikshus, bhiksunis, upasakas, and upasikas. There were great wheel-rolling kings, small wheel-rolling kings, and kings of the gold wheel, silver wheel . . . each encompasses by a hundred thousand myriad followers.

This continues for several pages, because, as one might expect, when the Buddha shows up, *everything* shows up—such lovely opulence and abundance is necessary in an effort to designate the field of dependent co-arising that is at work in and surrounds the cultivation of memory, and our always-finite task of following its vestiges.

We get, therefore, a double image. For Aquinas, as for us, our marshaling of memory in the face of the world is a more fragile and finite matter of becoming *someone*. But the litany of who stands up with Aquinas when he comes to speak is not just a list of voices housed, so to speak, "inside" of him, but a myriad of voices in which he himself is housed and kept (see Chapter 7, on the ecological character of one's "keep"). Through the cultivation of memory he, like us, becomes a wanderer in and through the world's embrace, and an affectionate and devoted student of its ways.

CHAPTER NINE

On the while of things

DAVID W. JARDINE

It's like making a path through the forest.
At first it's rough going, with a lot of obstructions,
but returning to it again and again, we clear the way.
After a while the ground becomes firm and smooth
from being walked on repeatedly. Then we have a good
path for walking in the forest.

— Ajahn Chah from Everything Arises, Everything Falls Away. (2005a, p. 83)

I

What is it that makes classroom experiences worthwhile? This formulation hides too much of the deep etymological inheritances of such a question: what makes a classroom experience worth, not simply zero-sum school-grade exchange, but *while*? What makes some experiences worthy of rest and repose, worthy of returning, worthy of tarrying and remembering, of taking time, of whiling away our lives in their presence? These questions are framed, for me, as a way to think through some of the classroom work I have witnessed over several decades of attention to a specific phenomenon: how, in vigorous and intellectually challenging and pleasurable classrooms, time and memory gather together, both things and thinking accrue and return, and there is a sense of plenitude wherein the panics of schooling are cooled in favor of good, worthwhile work.

Many of the tasks asked of students in schools are not worthwhile in this very particular sense: they are not worth lingering over, meditating upon, remembering, and returning to. They don't gather us together and demand gathering of us (an archaic way of saying "knowing") but rather they isolate and pathologize and accelerate attention into scatter-shot pursuit. And this pursuit is not of the marks and vestiges (L. *vestigia*, "tracks"—root of the work "investigation") of the topic under consideration but of the marks of schooling itself. In short, the purpose of, say, learning about a topic like "sovereignty" in Social Studies is not to articulate one's life and make it more knowledgeable and perhaps livable (sovereignty, after all, is part of the *topos* that we inhabit day to day, in multifarious ways) but to pass the upcoming examination.

With many examples of classroom work, no matter which aspect of which living discipline is under consideration, in schools, so often, the real topic is, as Ivan Illich told us over 30 years ago (1970), "school."

This helps us get a glimpse of why it is that many of the tasks asked of students are *purposefully designed* precisely to rebuke whiling away over. In light of provincial test scores, sovereignty, for example, *is* the definition that can be rattled off. It *is* (a) and (c) or "none of the above." In light of industrial images of timelines and efficiency and task management, whiling over such matters seems archaic, useless or, even worse, mere unproductive, hazy, liberal laziness. Many school tasks don't *need* a while because "needing a while" is understandable only as gumming up the works. Since most school curriculum is delivered in such a fragmented way as to not need a while, "needing a while" is understandable only as a "special need" (a need of what used to be called, ironically, "slow" children). Here, while is understood only as a slowed-down version of that which "normal" students can do quickly and efficiently (see Chapter 4).

The long and gathering while needed to properly take up a topic like democracy or sovereignty in and for one's own life, and shaping one's life in its witness and wake, is thus pathologized into the slow-wittedness of the one considering such a topic.

Given Fredrick Winslow Taylor's insinuation of the efficiency-movement industrial assembly line into the consciousness of schooling (Taylor 1906, 1911; Callahan 1964; Wrege and Greenwood 1991), students and teachers are, more often than not, living in the midst of industrial temporality and its measures. It is in light of these measures that most schooled tasks have been stripped of that character which would take a while. A "continuity of [our] attention and devotion" (Berry 1986, p 32) to some classroom work is very often not simply *unnecessary* but *impossible* because the school-matters at hand have been stripped of the very memorability and relatedness and demand that might require and sustain and reward such attention and devotion. From the point of view of efficiency and management, intellectual whiling in the leisures (*schola*) of school (see the Introduction) simply seems dense and unproductive.

Worth *while* instead of simply worth cramming-as-time-runs-out-for-upcoming-examinations speaks, therefore, to a sense of temporality. "While" and what might be worthy of it is about time.

One can't while over disconnected fragments. They don't ask this of us and will reject any such efforts at whiling.

There is thus a hidden ontology here, that *to be* worthy of while means not being disconnected and fragmented and distanced, manageable object, but to be lived with, "*lebensweltlich* (close to the living world)" (Ross 2004). Living disciplines full of topics that we are living in the midst of and to which we belonging in contested and multifarious ways—these things are worthwhile, worth whiling.

A side comment: whiling over a topic—working at it, composing it, composing ourselves over it, remembering, and cultivating one's memory of it—defines the work of hermeneutics.

Interpretation *whiles*.

And such whiling, I suggest, defines pedagogy at its best.

II

The way we treat a thing can sometimes change its nature.

Lewis Hyde, from *The Gift: On the Erotic Life of Property* (1983, p. xiii)

Worthwhileness is not simply some sort of objective property or set of properties pertaining to certain topics and not to others. We can't just get a list of "great classroom ideas" and splay them out for students or hand over to student-teachers some sure-fire "activities" that just need to be "done." This just leads, more often than not, to the complain that "it didn't work with my kids."

Worthwhileness has to do with a way of treating things, a way of composing our understanding of something, seeking its kinships (Wittgenstein 1968, p. 36) and verisimilitudes (Gadamer 1989, p. 21), and, in the same breath, composing ourselves, finding our composure in the face of what we have encountered. "Objectivity" and "subjectivity" are inadequate to this phenomenon. Such alternatives already bespeak the severing of the often hidden or occluded or forgotten, sometimes contested, sometimes revelatory kinships and "family resemblances (*Familienahnlichkeiten*)" (Wittgenstein 1968, p. 32) upon which whiling relies. Stripped of all their relations, fragments don't draw us in. Whiling, on the contrary pulls at us, because it seeks kinships, bloodlines. Whiling is the work of someone looking to be implicated in what they while over, looking to "recognize themselves in the mess of the world" (Hillman 1983, p. 49). ("we do not understand what recognition is in its profoundest nature if we only regard it as knowing something again that we already know. The joy of recognition is rather the joy of knowing *more* than is already familiar. In recognition, what we know emerges, as if illuminated. It is known *as* something." [Gadamer 1989, p. 114]).

More simply, yet more mysteriously put, when we experience something worthwhile, we experience something being *asked of us*. "Understanding begins when something addresses us" (Gadamer 1989, p. 299), or, as the old man put it in his 94th year, fragmented bits and pieces (like those requisite of assembly-schooling) are not in any living sense "the basics" (see Jardine, Clifford and Friesen 2008a): "something awakens our interest–that is really what comes first!" (Gadamer 2001, p. 50). In asking after worthwhileness, we are asked to find our measure in such things that awaken us and our interest. We are asked to learn and, in learning, to become something more than we had been before such encounters. A worthwhile matter "would not deserve the interest we take in it if it did not have something to say to teach us that we could not know by ourselves" (Gadamer 1989, p. xxxv). This breaks the spell of constructivism and its ancient Cartesian bloodline (see Chapters 2–4).

III

Part of my initial interest in these matters stems from this being the 12th year that I have taught a course that involves reading Hans-Georg Gadamer's *Truth and Method* (1989) cover to cover. This experience of re-reading—this experience of whiling away over this work for so many years—always ends up the same. Something always unanticipatedly *happens*, and a heretofore timid thread of Gadamer's work spins around and finds a face and faces me with something: the whiling time of works that Gadamer's text addresses, in combination with how many years I've lingered over this text. In this work, I was aided by happening upon Sheila M. Ross' brilliant article "Gadamer's Late Thinking on *Verweilen*" (2004). This text helps me see vestiges in *Truth and Method* that I had not experienced before, and yet, reading Ross' article was a peculiar act of recognition, of knowing something more in knowing the same thing.

This experiential sense of vestige links up with earlier work (see Chapter 8) on the composition of memory and how such composition involves the effort, not to "amass verified knowledge" (Gadamer 1989, p. xxi) but rather to *keep something in mind*. And the act of keeping something in mind is the act of shaping my life (*Bildung*) as one who carries himself this way, with this in mind. In such memorial whiling work, I become someone lodged in the multifarious memory of the world. I come upon myself making myself up, getting a hold of myself, composing myself in the middle of this worldly life.

There is something about such matters that provides clues to understanding an intimate form of classroom practice that sidesteps the panics of industrial time-consciousness and provides for whiling. And this interweaves with the opportunity I have had over the past year of working, in some small ways, with a group of wonderful teachers and students at a local high school. This has given me a site of meditation, a site of attention consider again the issue of worthwhile work in the face of the particular ways in which it arises in the work of students and teachers and the curriculum topics entrusted to them in schools.

I was recently a very small part of some conversations in a Grade Ten Social Studies class about British Minister Jack Straw's comments (from October 5, 2006 [see news.bbc.co.uk]; see Chapters 1 and 10) regarding Muslim women wearing the *hijab*. Minister Straw was suggesting that Muslim women unveil in his presence, and that their refusing to do so is nothing more than a way of cutting themselves off from British culture. One student's (a Muslim girl, wearing a *hijab*) comment was that it is often seen as "hiding something" and that, perhaps, helps start to explain the hushed conversations and stares on the bus on the way to school. I've wryly laughed since over the terrifying coincidence of George Bush's security fetishes and images of Texan wild-West outlaws with their faces obscured—bandannas, banditos ready to violate any and every border of civility—plundering, robbing us of house and home. The glare of the unobstructed, irresistible, you-have-no-say-in-it security gaze, and the demand to uncover, to strip down, is occurring precisely in a time of great secrecy and cover-up, a time of the deliberate and systematic "enfraudening" of the public sphere (Smith 2006a). Fredrick Winslow Taylor's security and surveillance-based lineups that underwrite much contemporary schooling have made us ripe for accepting and even embracing the contemporary zeal for entrenching of security paranoia. We've been *schooled* into experiencing a world that asks nothing of us beyond what we ask of it.

We've been *had*.

As I meditate upon Smith's words about the deliberate veil of enfraudening that has fallen over the public sphere, that Grade Ten conversations start to turn, to converse, to shape and form itself and seek verisimilitude ("the spontaneous and inventive seeking out of similarities" [Gadamer 1989, p. 432]). I start to "think it over," or "ruminate" or "worry" this bone of contention. Memory, in such a case, doesn't simply "store" these events and these ideational, image-filled speculations that they engender (including a terrible hesitation over the fact that Islam turns its back on the image in vital and telling ways). Memory "works" each event in relation to the other, working to "place" them properly and safely. This might sound a bit controlled, but consider: that link between Taylor's efficiency-movement schooling of our attention and contemporary security fetishes needs to be calmed down a bit, worked over a bit, not just blurted out. It needs to find its proper measure, its proper proportionality to the matters at hand that are emerging in memory and its ways.

The inventive seeking out of similarities is necessarily premised upon a slow and gathering memorial inventory, a "niche" where things are not simply stored but restored, measured, shaped, and formed in relation to and in the witness of each other. This leads to an emergent experience of the memorability of a place (a "topic") rather than to the simple memorization of fragments to which I bear no memorial obligation and which ask nothing of me in return. In this cultivated, worked and whiled-over space that develops "in between" (Gadamer 1989, p. 109), each initially seemingly "separate" tale becomes more than it might have been without the other. Oddly enough, in such memorial working, the "time" of each event changes as well. Each enters into the same *while* as I while away over them, caring for them, placing and replacing in the *invenio* memory- dance that is both inventive and inventorial (Carruthers 2003, p. 11). My "making something" of these events (my formative activity) is, at the same time, also "made" by the formative encounter with the fleshy "otherness" of the experiences undergone and remembered:

> Thinking is not a disembodied "skill"; there is no thought without matters to think with. People can only think with the contents of their memories, their experiences. And human memories are stored as images in patterns of places (or "locations" or "topics"). (Carruthers 2003, p. 89)

About a week after this class, one of those Grade Ten Social Studies students talked to me about how she understands that her *hijab* is seen by many as a form of oppression. She explained how, in her tradition, if you wear a *hijab* simply because someone tells you to, you might as well not wear it at all, but she understood how some Canadians, some of her classmates, have trouble understanding how anyone would *chose* such a thing. She admitted, as well, and without hesitation, that, of course, some in her tradition simply do what they are told. We commiserated a bit over how this is a deep kinship that many traditions share that we, here, share face-to-face, of mindlessly simply doing what you are told and remaining silent and silenced.

There is something, here, about the decision *to be regarded* a certain way and what that says about who you are in a profoundly worldly sense, here, in relation to, in standing with, others. There is also, echoing here, an issue of having to simply submit to another's demands for their right to have my self as the object of their unveiled regard, as with Minister Straw. It seems that Minister Straw did not while over those women who might visit his Ministry office. It seems that he did not ask himself what they might have to say about him and his unveiling presumptions. At least that is what the media has left us with—fragments of a fragmented story that flitters by our attention and leaves us flittering and, once again, bereft of the possibility of whiling except through great effort. These are faint echoes of that old Grade Ten Social Studies topic of (for Canadians especially, British) sovereignty and (American-style) self-sovereignty and the nature, occasion, and limits of submission.

Echoes, then, of a decision to be seen to belong in this multifarious world *this* way, veiled from something of its gaze and telling us something of the unremitting glare of that gaze and its pretenses.

That student also voiced a profound idea about herself and her classmates. Some of her female classmates believe that they are free to dress any way they want and if a boy ogles them, it is the boy's fault. She, on the other hand, suggested that how she is looked at, the gaze she attracts, affects who she is, and that it is her responsibility, at least in part, to protect how she is seen, because letting herself be seen a certain way is who she *is*. You become who you are in the witness of the world with which you surround yourself. If you surround yourself with ogling gazes, you become someone.

This, among, of course, clusters of other threads, is a reason for the troublesome demand to remove the *hijab*. This is also a troublesome reminder of the hollowing effect of being a young female who is *nothing but gazed at*—Paris, Lindsay, Britney, Nicole, and the Olsens come to mind, and the fact that this list will seem positively ancient and out of date by the time anyone reads this is, of course, *precisely the point*. We bounce, here, between anorexia and obesity, between too much and too little, between darkness and hiddenness and security threats, and paparazzi unveiled glare.

Again, "understanding begins when something addresses us" (Gadamer 1989, 299). But what occurs in such moment of address is that something starts to slow around these classroom events and the memorial ruminations they spawn, and memory starts to double in on itself and coalesces and becomes compositional. I want to *remember* this, but this remembering is not simply an issue of brute storage, but of exaggerating (Gadamer 1989, p. 115), forgetting (p. 15–16), seeking out resemblances or verisimilitudes or family resemblances as places to place such a memory safely, a place it can take root, be restored and recalled.

Something, in remembering, starts to form, to shape. This is what that whole "transformation into structure" section is about in *Truth and Method*, when the "to and fro" (1989, p. 114ff.) of play starts to become "a play," that is, a "work" that somehow begins to "stand there" with a life of its own, in "repose." This, too, is the *Da* of Heidegger's (1962) *Dasein* (see Chapters 5–7). But something else starts to happen in such memory work.

I gather things in memory, but then, as Clarissa Pinkola-Estes (1992, p. 27–8; see Chapter 5) describes so wonderfully, I also sing over these bones and something just might start to happen over and above simply structuring or creatively inventory-making. Something sometimes *wakes up* and starts to form a life of its own beyond my wanting and doing. There are echoes here, too, right back to the words of Hannah Arendt cited in our "Introduction," something of mortality and setting things right anew. We sing, and animation is invited though not caused by our singing. It is always only *possible* that it will arrive.

Right in the midst of dwelling on these old bones and worrying them in memory, something leaps up with a life of its own (which is precisely what the phenomenological presumption of hermeneutics pursues in its compositional work, an experience of the *lebensweltlichkeit*—the "life-worldliness" of something. Here is the great difference. For phenomenology, this life-worldliness is a given that is presented to consciousness is phenomenological reflection. For hermeneutics, it is not a given. It is "a task for consciousness and an achievement that is demanded of it" [Gadamer 1989, p. 127]).

Properly worried over, properly cared for and remembered, these things keep "coming up," erupting and interrupting of their own accord, asking for attention, needing something from me, it seems. This is a reason why Gadamer (1989, p. 366) suggests that understanding is "more a passion than an action. A question *presses itself upon us*," thus undermining the subjective-activity centeredness of constructivism and its consorts (see Chapter 3).

In a very literal and deeply bodily, deeply phenomenological sense, these events worry *me* as much as *I* worry over *them*:

> I am not anthropomorphizing. It's more like a thing is a phenomenological presentation, with a depth, a complexity, a purpose, in a world of relations, with a memory, a history. And if

> we look at it this way we might begin to hear it. It's an aesthetic appreciation of how things present themselves and that therefore they are in some way formed, ensouled, and are speaking to the imagination. This way of looking is a combination of the Neoplatonic *anima mundi* and pop art: that even a beer can or a freight car or a street sign has an image and speaks of itself beyond being a dead throwaway object. (Hillman 2006a, p. 33)

Thus, the image of being culpable for the gaze I attract—in remembering such an event, what begins is a shift in temporality and an ontological shift. What begins is a whiling over it, a whiling that seeks out the worth of that while (the keep-seeking of kinships and family resemblances that shape the inventorial, root of *invenio*) while, at the same time, makes the thing worthwhile through whiling (the inventive root of *invenio*).

What starts to occur is an experience of things that breaks the surveillance gaze and mastery pretensions of subjectivity (and its rude consort, "objectivity"). Whiling "breaks open the being of the object" (Gadamer 1989, p. 382) and we begin to experience how things are not simply arm's length objects in which we have no stake and we are not worldless subjects living inside our own experiences. Such a belief in the being of things and the nature of our selves is simply an outcome of how they have been treated.

Rather, in whiling, things start to *regard us* and tell us about ourselves in ways we could not have experienced without such whiling. And we become selves that recognize themselves in the recognition of the world:

> All things show faces, the world not only a coded signature to be read for meaning, but a physiognomy to be faced. As expressive forms, things speak; they show the shape they are in. They announce themselves, bear witness to their presence: "Look, here we are." They regard us beyond how we may regard them, our perspectives, what we intend with them, and how we dispose of them. (Hillman 2006a, p. 33)

But they will only regard us, speak to us, if we treat them properly. "Look, here we are" is not a phenomenological or ecological given. It is a task to be taken up, a dedication whose consequences must be suffered.

IV

Several weeks after that cluster of conversations and musings, I returned to a lovely website that houses "unpublished" work by Ivan Illich (www.davidtinapple.com/illich). I'd been reading Illich's work on fragmentation, commodification, and regimes of scarcity as a way of thinking through what might be meant by "curriculum in abundance" (Jardine, Friesen and Clifford 2006). All this was a follow-up to considering how classrooms might function as gift-economies (see Jardine, Clifford and Friesen 2008a, p. 211–22) rather than market economies where regimes of scarcity reign.

In such market economies, "time is always running out" (Berry 1983, p. 76; see Chapter 4). The time involved here, in the efficiency movement's fragmenting of the living disciplines entrusted to teachers and students in schools is not while-time simply sped up. Rather, this time is "empty"—"measuring time [as distinct from whiling time] requires a separation of the temporal units which measure from that which is measured; to separate time from its contents is to 'empty' it" (Ross 2004, discussing Gadamer [1970]). In light of such an empty measured-time, things are no longer understood to have a time of their own. Rather, things are rendered measurable by such empty, formal, clockwork temporality and thus things lose their while—things no longer *are* all of their relations and kinships and family resemblances, not any of the beckonings that might haunt us and call for our thinking (see Heidegger 1968). We can no longer say of something that "only in the multifariousness of voices [does it] exist" (Gadamer 1989, p. 284). Empty time, shall we say, pre-fragments things into its own clocked demands and therefore cuts any bloodlines that might not fall to this demand and reduces any unclockable multifariousness to singularity—the singular voice of empty, leveling, measurable surveillance.

Once time becomes detached from that which it measures, quite literally nothing holds time at bay, nothing can cause it to linger or tarry. Worse yet, once time becomes thus clocked independently of that which it measures, this temporality of industrial fragmentation *demands the fragmentation of that which it measures* and measures the truth of things by the ability to control, predict, and manipulate such fragments. This is why, following James Hillman's admonition cited above, that we might suggest that such empty time is a form of anthropomorphism, but it is a special form. It isn't the living, Earthly body (*morphos*) of humanity or the Earth-bodies of things that are the measure. It is the morphology of an abstract idea into which we have shaped ourselves: clock-watchers whose lives have become machined. *Anthropos* has rendered itself into surveillable DNA sequences, or into the image of computer storage and retrieval, or scannable identity cards and the like. As many teachers have said, in one way or another, we and our students and the disciplines entrusted to us all become rendered to fit the institutional machine of schooling.

Once it is compositionally and topically unheld, fragmented time can only try to become fulsome through *accelerating* (this again is a lived-experience in schools caught in empty time and its effluence). Cut off from the while of things, there is nothing to hold memory and attention and experience in place, nothing to call it to collect itself or attend or return. Time speeds up. Whiling appears as a luxurious waste of time that many teachers have told me they would pursue with their students if it were not for how many fragmented things needed covering and the fact that time's running out.

To repeat, there is something worse yet. We start to believe that we live in a world where *nothing requires a while*. We experience a world in which nothing is asked of us beyond what we ask of it:

> The Gadamerian dystopia is not unlike others. In his version, to be glib, little requires human application, so little cultivates it. Long alienated from abiding in inquiry as a form of life and a way of being, a restless humanity defers to models, systems, operations, procedures, the ready-made strategic plan. (Ross 2004)

The time things need from us is forgone in favor of the time we have to "cover" them in class, and in such measured time, as every teacher has experienced in the institution of schooling, there is never enough time to take a while over something and make it worthwhile. Thus rendered under the demand of another, measured-time becomes akin to the Straw-gaze that Muslim women were asked submit to. It *renders*.

The sovereignty of the fragmented, measured-time curriculum disassembly is, of course, on behalf of the ease of management and surveillance. In measured time, ideally, nothing *happens*. Things just occur according to the rules that measured time has measured out for things, or they deviate from such a measure and need realignment. In such a light, whiling now appears as a potential threat to the security and orderliness and manageability and surpriselessness that measured-time demands of that which it renders.

In whiling, you can happen upon something unanticipated.

Insurgency is possible. Something can "come up" of its own accord, "over and above our wanting and doing" (Gadamer 1989, p. xxviii). Whiling is *epiphantic*, and, thus, because it cannot lay out in advance what will happen, it appears veiled and suspicious.

After all, the voices say, what are those teachers and students up to who while over the *hijab* even though the curriculum guides don't say that it needs to be covered? (A pitiful pun, I know).

V

On this Illich-related website, there are two papers I spotted that I hadn't quite seen before. My susceptibility to seeing them was a vestige of memory and its composition. Their titles have now become full of address: "Protecting the Gaze in an Age of Show (2001)" and "The Scoptic Past and the Ethics of the Gaze (2001a)." In these papers, Illich speaks of what he names, in another context (2005, p. 108), the "*custodia oculorum*, the guarding of the eye" that was once a commonplace idea in European thought (and clearly, from that Grade Ten conversation, an idea borne somewhere near the heart of Islam):

> Until quite recently, the guard of the eyes was not look upon as a fad, nor written off as internalized repression. Our taste was trained to judge all forms of gazing on the other. (Illich 2001a, p. 5).
>
> In 726, the emperor Leo III had the icon of Christ torn from the tympanum of his palace's bronze gate, to be replaced by a naked cross. In this event, three distinct currents find a common expression: the Old Testament awe rejecting any visualization of the Word of God that touches the flesh, the heart of the believer; the later Muslim exaltation of the sound of the Koran with whose majesty and beauty no picturing of the Almighty

> could possibly compete; and, of course, the Greek Ikono-skepsis, the philosophical hesitancy in giving the weight of truth to representations. (Illich 2001b, p. 7)

Like any of the good fields (*silvia*—see Chapter 8) entrusted to teachers and students in school, (curriculum) topics emerge and show their fullness and richness and abundance if they are worked carefully and in ways proper to them and their (sometimes contested, sometimes contradictory, sometimes worthy of repudiating or valuing or re-evaluating in light of new circumstances) familial limits. After all, who would have imagined on September 10 that the vitality and difficulty and particular ancestries and worries about a Canadian Social Studies curriculum topics like "multiculturalism" or "sovereignty" would have turned out quite like this? They need our while anew.

If we are surrounded, not by the living world but by surveilled and manageable fragments rendered by measured-time, this has an effect. As with the zero-sum scarcity regimes of market economies, "it nullifies precedent, it snaps the threads of memory and scatters local knowledge. By privileging individual choice over the common good, it makes relationships revocable and provisional" (Gray 2001, p. 35–6). We become something under the gaze of such revocability. If we surround ourselves with fragments, we become fragmented, isolated, entrenched, tribalized, paranoid, and any sense of relatedness or worldliness is simply a site of a possible security breach. If we surround ourselves with things that are trivial and cheap, our lives become trivial and cheap. If learning becomes just "for show" on an exam and no longer about the formation of our lives, our lives become susceptible to the trivializing and infantilizing flicker of the business of show (this hides the great critiques in hermeneutics of the metaphysics of *presence*). In being formed by such flickering, I become

> the ideal-type channel-hopping MTV viewer who flips through different images at such speed that she/he is unable to chain the signifiers together into a meaningful narrative, he/she merely enjoys the multiphrenic intensities and sensations of the surface of the images. (Usher and Edwards 1994, p. 11)

This was written in 1994. The enjoyment of such multiphrenic intensities and sensations of the surface of things is now, post-9/11, underwritten by a paranoia about what is hidden behind the imaginal veil. And it links back, too, to those older musings about regimes of scarcity and market economies:

> People whose governing habit is the relinquishment of power, competence and responsibility, and whose characteristic suffering is the anxiety of futility, make excellent spenders. They are the ideal consumers. By inducing in them little panics of boredom, powerlessness, sexual failure, mortality, paranoia, they can be made to buy virtually anything that is "attractively packaged." (Berry 1986, p. 24)

Illich (2001a, 3) asks us "'What can I do to survive in the midst of show?' not 'how do I improve show business.'"

> Tarrying, involving the "temporal structure of being moved" and occasioning "durationaless" time . . . suggests a most practical and accessible solution [to this issue of how to survive], demonstrating how practice is a solution. "The *Weile* [the 'while' in *Verweilen*, tarrying] has this very special temporal structure" (Ross 2004, citing, at the end of this passage, Gadamer 2001)

VI

Obviously such streams of consequence and gathering get out of hand very easily when whiling is trying to be portrayed in narrative form, because each of these incidentals and their "interweaving and crisscrossing" (Wittgentein 1968, p. 36) is only especially sensible if such matters are compositionally *experienced* and *undergone*, not simply rattled off in some "brainstorm" wherein none of the possibilities tossed around are taken especially seriously. That is what is meant by suggesting that the scattershot fragmentation of attention has a practical solution.

Whiling must be *practiced* in order to be understood. This is why hermeneutics cannot be adequately described procedurally and why the proper first response to the question of "How do you do hermeneutics?" is "What is your topic?" (see Chapters 5 and 8). Without the worldly resistance of a topic and the topical work of memory, composition, and composure around *this* or *that* topic—without the "fecundity of the individual case" (Gadamer 1989, p. 37)—hermeneutics doesn't "work" because it has nothing to work in concert with, no "other" to heed, no vestiges, no need to compose myself, nothing over which to while.

Equally obvious is that what starts to occur in the task of whiling is that we begin to experience the matters we are whiling over as something that "outplays" us. We begin to experience the fact that the thing under consideration is *itself* and not us. With measured time, the thing measured comes more and more into our purview, under our gaze, in our control and subjected to our demands. With spending time over things that are worthwhile, something else occurs:

> When any of us think of those things in the world that we dearly love–the music of Duke Ellington, the contours of a powerful novel and how it envelopes us if we give ourselves over to it, the exquisite architectures of mathematical geometries, the old histories and stories of this place, the rows of garden plants that need our attention and devotion and care, varieties of birds and their songs, the perfect sound of an engine that works well, the pull of ice under a pair of skates, and on and on—we understand something in our relation to these things about how excessiveness might be basic to such love. We do not seek these things out and explore them again and again simply for the profit that we might gain in exchanging what we have found for something *else*. What we have found, in exploring and coming to understanding, to learn to live well with these things is not an arms-length commodity but has become part of who we are, and how we carry ourselves in the world. We love them and we love what becomes of us in our dedication to them. And, paradoxically, the more we understand of them, the better—richer, more intriguing, more complex, more ambiguous and full and multiple of questions—*they* become, and the more we realize that gobbling them up into a knowing that we can commodify, possess and exchange is not only undesirable. It is impossible. We realize, in such knowing, that the living character of the things we love will, of necessity, outstrip our own necessarily finite and limited experience, memory, and exploration. (Jardine, Clifford and Friesen 2003, 208)

VII

> So long as [these curriculum topics are] not placed in the object-world of producing and marketing [the object-world, of course, of measured time, not of while], [they are able to] draw us entirely outside of ourselves and impose [their] own presence on us. [They] no longer [have] the character of an object that stands over against us; we are no longer able to approach this like an object of knowledge, grasping, measuring and controlling. Rather than meeting us in our world, it is much more a world into which we ourselves are drawn. (Gadamer 1994, p. 191–2)

This final section is, in part, a memo to myself as a teacher. I have witnessed, over and over again, the profound thoughtfulness that teachers and students can display in their whiling over the world, if their time and the topics they while over are treated properly and they are allowed to become untethered from the time-measured panics of schooling. Such untethering is difficult, lifelong work and, given the pervasiveness of the spells of measured time, engaging in such work is not necessarily viewed as honorable by one's colleagues. This, again, is Gadamer's version of dystopia: in the day-to-day work of most schools, "little requires human application, so little cultivates it" and and those who pursue such whiling cultivation can seem pretentious, perhaps even mad.

I have witnessed, too, over the 20 years I've worked in schools in the Calgary area, how intellectually vigorous and sound is the work so many teachers and students have done once they are able to get their bearings in the often-wild whiles of things. The intellectual and spiritual pleasure to be experienced, and the honorability of the suffering such whiling requires, is beautiful and true.

Finally, there is another connection that links up some of the phenomenological rootedness of hermeneutics with what I believe is a profoundly ecological idea. Here is a difficult hint in a commentary by Hans-Georg Gadamer on the work of one of his great teachers, Martin Heidegger:

> The existing thing does not simply offer us a recognizable and familiar surface contour; it also has an inner depth of self-sufficiency that Heidegger calls "standing-in-itself." The complete

> unhiddenness of all beings, their total objectification (by means of a representation that conceives things in their perfect state [fully given, fully present, fully presented, finished]) would negate this standing-in-itself of beings and lead to a total leveling of them. A complete objectification of this kind would no longer represent beings that stand in their own being. Rather, it would represent nothing more than our opportunity for using beings, and what would be manifest would be the will that seizes upon and dominates things. [In whiling over something rather than rendering it in measured time] we experience an absolute opposition to this will-to-control, not in the sense of a rigid resistance to the presumption of our will, which is bent on utilizing things, but in the sense of the superior and intrusive power of a being reposing in itself. (Gadamer 1977, p. 226–7)

Worthwhile things are thus experienced as standing-in-themselves, "over and above our wanting and doing" (Gadamer 1989, p. xxviii). As anyone rapt of the Earth's ways will understand, it takes quite a while to experience the while of the Earth and its ways.

As hinted at above, having become more experienced about something through whiling our time away over it has a strange result: *what is experienced* "increases in being" (Gadamer 1989, p. 40), while our knowledge of such things becomes more and more incommensurate with the thing itself. Things become experienced as having their own measure. We begin to experience them as *there*. Understanding such things is no longer a matter of mastery and control which forces things to face this way and unveil. Things reposing in themselves do not just face this way.

But we must work to cultivate an experience of such repose. It takes time and practice to learn how to treat things well. It takes a while to let things repose ("letting things be" is how Heidegger [1962] defined phenomenology; see Chapter 11). Even here, in the meager beginnings of ventures in this paper into the gaze, into sovereignty and the strange positioning of Islam in the iconophilic midst of a contemporary Canadian high school, we can start to recognize ourselves in this mess of the world. We can start to experience ourselves, not as having such matters belonging to us, but as *belonging to and implicated in such matters*. This is what is meant by something being worthwhile.

This constitutes an *ontological* assurance about the abundant while of things and about the worthwhileness of treating things with such soft and loving assurance. This love of the while of things is a frail and finite assurance around which pedagogy, hermeneutics, and ecology turn, and around which there might be a pedagogy left in peace.

CHAPTER TEN

Learning not to speak in tongues

DAVID W. JARDINE & RAHAT NAQVI

In the Koran, the first thing God said to Muhammad was "Read."

— *Alia Muhammad Baker, from the* New York Times, *July 27, 2003*

I

The passage cited above forms the frontispiece to a wonderful new children's picture book written and illustrated by Jeanette Winter (2005) entitled *The Librarian of Basra: A True Story from Iraq*. At the early outset of the invasion of Iraq by the United States, the librarian in question, Alia Muhammad Baker, takes it upon herself to protect the 30,000 books in the library in Basra, Iraq, where she has worked for 14 years. The library had been "a meeting place for all who love books" (p. 2), but now, the only talk was not of books but of impending war: "Alia worries that the fires of war will destroy the books, which are more precious to her than mountains of gold . . . books in every language, new books, ancient books, even a biography of Muhammad that is seven hundred years old" (p. 3). After being refused official permission to act, she secretly begins putting books into her car and taking them, first to a nearby restaurant belonging to her friend Anis, and then, eventually, after the library is burned to the ground, to her home and the homes of her friends.

At first blush, it is difficult to avoid parallel thoughts of Hypatia (c. 350–415 CE) and her failed attempt to protect the Library of Alexandria from ruin (see also Smith 2006b). The ruin of the Alexandrian library is often cited as one of the initiating gestures of what later became known as the "Dark Ages" (Humphreys 2004). Jeanette Winter's seemingly simple tale thus involves profound questions and images regarding the nature of knowledge and its safe-keeping. It evokes thoughts of the ravages of war not only regarding the materiality and flesh of our lives but also regarding the fragility of knowledge itself and how often it has been both the ideological motive and innocent victim of embattlement and war.

What we, as educators, have here with this simple children's book is an image of taking care of knowledge in difficult and dark times, our time, this time, under the current shadow of war consciousness (see Chapters 1–3).

II

> It occurred to me to look into my copy of St. Augustine's *Confessions* where I first fixed my eyes it was written: "And men go abroad to admire the heights of mountains, the mighty waves of the sea, the broad tides of rivers, the compass of the ocean, and the circuits of the stars, yet pass over the mystery of themselves without a thought."
>
> Petrarch (1304–47), from *The Ascent of Mount Ventoux*, A Letter to Dionisio da Borgo San Sepolcro, April 26, n.d., Malaucene (from Fordham 2007)

"The Dark Ages" was a term first coined by Francesco Petrarca (L. Petrarch 1304–74) around 1330 CE to describe the period between roughly 476–1000 CE. In this time period, intellectual pursuit and the great wisdoms of ancient Greece and Rome were lost, sometimes deliberately and systematically, to Christian-European consciousness:

> Petrarch revived, after a lapse of 1,000 years, recognition that a poet and intellectual was an important member of society. Petrarch had perhaps his most enduring influence by his re-initiation of humanistic studies. Traveling widely as an ambassador and celebrity, he collected manuscripts that led to the recovery of knowledge from writers of Rome and Greece. (http://www.humanistictexts.org/petrarch.htm)

Petrarch wrote of feeling "*surrounded by darkness* and dense gloom" (cited in Mommsen 1942, p. 233). His great efforts initiated a revival of knowledge from under the severities of literalism, Church oppression, and simple neglect. And it was not just knowledge that dimmed:

> The seventh century [in particular] is justifiably regarded as a "dark age." In all parts of the Mediterranean, economic decline accompanied political instability. Levels of culture and standards of literacy fell as people ceased to learn, build, paint, and write in the traditional fashion. (Herrin 1987, p. 133)

As these passages suggest, however, "Dark Ages" is a clearly geographically located and (debatably) appropriate description of a dark time. We must ask of the passage cited above regarding Petrarch's accomplishments, from whom did he collect such manuscripts and precisely upon whom had such a Dark Age fallen? There are tales of both Islamic and Christian warriors who, when passing the Islamic Libraries of Northern Africa and Southern Spain, wherein, they declared, in various yet similar ways, that if the library contains knowledge that is *identical* with "The Book" (the Qu'ran/The Bible) then its contents are redundant, and if it contains knowledge that is *different*, its contents are heretical. In either case, burning down the Library makes perfect sense once knowledge is constricted in such a fashion, under the logic of identity and difference (something either is A or it is not-A). Ironically, this is a terrible kinship that two seemingly "different" traditions share (since a kinship, which belies the logic of identity and difference, is what these traditions share). As a colleague of ours, Matthew Zachariah, once noted, the fundamentalists across different traditions have more in common with each other than they do with moderates in their own tradition (see Naqvi and Jardine 2008).

As an aside, we can't help but indicate how, in North America, educational scholarship itself is in a state of embattled darkness:

> In spring of 2002, for example, leaders of the Bush Department of Education issued orders to delete material from the thirty-year-old Educational Resources Information Center (ERIC) database that doesn't support the general philosophy of NCLB [No Child Left Behind]. Every assistant secretary of education was directed to form a group of departmental employees with a least one person who "understands the policy and priorities of the administration" to scrub the ERIC website. Such action runs counter to the original intent of the website established in 1993 to construct a permanent record of educational research for students, teachers, citizens, educational researchers, and other scholars. Concurrently, such information deletion raises the stakes of right wing knowledge politics to a new level, as individuals will only have access to public data that supports particular ideological agendas. (Kincheloe 2006, p. 41)

The parallels between the destruction of the Basra Library and the purging of educational research in America post-9/11 should give us pause. Given such actions, the darkness of the current age needs careful thought and consideration.

III

Admittedly this loving and protecting of knowledge witnessed by the librarian of Basra during recent troubles in Iraq and what this has to say to us as scholars and teachers in education about our own work—all of this doesn't exactly fit with the popular, televised image that is afoot in these post-9/11 times of Islamic education. We don't get much in the way of the great pleasures and freedoms, the deep obligations and responsibilities, or a sense of intellectual ancestry that comes from the veneration and pursuit of knowledge. Current images are much more centered around Taliban-like schools full of obedient rote repetition and, as is often the (not wholly or always groundless) accusation, mind-numbing indoctrination that sometimes goes as far as not only discouraging questioning and thoughtfulness and meditation but in fact disparaging such things and demonizing them. We are inundated with images of repressive authoritarianism, violence, intolerance, and hatred, wherein knowledge itself has become endangered on *both sides* of the "for us or against us" ledger. After all, so-called traditional Western schools like Foundations for the Future in Calgary provide teachers with unalterable scripts and children with no voice of dissent or disruption or difference. In such schools, the very terrorizing obedience we distain in "them" is never raised regarding "us." "We" are just going "back to the basics" (see Jardine, Clifford and Friesen 2008a). *They* are indoctrinating and refusing freedom.

The *Librarian of Basra* thus begins to appear as little more than a quaint and unruly exception to the rule.

Once this image- and media- and prejudice-driven situation is added to what David G. Smith (2006a) has described as the systematic "enfraudening" and "veiled innuendos" (p. 1) that are rife in American foreign policy, we might even go as far as to lament that "knowledge becomes, as John McMurtry [1998] describes it, 'an absurd expression' (p. 192)" (Smith 2006a, p. 1). Once we hear that, in 2003, 48 per cent of Americans believed that Saddam Hussein was "personally involved" in the 9/11 attacks (Feldman 2003) and that it wasn't until March of 2006 that a very slim majority of Americans believed that weapons of mass destruction were indeed *not* found in Iraq (Teixeira 2006), knowledge, absurdity, opinionism, and deliberate enfraudening start to grotesquely intertwine. And, as Smith (2006a, p. 1) goes on to say, in such an endarkened milieu, very task of education itself becomes jeopardized: "When the lines between knowledge and misrepresentation become completely blurred in the public mind, then education as a practice of civic responsibility becomes very difficult."

All this, of course, is nothing especially new, nor, as Smith suggests, are these issues especially Islamic in their manifestation. It makes some terrible sense that, in times of threat, imaginativeness and exploration and intellectual pursuits give way, in a great paranoid rush, to the tried and true, to efforts of fixed and ensuring surveillance and the like. As Ivan Illich (1992) has suggested, war makes cultures more alike in these matters (we've seen how both "sides" have marshaled their most paranoid and unforgiving and unresponsive faces in the current conflicts in the Middle East), whereas in times of peace, differences and multiplicity and intellectual vigorousness and imagination are able to flourish.

This is another reason that this tale of the *Librarian of Basra* is so telling. We have this children's picture book (part of whose proceeds, incidentally, are donated to a fund, administered by the American Library Association, to help rebuild Basra's Central Library), with Alia and her friends loading up her car to protect the library's books—to protect the flourishing of knowledge—in a time of great impending darkness. One might even think of this true story allegorically, as full of images of taking knowledge to heart, taking knowledge to hearth and home, making a place for it where it can be nurtured and protected and allowed to flourish. A place where it can be "left in peace" (Illich 1992, p. 16) and wherein we can find comfort (common fortitude or strength) in its cultivation.

IV

There is another form of darkness that can come over the face of knowledge that is not born of embattlement but, in a sense, out of the opposite. When a culture is "left in peace" and becomes familiar and dominant, it can often lose from explicit memory and articulation the character and ancestry and bloodlines of that familiarity. What "we" do becomes simply obvious, and when our "doings" are interrupted, we don't necessarily feel enticed to self-knowledge. As an immigrant to Canada, I (R.N.) can attest to meeting looks of bewilderment or aggravation at such moments. We both wonder, then, about George W. Bush's (and his father's) admonishment that, in the face of international questioning, how "the American way of life is not up for negotiation" (Rasmussen 2003) has come to mean that it is not, in many quarters, up for examination and thinking *at all*. As a dominant force in the world, we have witnessed how often attempting to think about the events of 9/11 are taken to be nothing more than unthinkable acts of failed patriotism:

> How can any teacher teach in the name of democratic pedagogy . . . when the new politics is imbricated in exactly the opposite direction? If unilateralism and monological decision-making mark the character of political leadership, what

> becomes, for teachers and students, of the relationship between thought and action, of my belief as a teacher that indeed, what I and others may plan for tomorrow may bear an expectation of being brought into effect? If bullying, both domestically and internationally, is legitimized publicly (albeit euphemistically), how as a teacher can I council my students against what has become one of the greatest scourges in the contemporary schoolyard? If lying, duplicity and deliberate misrepresentation are acceptable strategies by which to operate in the name of Truth, what is the basis upon which any human relations may be trusted? If the academic fields of child development and child psychology can be legitimately co-opted for commercial control of the minds of the young, what becomes of intellectual liberty at even the earliest stages of new life, to say nothing of the problem of children learning early that exploiting others for personal gain is 'the way to go'? (Smith 2006a, p. 11)

There is another, equally disturbing and pernicious manifestation of this dimming of knowledge that is not simply the outcome of deliberate suppression or deceit. Hans-Georg Gadamer (1989, p. 133) hints at this phenomenon when describing the work of the artist: Belonging to a tradition in no way necessitates the *understanding* of that tradition and the conditions, nature, history, and limits of that belonging:

> The artist . . . stands in the same tradition as the public that he is addressing and which he gathers around him. In this sense it is true that as an individual, a thinking consciousness, he does not need to know explicitly what he is doing and what his work says.

Likewise, under conditions of (pre)dominance, taken-for-granted images, understandings, ideas, and practices become simply "obvious" and such obviousness need not give an account of itself to those who stand in the same tradition *or* to those emigrating into that dominant tradition. There is no compulsion, in convivial life as lived, for that life to understand, experience, and articulate itself. One could even go as far as to say that, to those within a tradition, "it goes without saying" and "it is beyond question" are signs of such belonging. In such instances, what appears to someone not fully at-home in this dominant culture is a hard, not especially knowledgeable surface of "givenness" that no longer seems tethered to any roots, ancestries, or bloodlines, and no longer brooks any question of how such matters *came to be given*. "Left in peace" *can be* a place of complacency, where the actual living conditions of that peace are not cared for or understood, but rather flattened out into familiarity. Once this occurs, *disturbing* this flatness on behalf of an attempt to understand, experience and cultivated and care for our convivial living is experienced as a threat to the peace of familiarity.

This passage from Gadamer's *Truth and Method* regarding the artist and his or her works thus speaks also to a more difficult truth, especially when we consider the burgeoning multicultural face of Canadian culture. Belonging to a culture and its forms of language and forms of life (Wittgenstein 1968) by no means entails that one needs to *understand* these matters or be able to articulate their nature and origins. *Belonging* and *understanding that belonging* are not identical. But here is the rub. If one enters Canada as part of a minority, one is being constantly called upon to understand and articulate one's culture of origin while at the same time facing a profound inarticulateness from the predominant culture into which one has emigrated. In other words, a predominate culture is rarely required to give an account of itself while, at the same time, requiring an account of those who are otherwise. Only when the condition of belonging is somehow *interrupted*, and only when the everyday familiarity of belonging becomes strange and estranged are we called upon to think about that belonging and its character.

The real issue, here, is this. In light of the question of what constitutes a livable pedagogy—a pedagogy left in peace—how can we interrupt familiar belonging in order to understand our convivial living without inducing the sorts of threat-based contractions which shred that familiarity in favor of those understandable but ontologically impossible enclosures into "us" and "them"?

V

"Mum look what I got for you from school." said my (R.N.) 7-year-old daughter, as she entered the house excitedly. She shoved an oval object into my hand as she spoke. I probably looked a little lost and she added, impatiently.

"Mum it's an Easter Egg."

As she moved around the house excitedly humming an unfamiliar tune I stared at this object on my kitchen counter that now had a name. Under the fading twilight, the bright blue and pink on the egg shone, staring back at me. At that instance, I am not quite sure what happened but whatever it was prompted me to explore the premises of this tension that I was experiencing as an immigrant parent.

This was by no means the first or final instance of such strangeness arriving in my daughter's life, arriving as it did with a sense of assured familiarity and normality. On another occasion, when I went to pick up my younger daughter from preschool around the same time as the arrival of Maria's egg, her teacher arrived at the door wearing rabbit ears.

Like so many others, I immigrated to Canada like with my husband almost 10 years ago. We have two children both born in Canada. As Muslims living in Canada, we are constantly negotiating questions of identity. Who are we in the midst of all this diversity and more than that who are our children and what they will become in what Judith Butler (2004) has called "precarious times." "Precarious"—"the position of being held through the favor of another" (OED) (see Naqvi and Prasow 2007).

As an immigrant attempting to enter into the life of a dominant culture other than my own, my family and I face an interesting reality. With bunny ears, and pinks and blues and yellows (just like the reds and greens and trees and lights around December), such matters are so familiar to those who belong to such familialness that articulation is not simply unnecessary. Asking for an articulation is precisely a sign of "not belonging." In fact, such asking is often greeted with "Who do you think you are?" and sometimes even "Why don't you go back home?" These are good questions even though they weren't meant to be. "It's Easter" or "This is what we do" or "You know? Red and green? Christmas?" are fully adequate answers from within the condition of belonging, and an immigrant voice from outside of that sphere sounds almost inevitably "out of place." Who *do* we think "we" are? Where precisely *is* "home"?

It is clear, also, that our family traditions that stretch out across India, Iran, Afghanistan, and Saudi Arabia, and the complex stories about our family lineage and our Muslim heritage are themselves intimately familiar to us. There is little doubt that if this teacher with the bunny ears, or the one who sent home the Easter egg, moved to our countries of origin, they, too, as people other-wise to such places, would run into precisely the same incredulousness, the same silent, strange and estranging, taken for granted practices. We thus share an ephemeral kinship.

I didn't ask her about the rabbit ears. She may have welcomed such a question with open arms. She may have had much to say about such matters, much knowledge to impart, many questions to ask. This is the most difficult of places to inhabit: shall I move outward toward asking and engaging and risk the bewildered stares? Or should I just forgo for now? Pile up knowledge and its pursuit away from sites of possible embattlement? Should I, this time, pull back into reserve and silence?

Feelings of separation and loss and estrangement are inevitable. And some of this sense of separation occurs, of course, between generations—between parents who visit here from Pakistan and ourselves, between us and our children, and so on. Here is the duplicity that comes from being an immigrant. By the very nature of its population makeup, immigrants to Canada have to embody many cultures from the moment they settle within its borders. A person like myself of Asian descent is already multicultural of necessity when he/she arrives in Canada. This is precarious because one's own culture remains the culture of one's origin, even though, with me and my husband and our two children, our own culture is Canada.

White Anglo-Saxon culture in North America seems premised on a strange and silent distance from its own ancestral roots. It seems that the strangest and most estranged thing in Canada isn't, for example, Islam or Pakistan, but those silent yet predominate things that "go without saying."

VI

My (D.J.) mother, whose cultural background is, through her father, French-Canadian (Terriault) back to about 1640 in Quebec, and Norwegian (Hendrickson) through her mother, always called herself English because she spoke English. Her father's family (under, I suspect, lost-track-of religious and cultural pressures), anglicized their name to "Terrio" around 1850 (only the boys names were thus changed, since the girls would, if they married, "lose" the French name). It was further anglicized by my grandfather, Gardner, to "Terrie" when the family moved from Joggins, Nova Scotia, to Toronto, Ontario, in around 1925, where "Terrio" made folks think they might be Italian.

My brother's first name is Terry. No one in my family ever spoke of these erasures of memory. That is, these erasures, for the most part, *succeeded*.

VII

In his article "'The Farthest West is but the Farthest East': The long Way of Oriental/Occidental Engagement," David G. Smith (2006b) demonstrates how the entrenchment of East and West into separate and separably definable traditions is an illusion and a dangerous one at that. In times of embattlement, such entrenchment into "us and them"—wherein our interrelatedness seems to be "revocable and provisional" (Gray 2001, p. 35–6)—this might make a terrible sort of sense. However, as Gadamer (1989, p. 284) suggests, "only in the multifariousness of voices" does any tradition exist. It is precisely this situation of "mutuality" (Smith 2006b; see also Clarke 1997, for an exploration of how Asian traditions entered into European imagination regarding the Enlightenment) within which both East and West are what they have become only because of the other. It is not simply that without those that are other-wise, we might never have occasion to think about our own familiar belonging. It is, rather, that that very familiar belonging has become what it is because of its often long-lost mutuality with those who seem simply "other."

"The Dark Ages" is but one timely example of such mutuality. What was, for Petrarch, a great Dark Age was, for Islam, an age of intellectual flourishing:

> By the 10th century, Cordoba had 700 mosques, 60,000 palaces, and 70 libraries, the largest of which had 600,000 books, while as many as 60,000 treatises, poems, polemics and compilations were published each year in al-Andalus. The library of Cairo had more than 100,000 books, while the library of Tripoli is said to

> have had as many as three million books, before it was burnt during the Crusades. The number of important and original Arabic works on science that have survived is much larger than the combined total of Greek and Latin works on science. (http://en.wikipedia.org/wiki/Islamic_Golden_Age)

Petrarch's recovery of the ancient texts of Rome and Greece was abetted by a flourishing Islamic intellectual tradition. As with the *Librarian of Basra*, a whole array of scholars took good care of "the books" in a time when Europe fell into darkness and embattlement.

It is impossible to give a full account of such matters in the present context. We would like to simply refer readers, as a starting point, to the wonderful website *Islamica Philosophica* (www.muslimphilosophy.com), as well as the online *Catholic Encyclopedia* (http://www.newadvent.org/cathen/index.html) (and countless other wealths of information). Here we will simply thread out one small line of thought that helps us understand this Librarian and her work. To preface this thread we need, first, to recall that the works of Aristotle that underwrote much of later Middle Ages European philosophy and theology were an inheritance indirectly from knowledge protected by and commented upon by Islamic scholars:

> Aristotle was understood to be a philosopher who belonged more to the Arab than the Christian world. Running against the grain of tradition and at the risk of condemnation, Abelard, Albertus Magnus, and Thomas Aquinas drew upon Aristotle's thoughts. Indeed, Aristotle's writings on metaphysics and logic were studied in Baghdad well before they were translated into Latin in Muslim Spain; then, from Toledo, they arrived in Paris by the end of the twelfth century. (Dussel 2000, p. 466)

Parenthetically, here, Hans-Georg Gadamer (and Palmer 2007, p. 421) muses upon the fact that "it is certainly no accident that in the passage of Aristotle through Arabic culture one finds many traces of that culture echoing through our language." He specifically notes how Arabic numerals arrived in Europe and how their arrival made possible an algebra that is simply impossible with Roman numerals. The world of mathematics—that very world entrusted to teachers and students in contemporary schools—thus shifted under Arabic influence. He notes as well, regarding the translation of Aristotle from the original Greek, that "Not every language is as logical as Latin. In Latin, things get weaker, paler. The whole fate of Western civilization is foreshadowed here." These tantalizingly brief comments, made when Gadamer was 96 years old, open a path for thinking about the threads of influence and inheritance that come from our *shared* Islamic past.

Al-Farabi (*c.*870–950) was known as "the Second Master" following Aristotle, and his work was one of the first to incorporate Aristotle's idea of emanation. Simply put, this idea means that the world can be understood as an emanation, a pouring forth, a "gift," one might say, of God. As such, the world holds in its multifariousness and complexities signs of God's hand; moreover, the human spirit is ensouled and therefore humanity, at its best, shows signs of God's character. Therefore (and especially of interest to educators) the task of coming to know about the world (and to not simply live in it in sleepy familiarity and belonging) is itself a venerable task and one to which it is worthy of dedicating one's life (see Netton 1998). Pursuing knowledge of the world is not antagonistic to faith but in fact a way to deepen it. (This is clearly a by-no-means uncontentious position within the history of Islam or Christianity—we point, here, not only to the fear and paranoia of fundamentalism regarding knowledge, but also to the dangerous hubris that can come with the pursuit of knowledge, a danger understood and shared by many religious traditions.) In light of the veneration of knowledge that is also commonplace in most religious traditions, the *Librarian of Basra* is not demonstrating infidelity by protecting the books but rather fidelity. In this light, too (and equally contentiously), the living disciplines that have been entrusted to teachers and students in schools, and how we might take care of those disciplines even in times when knowledge is embattled, become fascinating gifts and difficult tasks to ponder.

One of the greatest figures in this line of Islamic ancients is Ibn Sina (L. Avicenna) (980–1037) born near Bukhara in Central Asia. Here we have another generation of the wisdom of ancient Greek philosophy:

> He maintains that God, the principle of all existence, is pure intellect, from whom other existing things such as minds, bodies

> and other objects all emanate, and therefore to whom they are all necessarily related. That necessity, once it is fully understood, is rational and allows existents to be inferred from each other and, ultimately, from God. (Kemal 2007)

Avicenna elucidates the possibility of inference from God and his Word to God and his works—the *ens creata*, that which God created—and this once again ennobles the pursuit of knowledge of the created world as part and parcel of a knowledge and veneration of God. Unlike many Islamic and Christian fundamentalists who cleave solely to "The Book" and who thus set up a state of embattlement between worldly knowledge and faith, the whole of the world, in Avicenna's work, is such a sacred text. Avicenna's work on science, logic, and mathematics, as well as his careful commentaries on Aristotle, proved to be a major influence on Duns Scotus (1265–1308), thus portending a whole bloodline of Christian scholarship.

Finally, for now, we have The Great Commentator, Abul-Waleed Muhammad Ibn Rushd (L. Averroes) (1128–98), born in Cordova, Spain. Averroes' commentaries on Aristotle were a central influence on the Angelic Doctor, Thomas Aquinas (1225–74) and, therefore, his work helped theologically found contemporary Roman Catholicism (Zahoor 1997). One needs to simply glance at the grand breath of St. Thomas' *Summa Theologica* and the cascades of detailed scholarship that follows upon it to understand how profound was this knowledge kept safe by Islamic scholars. It is up from Aristotle, through Averroes to St. Thomas, in fact, that educators, directly or indirectly, inherit the very idea of "disciplines of knowledge," "subject areas" (see Thomas's "division of the sciences" [1986], which is itself of Aristotelian origin), one might say, and the rationale for their order and character. In the very mundaneity of Alberta's Program of Studies and its orderly laying out of disciplines lurk old and silent familiars. Differently put, the Alberta Program of Studies is, for good and ill, in part an Aristotelian and Islamic inheritance. Even when we heard, in Calgary, Alberta, of the ways in which the Calgary Board of Education has recently been organized around the "ends" of education, this teleological discourse is, in ways that are left completely in darkness, Aristotelian in origin, Islamic in its articulation, and eschatologically both Christian and Judaic in its character.

We've threaded our way through these authors, not in order to even begin to pretend to be authoritative in such matters, but in order to simply demonstrate how much stumbling-around-in-the-darkness we ourselves are experiencing in walking these terrains for the first time and finding ourselves so profoundly bereft. It is, frankly, humiliating in that lovely way that is the way of scholarship. Moreover, this skirting through history shows a great bias that points the knowledge protected by Islamic scholars in relation to very specific and limited Christian and Enlightenment-European traditions that were to come. One can see, for example, in the Abu Hamid al-Ghazali (1058–1111) a move away from the logic, rhetoric, and intellectualism of Aristotelianism and its emphasis on the structure and formalities of knowledge, toward poetry, imagination, creativity, and reflection. Al-Ghazali was interested in "actively considering how knowledge is *made*, rather than viewing it passively" (Moosa 2005, p. 38). Moosa goes on (p. 38) to contend that "Ibn Rushd's [L. Averroes']" extremely negative and mocking "observations [regarding al-Ghazali]. . .blissfully skirted. . .the essence of all knowledge: invention." Mossa notes (p. 38), however, that this character of al-Ghazali's work links him up, for example, to Giambattista Vico's (1668–1744) later work on imagination and *sapientia poetica* (poetic wisdom [see Vico 1984, Book Two]) as a source for how knowledge is actually *created*, and, from this thread, through to Hans-Georg Gadamer's drawing on Vico's work on images and memory in his formulation of philosophical hermeneutics (see Jardine 2006d). Even here, we can hear echoes of the subdivides of arts and sciences in contemporary schooling, and those long and heated arguments about "core curriculum" and what it means. We can hear echoes, here, too, of our images of children as active and inventive beings who must "make" something of their world in order to "know" about it (a gloss on the shallows of the educational practice of contemporary "constructivism" [see Chapter 3]).

We can hear, too, even in this emphasis by al-Ghazali on the creation of knowledge, echoes of Aristotelian emanation. In the image of God, and by analogy, the creativity of human knowledge reflects God's creative will. In our frail and finite ways, of course, we, unlike God, cannot create *ex nihilo*. Our inventiveness needs something to be invent *with*—an "inventory" of material to think and create with (invention and inventory are two etymological offshoots of the Latin term *invenio*). However, even here, an analogy, a likeness, a kinship, persists.

What was, for Christendom and Europe, a Dark Age proves to be a different story in certain threads of Islamic intellectual ancestry. In a wonderfully parallel way to that simple children's picture book by Jeannette Winter, these threads show how knowledge was protected in a "Dark Age." Similarly, *The Librarian of Basra* proves to be something more than simply "A True Story from Iraq" (a true story which, notably, never names those who set fire to the library, never names the invaders). It is, in its own way, a reminder of something nearly lost to memory and certainly endangered in contemporary over-simplified and frightened disparagements of Islam and the full breadth of its ways.

It is a reminder, too, of something far more simple and immediate. Aristotelian and Neo-Platonic theories of emanation seem so distant from the everyday world of school and schooled knowledge. But this hint, from al-Ghazali and from his confrontations with Averroes, are an ancient playing out of the contemporary educational conversations and confrontations between knowledge as structured and methodological, and knowledge as a poetic and creative act.

We find some of these long and tangled threads right in the midst of some work that Maria did at the local Mosque school (she would have been in around Grade One at the time in her "regular" school). She was given a worksheet to color in and learn about, and this work became the basis of long and ongoing conversations between children and teachers and parents. The sheet portrays the Qu'ran at the top of the page, and, in Arabic script on the right side, and English on the left, the opened pages say:

"And recite the Qu'ran clearly, beautifully."

Below this are pictured three other books, one about animals, another about birds, and a third about flowers. Underwriting this is what is called a "Do'a [prayer] before studying." It is first written in Arabic script, then transliterated into English:

> Allaahumma infa'nii bimaa alamtanii wa'alimnii maa yanfa' unii.

Then, there is an English translation in which echoes of Averroes and Avicenna can still be heard:

> O Allah. make me useful to the society with the knowledge that You have granted me and grant me the knowledge that is useful to me.

As I look back over the picture, the Qu'ran is picture sitting up, open on a stand and the bottom of the support seems to open wide, almost sheltering or housing the books pictured below it. Birds, animals, flowers. A Grade One child's simple work, with the Qu'ran pictured somehow "emanating," an embrace descending outward into worldly knowledge and a prayer regarding knowledge and being of service and use to the world with the gift of such knowledge. When D. J. came over to my house late last year, we had talked about the Qu'ran up on top of my (R.N.'s) refrigerator, open on a stand, place up high, above the frays of daily life and the fridge-magnets that pinned Maria's worksheet up for all to see.

VIII

> [I carry] a general skepticism toward all ideas which are used as sources of legitimacy by the winners of the world. I should like to believe that the task . . . is to make greater demands on those who mouth the certitudes of their times and are closer to the powerful and rich, than to the faiths and ideas of the powerless and marginalized. That way lies freedom, compassion and justice. (Nandy 1987, p. 123)

During the invasion of Iraq in 2003, reports came out of Baghdad of the American Army setting up guard outside the head offices of various oil company buildings in order to protect what were euphemistically called "American interests." At the same time, reports spread that the American administration had refused to believe the warnings that Iraq's cultural wealth would need protection if the city were to fall:

> From April 10 to 12, 2003, during the mayhem that followed the collapse of Saddam Hussein's regime, looters entered the Iraq National Museum in Baghdad. They stole and destroyed artifacts and caused damage to the museum. Seizing upon tiny bits of available information, Western archaeologists created their own

> narrative of events and aggressively promoted it through the world media. (Joffee 2004, p. 1)

Although that it is true that American troops were dispatched to protect oil company buildings in Baghdad, and it is equally true that they were not dispatched to protect the National Museum, it seems that the main thing "lost from the Baghdad museum: truth" (Aaronovitch 2003).

It was initially reported that over 170,000 items were stolen or destroyed and the ancient depth of despair sounds eerily familiar:

> The looting of the Iraq Museum (Baghdad) is the most severe single blow to cultural heritage in modern history, comparable to the sack of Constantinople, the burning of the library at Alexandria, the Vandal and Mogul invasions, and the ravages of the conquistadors.
>
> *The American Schools of Oriental Research*, April 16, 2003 (cited in Joffee 2004, p. 1)

Claims were made that the items stolen were so specific and targeted that the looters could not have been simply people "off the street" but had to be well-informed and selective agents who had planned ahead-of-time a strategic heist. "Nothing was accidental about it. Rather, it was the result of a long planned project to plunder the artistic and historical treasures that are held in the museum" (Talbot 2003, p. 1). Talbot goes on to talk about how the British press had suggested that "the ACCP [the American Council for Cultural Policy] may have influenced US government policy on Iraqi cultural artifacts" (p. 3):

> The ACCP was formed in 2001 by a group of wealthy art collectors to lobby against the Cultural Property Implementation Act, which attempts to regulate the art market and stop the flow of stolen goods into the US. (p. 3–4)

Later reports attempted to quell these claims. Far fewer items seemed to be missing. Vaults were discovered where items had been stored precisely because of knowledge of impending threats to security (shades of Alia's car-trunk). Talk came of "inside jobs" (Joffee 2004, p. 5–6)—"the work of newly deposed Baathist officials, who had been selling of our patrimony as they saw their days were numbered. As the regime fell, these Baathists went back for one last swindle" (Joffee 2004, p. 5, citing Makiya 2003). In the midst of this swirl of suggestions and accusations, David Aaronovitch (2003 p. 4) proposed that what might be at work here is a simple (albeit perhaps understandable) political presumption: "these days—you cannot say anything too bad about the Yanks and not be believed" (Aaronovitch 2003).

We will leave this foray for now with a troubling reflection. As teachers and scholars, our work involves thinking and seeking out the truth of things and this statement seems profoundly and irretrievably naïve in these post-modern times of slippery signification and political and media manipulation. David Smith (2006) suggests that our work, now, is occurring in "a season of great untruth" in which "the truth of things" is simply a manipulable item in the sway of public opinion. He speaks (2008) about the influence of Leo Strauss on contemporary Neo-Conservativism and how they took from Plato the idea of "the noble lie," where "the untrue becomes true if it helps you manage [the ignorant masses] better" (Jardine 2006a, p. x) (of course and always "for their own good" [Miller 1989]):

> But Strauss is not a nihilist if we mean by the term a denial that there is *any* truth, a belief that everything is interpretation. He does not deny that there is an independent reality. On the contrary, he thinks that independent reality consists in nature and its "order of rank" – the high and the low, the superior and the inferior. Like Nietzsche, he believes that the history of western civilisation has led to the triumph of the inferior, the rabble – something they both lamented profoundly. (Postel and Drury 2003)

The trace lines are deep and wide: Paul Wolfowitz and other members of and advisors to the Bush administration are students of Strauss's work, and Strauss's ideas are a central guiding concern in the Department of Political Science at the University of Calgary—Stephen Harper's *Alma Mater* (Smith 2008).

"A season of great untruth?" Should we suspect that Alia Muhammad Baker's efforts—whether *our* efforts—are simply attractive and convincing shadows on the cave wall? That we have been manipulated into something laughably ridiculous—all the sort of laughability that underwrites the anti-intellectualism of the previous American administration? That we've been fed a book that simply charms and spellbinds those who might venerate knowledge into believing a convincing, noble lie?

Even if it is a "true story from Iraq," what its truth is and whether we, as educators, might or should or could stand by such a truth—all of this is part of what this "simple" children's book now asks of us.

IX

Many stupid and violent things have been done in the name of Allah, and in this regard, Islam shares a terrible kinship with its two Abrahamic forbearers. Admitting this kinship can provide a certain relief.

That is why it was especially disingenuous of Benedict XVI to not admit of the violence and stupidities perpetrated in the name of the Roman Church in what turned out to be an incendiary speech given on Tuesday, September 12, 2006. The media-version of this speech—"Faith, Reason and the University: Memories and Reflections" (Benedict 2006)—focused on how the Holy Father had emphasized that, as he put it, "for Muslim teaching, God is absolutely transcendent. His will is not bound up with any of our categories, even that of rationality . . . . God is not even bound by his own word" (p. 2). Benedict cites an edition of dialogues edited by Theodore Khoury of Munster, in which, "perhaps in 1391 in the winter barracks near Ankara" (p. 2) the Byzantine Emperor Manuel II Palaiologos was arguing over the topic of "holy war" with "an educated Persian" (p. 2). If God is wholly transcendent to the world and to human categories, then there is nothing in human affairs that would prevent, curb, or discourage violence being perpetrated in the name of the faith. We are not called upon to be generous or reasonable because of some analogy to God. Manuel II argued that "not to act in accordance with reason is contrary to God's nature" (p. 2), but it seems that his Persian interlocutor disagreed. As Manuel continues in this line of argument, the cited text that caused Benedict XVI so much grief emerges. Manuel II says to his guest: "Show me just what Mohammed brought that was new, and there you will find things only evil and inhuman, such as his command to spread by the sword the faith he preached."

We'll leave, for now, the almost-overwhelming urge to speak about how Christianity's skills with the sword are themselves quite practiced, let alone the violence of a faith that created and perpetuated Residential Schools, again, for the good of godless "Indians." For now, we're fascinated by *precisely who it is* that Benedict XVI chose to cite in the history of Islamic thought—not al-Ghazali, not al-Farabi or Ibn Sina or Ibn Rushd, but Ibn Hazm.

Ibn Hazm (994–1064 CE), more fully Abu Muhammad 'Ali ibn Ahmad ibn Sa`id ibn Hazm, was born in Cordova in Southern Spain. He grew up in a time of difficult and violent ethnic and clan rivalries and war. His work is thus born and thus betrays a sense of threat, retrenchment, and embattlement. Unlike al-Ghazali, al-Farabi, Ibn Sina, or Ibn Rushd (of whom, of course, Benedict XVI, as a scholar and intellectual knows full well), in Ibn Hazm's work, the kinship between God and his creation has been severed. God is wholly Transcendent. Therefore, all we have to go on is the literal words of the Qu'ran:

> He argues that people are bound to obey only the law of God, in its *zahir* or literal sense, without restrictions, additions, or modifications. He takes the position that language itself provides all that is necessary for the understanding of its content and that, therefore, God, who revealed the Qu'ran in clear *(mubin)* Arabic, has used the language to say precisely what he means. From this position, it follows that Ibn Hazm strongly criticizes the use of reasoning by analogy *(qiyas)*. Ibn Hazm does not deny recourse to reason, since the Qu'ran itself invites reflection, but this reflection must be limited. Reason is not a faculty for independent research, much less for discovery. By submitting humans exclusively to the word of God, Ibn Hazm's literalism frees them from any choice of their own. (Arnaldez 2006)

Roger Arnaldez (2006) goes on to suggest that Ibn Hazm's work constitutes one of the "most original and important monuments of Muslim thought." Benedict comments indirectly on this originality. It has to do, according to Benedict, with the erasure of Hellenic/Greek thought from threads of Islamic thought, erasure, therefore, of any signs of Aristotelian or Neo-Platonic emanation and therefore of any sense of an analogical intimacy or kinship between God and his creation. Thus evacuated from the world, the only recourse to knowledge is *literal*—the letter of the Book. Reasoning and thoughtfulness about the living convivialities and kinships of the world thus give way, in the contemporary imagination, to Taliban-like rote repetition of the letter, and incitements to violence against those who do not follow that letter—common incitements in all forms of fundamentalism. (Here is one more source, too, of the anti-intellectualism that sometimes infects, of all things, education itself.)

Despite the clumsiness with which Benedict XVI fumbled these matters, the work of Ibn Hazm is not without importance. Those Muslim and Christian warriors who burned libraries that contained anything but "The Book" have Ibn Hazm as an ancestor. And, as we have been suggesting all along, under threat, retrenchment, the severing of convivial ties to the living world, and the attempt to secure us from them, holds sway. That Benedict chose *this* way to unfold the Church's relation to Islam was not accidental.

Later in this speech, Benedict goes on to discuss the issue of the de-Hellenization of Christianity in a way that further betrays precisely how odd and selective was his choice of Ibn Hazm alone to cite under the blanket of "Muslim teaching":

> It is often said nowadays that the synthesis with Hellenism achieved in the early Church was a preliminary enculturation which ought not to be binding on other cultures. The latter are said to have the right to return to the simple message of the New Testament prior to that enculturation, in order to enculturate it anew in their own particular *mileux*. This thesis is not only false; it is coarse and lacking in precision. The New Testament was written in Greek and bears the imprint of the Greek spirit. The fundamental decisions made about the relationship between faith and the use of human reason are part of the faith itself; they are developments consonant with the nature of faith itself.

Again, we cite that our ancestral memory of this Greek consonance has threads of Islam as its kin and its protector through a Dark Age. Although our thoughts return to the *Librarian of Basra*, the Holy Father's final incitements are important: "listening to the great experiences and insights of the religious traditions of humanity, and those of the Christian faith in particular, is a source of knowledge, and to ignore it would be an unacceptable restriction of our listening and responding." Indeed. Would that he had been more careful in laying out a kinship of "listening and responding" between Islam and Christianity. This would not only include meditations, for example, on Averroes and Avicenna wherein there is an affinity regarding the use of human reason between these two faiths. Important, also, would be some consideration and admission of how Christian faith itself has historically been quite amenable to spreading the faith through violence (and quite amenable to forms of education that are quite Talibanic in their closed-mindedness and literalist/fundamentalist paranoias). Then, perhaps, his sentimentalized journey through the Universities of Germany of his youth might have been, as the title of his journey declares, truly "Apostolic" and Ecumenical, and not quite so incendiary.

Conclusion

We end these mediations on the *Librarian of Basra* with a fascinating incident whose meaning goes far beyond its intent. Early in 2007, Rahat Naqvi, Helen Coburn, Sally Goddard and Laureen Mayer submitted an article (2007) to the *Alberta Teacher's Association Magazine* entitled "What Do I Do When 80 percent of My Students Don't Speak English?" This brief research report spoke of work done on dual language books being used in a local Calgary, Alberta Elementary School.

The paper passed into the adjudication and editorial process and nothing more was heard of until the printed magazine arrived in R.N.'s campus mail. Along with R.N.'s discovery of Jeanette Winter's children's book, this is the moment at which this chapter of ours began. Unknown to its authors, the paper had been retitled. Although the subtitle remained as the authors had written it, the main title now is "Speaking in Tongues." Along with this, there was a photograph of seven girls, each one dressed up in what appear to be "ethnic costumes."

Clearly, on the face of it, this new title probably seemed simply more "catchy" than the authors' original title. It has since caught the eye of many readers who have contacted the authors about their work. It serves, however and also, as an opportunity to think—about Al-Ghazali, for example, and his intimate connection with Sufism which references a phenomenon similar to "speaking in tongues." However, this precise phrase is peculiarly Christian in its origins and contemporary face:

> Many Christians believe that speaking in tongues is the fulfillment of the Latter Rain promised in Joel 2:28–29 and that it is the final manifestation of the Holy Spirit before the Second Coming of Christ. It is also commonly taught that you are not saved unless you have demonstrated the gift of speaking in tongues. (www.speaking-in-tongues.net)

As we've suggested, this editorial change is more meaningful than it was meant to be. This is always the way in an interpretable world (see Chapter 5). Containing meaning within an author's (or editor's) intention (*mens auctoris* [see Gadamer 2007b, p. 57]) is one more vainglorious attempt toward enclosing the world into the terrible, literal logic of identity (A=A) that is born of threat. Instead, this innocent re-titling opens gaping holes in what we thought we knew and disturbs a sense of familiarity and belonging. It is a perhaps-unintended gift that once again calls for thinking.

However, we will leave this meditation for another time.

CHAPTER ELEVEN

“Take the feeling of letting go as your refuge”

DAVID W. JARDINE

It’s like the water of a river. It naturally flows down the gradient; it never flows against it; that’s its nature. If a person were to go and stand on a riverbank and, seeing the water flowing swiftly down its course, foolishly want it to flow back up the gradient, he would suffer. Whatever he was doing his wrong thinking would allow him no peace of mind. He would be unhappy because of his wrong view, thinking against the stream. If he had right view he would see that the water must inevitably flow down the gradient, and until he realized and accepted that fact, the person would be agitated and upset. The river that must flow down the gradient is like your body. Having been young your body has become old and now it’s meandering towards its death. Don't go wishing it was otherwise, it's not something you have the power to remedy. The Buddha told us to see the way things are and then let go of our clinging to them. Take this feeling of letting go as your refuge.

— (Chah 1987)

I

The very experience that too easily results in or is premised upon a clinging threat-retraction is the one that is *sought out* by hermeneutics, Buddhism, and ecology, again each in their own way: the experience of interpretability, the experience of impermanence and the dependent co-arising of things and selves, the experience of earthy intimacy and how all things and selves are part of a fabric of interrelatedness and dependency. What comes from seeking such experiences is a sort of surge of being part of something that of necessity goes beyond our wanting and doing and the limits of our command and control, something that has "*always already everywhere inhabited*" (Smith 2006c, p. xxiv) and shaped our lives and into which we step, in pedagogy, with the task of coming to know and setting right anew:

> Our knowledge of the world instructs us first of all that the world is greater than our knowledge of it. To those who rejoice in abundance and intricacy, this is a source of joy. To those who hope for knowledge equal to (capable of controlling) the world, it is a source of unremitting defeat and bewilderment. (Berry 1983, p. 56)

Each in its own way points toward a sort of letting go of the deluded ontology of self-containedness that wants to get out front, or in behind, this belong and render it into an object under control and therefore no longer a real or perceived threat. Each points to an experience of coming to understand the convivial, dependent co-arising of the world and my self. Each thus is especially telling in the contemporary atmosphere of perpetual war against the very idea of threat itself. And this both inside and outside of the world of education.

Each points, too, to how, under threat, a mechanism ensues: like trying to grab cornstarch dissolved in water, the faster and harder and more desperately we try to seize these matters and cling to something permanent, the more substantial they *feel* and the more is aggravated our desire to grip even tighter (this is why all the talk radio blur of people saying how they feel is so disturbing a closed-circuit and how equally disturbing is the ease with which this felt-world can be manipulated and teased into seemingly important and seemingly well-meaning compliances). But it never *is* thus, and a pedagogy built on this grip becomes exhaustedly caught either in the building of unbreachable battlements or in the sad laments of "if only."

There is no real refuge in such delusional pursuits.

Put this way, however, all this sounds far too grandiose and impractical and unpracticable and frankly rather philosophically psychedelic. This is one of the great secrets of a pedagogy left in peace, because it is *precisely the opposite*. Understanding this requires reiterating two caveats that have been at work in our explorations.

First, a recitation of a passage discussed in Chapter 5 in relation to hermeneutics and its practice and the links of this to an error that sometimes arises in ecological thinking:

> This is one of the secrets of ecological mindfulness. To understand what is right in front of us in an ecologically sane, integrated way is to somehow see this particular thing *in place*, located in a patterned nest of interdependencies without which it would not be what it is. Differently put, "understanding 'the whole'" involves paying attention to *this* "in its wholeness." This rootedness in the particular is what helps prevent ecology from becoming woozy and amorphous–a disembodied idea that misses the particularities in the flit of *this* Ruby-Crowned Kinglet pair in the lower pine branches and how this movement is so fitting here, in the coming arch of spring in the Rocky Mountain foothills. (Jardine 2008b, p. 143)

This is what is meant by Hans-Georg Gadamer's insistence (1989, p. 307ff.) that understanding is always application—it is always, as his teacher Edmund Husserl insisted, the *understanding of something* and, moreover, that that "something" will have something to say about the worthwhileness of our exploration of it. The first caveat, then, is that a pedagogy left in peace is not pointing to some large and grand insight, but to something local, immediate work that needs to be done. It is only in the fabric of *actually working through a topic* and opening up its particular possibilities and free spaces that a sense of the interpretability of the world and ourselves arrives. Untethered from (as Gadamer's teacher called it) "the thing itself" (Husserl 1970) and the way that tether holds attention to account, interpretation becomes either reckless like a post-modern scatter-shooting of proliferating, accelerating connectionism (what a colleague and I have jokingly called "brainstem-storming"—this is connected to that, and this to that and endlessly so on, which can too easily eventually "exhaust itself in inglorious compromise" [Kermode 1980, p. 80, citing Paul Ricouer]), or reclusive, pulling inward away from the world. This is why hermeneutics insists that the individual case is always "fecund" (Gadamer 1989, p. 38) in the letting-go of the deluded ontology of self-containedness and the beginnings of an interpretation of some worldly phenomenon. It is the wholeness of *this particular topic* entrusted to teachers and students in schools that is at issue. The real work, therefore, is always in this sense "local." By analogy, it is not about "saving the environment" but knowing about, learning about, and doing the specific work that is needed here, setting *this* right anew. This is not a matter of just working locally and thinking globally. This skips over what is the most difficult matter: thinking locally, coming to know about *this* and not just "acting locally" having *thought* only globally. Therefore, application, in this hermeneutic sense, does not mean taking fully understood general laws, methods, or principles and simply aiming them at a particular case. It means doing the work of tracing out how the particular case can have something vital to say about what we have heretofore understood those laws, methods, and principles to be. As we saw, right at the beginning of our "Introduction," in that long passage from Gadamer's speech in 1986, when these "individual cases" first arrive, they first seem to believe that anything is possible, that all of the convivial threads of the past can and should be simply overturned, that they should be listened to without constraint or resistance or work. The work of a pedagogy left in peace is the slow work of finding out, in concert with the young, what possibilities are truly open and then, from there, building new solidarities.

But still, this sounds too woozy and huge. As I was in the process of finishing this chapter, I received an e-mail from a former MA student, a high school English teacher in Calgary, Alberta. She sent me a passage from a Canadian novel she had been reading and had sent copies to a common acquaintance and friend, a high school Mathematics teacher in the city, with the request to forward it to yet another acquaintance and friend who is also a high school Mathematics teacher in Calgary. I mention all this because it is a real and local instance of what Gadamer (1986, p. 59) called a "chain of generations" that we all understand, often in ways unspoken, is then, in some measure, handed along to our students in class after class, year after year, in each of our classes no matter what the course might be. "Understanding and interpretation are not constructions based on principles, but the furthering of an event that goes far back" (Gadamer 1989, p. xxiv])—with the understanding, too, that such furtherance requires, of necessity, "set[ting] right anew" (Arendt 1969, p. 192), not simply the numbing repetition of the same.

> The ordering of life by rules of law . . . is incomplete and needs productive supplementation. At issue is always something more than the correct application of general principles. Our knowledge . . . is always supplemented by the individual case, even productively determined by it. The judge not only applies the law *in concreto*, but contributes through his very judgment to developing the law. [Our knowledge] is constantly developed through the fecundity of the individual case. (Gadamer 1989, p. 37)

(Compare this, if you will, to the image of the judge in Immanuel Kant's *Critique of Pure Reason* [1964, p. 20; see also Chapter 3.)

Here is the passage that came by e-mail:

> The first dwellers of the prairie addressed themselves to an original wholeness when they came to the Dirt Hills. I come here to convince myself that we have not yet erased all vestiges of that organic unity, that we may still take counsel from the circle. The unbroken arc has, at one time or another, entered the

> cosmologies of all religions, all civilizations east and west. My own culture at its forgotten core recognizes too that life sustains itself in a circle of wholeness. There is a harmonic in the English language that runs from the circle to the ideal of beauty through the words *wheel, whole*, and *health*. It goes like this: a circle is a wheel, a wheel is a whole- the two words echo one another. *Whole* comes from the Old English *hal*, and *hal* is the root of *heal* and *health*. Beauty, by the standards of nature and any sane culture, is nothing more and nothing less than health, wholeness. Robinson Jeffers, a West Coast poet, bypassed all this etymology and said it as a simple truth: "The greatest beauty is organic wholeness." Standing here, my vision pulled along lines that run to the hundred-mile sweep of horizon, there is no avoiding another voice of the western part of this continent and what he had to say about lines, circle, and man on the prairie. In *Wolf Willow*, Wallace Stegner described the Northern Great Plains as "a country of geometry" where a "Euclidean perfection abides." (Herriot 2002)

In reading this happenstance arrival, the images cited in Chapter 5 from Wendell Berry about health and healing and wholeness (Berry 1986, p. 103) arise all over again and freshly re-readable, in *need* of re-reading; reminders that the geometries of circles and arcs are not isolated bits and pieces of some curriculum guide to be simply memorized, but are also abundantly earthly in their experienceability. They are festive memorials such that, even in their abstract formulation, they can be *remembered* not just *memorized* (see Chapter 8). The seemingly isolated and pristine and self-contained abstractions of the geometries of circles don't then disappear from view. They simplly "let go" of their memorizable self-containedness and become visible in the keeps of their arrival *from which* they might be abstracted (see Chapter 7). Every mathematical formula, shall we say, breaks forth as if from a center and causes whole worlds of relations, cultures, locales, and ancestries, to be summoned.

But then (and here is something often overlooked), when we now go back to those abstract formulae, we can experience how they "contain" myriads of worlds (see Friesen and Jardine 2009). They become radiant and beautiful and their power and reach, along with the specific nature and limits of our human ability to abstract, all this starts to come into view. We find ourselves in the field of what mathematics actually *is*: a living discipline in and of the convivial world, in which particular doings of being human are hidden and at work. Even at their most abstract, arcs summon circles, circles summon centers and peripheries, and so on. "In each dust mote is vast abundance" (Hongzhi 1991; see Chapter 4) and likewise, too, in each seemingly self-enclosed formula or rule.

Actual, practical, practiced, ground-level workings of the world is where a pedagogy in peace finds its real refuge. A student from another graduate course has since been pursuing a graduate degree at Waterloo University in Ontario, Canada. About a year ago, he sent me links to a project he recently completed for a course University of Waterloo's Master of Mathematics for Teaching program, *History of Mathematics 680*. At the core, Adam Sahib (2011) blends together two beautiful things: first, the need, as a Muslim, to face Mecca for prayers each day, combined with the peculiarly complex issue of living, as a Muslim, on a sphere whose geometry and directionality can be investigated. More simply put, how do you know you are facing Mecca if the earth is a sphere? Adam and I joked that if you face directly east from here in Calgary, Alberta, it means that you're facing somewhere near Kiev, Ukraine, 29 degrees north of Mecca (Okay, altogether now! If you are 29 degrees from a point on a sphere, and the sphere has a circumference of approximately 25,000 miles, about how far away are you?). He produced a brilliant six-part YouTube video entitled *Determining the Direction of the Kaaba* (Sahib 2011) which he has said, with genuine modesty, is simply a first venture to try to understand these matters as a mathematician and a Muslim.

When I showed this video to yet another graduate class, a teacher almost instantly sent me a link (see Arab [2011]) to a project done by a group of Grade Seven students in the Spanish/English bilingual program in their mathematics class: *Arab Influence in Mathematics and Hispanic Culture*.

Patterns. Repetitions. Familiarities. Family resemblances. Things belonging together in relations of kind. In the past year, these threads got woven into my undergraduate Math/Science Curriculum class first to the peculiarities of birding guides like that of Roger Tory Peterson (1980; see Jardine 2008a), and what makes them accessible, useful, searchable, informative, earthly, and immediate. Meditations on the ways of scientific description and what it looks like when it is done well. From there, leaps to websites full of the work of Earnest Haeckel (1900), who influenced Jean Piaget (and then, in fact, Benjamin Spock) to say that the life of the developing child recapitulates the life of the developing species (ontogeny recapitulates phylogeny; see Chapter 3, for details on this vestige). When we were exploring the patterns and repetitions that organized those birding guides, up came in seconds Haeckel's (1862) work *Die Radiolarien (Rhizopoda Radiaria)* (e.g. http://caliban.mpiz-koeln.mpg.de/haeckel/radiolarien/) and another even more astounding work also produced an astounding work entitled *Kunstformen der Natur* (1900) (see http://caliban.mpiz-koeln.mpg.de/haeckel/kunstformen/natur.html) in which some of the symmetries of biological species are cataloged. In my undergraduate class, this made Roger Tory Peterson's text understandable and experienceable in a new way. It was as if finding Haeckel's work "set right" what we had already experienced, opened it up from its sense of impending finality, and made new things imaginable and perhaps possible in the classrooms we inhabited. We had lovely speculations of how a Grade Three class might be totally transformed if we projected these beautiful, slightly disturbing Haeckel oddities around the room and began conversations about the bewildering abundance and recognizable resemblances of the world and its creatures (irresolvable to either of the extreme simplifications of identity or difference—Jean Piaget [1965, p. 6] noted Henri Bergson's early twentieth century "surprise at the disappearance of the problem of 'kinds' . . . in favor of the problem of 'laws'").

Here again, too, echoes of Ludwig Wittgenstein's (1968) talk of the fabric of language being constituted, not by laws of identity and difference ("we can draw boundaries,") but by "kinships" (p. 36) and "family resemblances" (p. 32). How we can draw boundaries but not give them (p. 32). Hans-Georg Gadamer's thoughts (1989, p. 114) on "verisimilitude"—"likeness." Not surprisingly, there is a "kindness" at the heart of a pedagogy left in peace. And this is where that seeming exaggeration of things becoming "radiant" in their simplicity comes true. A student in that undergraduate class talked to us about going back to her practicum Grade One class and seeing the children deeply engrossed in something she had seen many times before but yet not seen: *pattern blocks*. Blocks that seemed so trivial before now "shine" with significance and bristle with real, practical, and practicable possibilities.

Arcing back, then, to high school English and e-mail messages that arrived, I've sent these passages back in response and appreciation for this passage from Trevor Herriot:

> The rhythm of a song or a poem rises, no doubt, in reference to the pulse and breath of the poet. But that is too specialized an accounting; it rises also in reference to daily and seasonal and surely even longer rhythms in the life of the poet and in the life that surrounds him. The rhythm of a poem resonates with these larger rhythms that surround it; it fills its environment with sympathetic vibrations. Rhyme, which is a function of rhythm, may suggest this sort of resonance; it marks the coincidences of smaller structures with larger ones, as when the day, the month, and the year all end at the same moment. Song, then, is a force opposed to specialty and to isolation. It is the testimony of the singer's inescapable relation to the earth, to the human community, and also to tradition. (Berry 1983, p. 17)

Or, pushed further by Gary Snyder (1980, p. 48):

> I'm farming all the time: cutting six cords of firewood for the winter, planting fruit trees, putting in fencing, taking care of the chickens, maintenance on the car, and maintenance on the truck, doing maintenance on the road. There's an enormous amount of physical work to be done. That's a kind of work rhythm to be sure . . . which is just good old rural life work rhythms. Though I think probably the rhythm I'm drawing on most now is the whole of the landscape of the Sierra Nevada, to feel it all moving underneath. There is the periodicity of ridge, gorge, ridge, gorge, ridge, gorge at the spur ridge and tributary gorges that make an interlacing network of, oh, 115-million-year-old geological formation rhythms. I'm trying to feel through that more than anything else right now. All the way down to some Tertiary gravels which contain a lot of gold from the Pliocene. Geological rhythms. I don't know how well you can do that in poetry. Well, like this for example. Have you ever tried singing a range of mountains?

Or further:

> Rhyme leads one no doubt to hear in language a very ancient cosmology. Rhyme is not only an echo from word to word.

> Arrangement for arrangement, the order of language, being an order in language, evokes and mimes a cosmic order. In realizing itself, rhyme is tuned in to [this cosmology]. Rhyme and meter are praise. An indirect theology. (Meschonnic and Bedetti 1988, p. 69)

One last one for now:

> There are lots of sounds that we haven't heard that the birds know about. There are lots of rhythms that we haven't heard that the trees know about. It's not only the sounds in *your* environment. (Addy 1992)

And thus the great arc back through language and grammar and poetry to those birding guides and these Pine Grosbeaks at the feeder.

Interpretation (as with ecological consciousness and the actual practice of Buddhism), then, works down at the ground level so to speak, even though the attempt to articulate the ontological gesture of this work is highly arcane. It is interested, in its investigations, in *vestigia*—"tracks" and the particularities of their pursuit. It is at *this* level that the false ontology of self-containedness is belied and, thread by thread, undone. There is something misleading, here, about simply casting out these passages one after the other, because each one points to "possible ways of shaping our lives" (Gadamer 1986, p. 86)—possible ways, in fact, that our lives have *already been shaped*. So eating up these passages and gorging on the connections can simply aggravate the delusion that a pedagogy left in peace is meant to unwind. Letting go and actually working through what becomes of my life when I read "It's not only the sounds in *your* environment" is worth the while of a lifetime.

Thus, as mentioned above, hermeneutics, Buddhism, and ecological consciousness, each in their own way, seek out and take up the suffering caused by and codified in the false ontology of substance and self-containment. Each in their own way provide ways to unwind this deluded sense of self-containment out into all its relations, letting ourselves go out into the flowering and flourishing of relations that arrive when things and our selves are left unthreatened and in peace. Every topic entrusted to teachers and students in school *is* empty of self-existence.

Hence the second caveat in this proposal of a practicable pedagogy left in peace. It is connected to the first caveat but extends it. A pedagogy left in peace is ground level, tough, pleasurable work. It is the deep pleasure of *scholarship*. And every time one topic starts to give way and become full of rich fields of possibility, the next topic seems to arrive as hard as nails—flat, uninteresting, with no prospects of invitation. So the process always must start again, with *this* site of the tough-yet-false semblance of self-containedness. Right after the eventually exhilarating work over scientific description and patterns, you're asked to teach commas and semicolons to a Grade Five class, and the work starts all over again.

Thus, the second caveat of a pedagogy left in peace. This sort of work involves a recurring experience: it's too much, it's overwhelming. Panic sets in. I haven't read enough. I don't know enough. I'll never know enough. It's too late. Maybe later. Threat. Withdrawal.

When my student-teachers sometimes feel overwhelmed by the wealth of knowledge that has been entrusted to them and their students, we often and repeatedly go through a meditative exercise. I call it this because "meditation and [cultivating] familiarity are synonymous" (Pabongka 2006, p. 561). (These meditations are as much for me as they are for them.) I bring in a globe and point to the lines named Tropic of Cancer and Tropic of Capricorn. It doesn't matter, now, if you don't know what these mean, if you don't have knowledge of them and their significances and possibilities. You can rest assured that, despite this feeling of lack, knowledge will be there when and if you go to these things and begin investigating their ways. They will have relations, histories, possibilities real and imagined—there will be maps and astronomies and names and stories waiting patiently for your arrival.

Relax. Even though it will take some work, the embrace of the world will start to hold up and make buoyant your efforts. You don't and won't need to hold the whole world aloft by your own wanting and doing.

This is, of course, not the assurance that comes from having somehow sated the prospect of coming to know and put an end to it by feeling full enough and in command of all future possibilities and prospects. What has become familiar, here, is not just the nests of relations that dependently co-arise around *this or that particular topic* (what, in hermeneutics, would be designated as an ontic knowledge [see Heidegger 1962])—knowledge of a particular existing thing (Greek *onto*)—for example, birding guides, or Haeckel or rhyme in poetry and so on, and all the resembling familiarities between them. What also becomes familiar is a deepening understanding that *this (empty of self-existence and instead dependently co-arising) is how all ideas, images, things, and selves exist.* This *ontological familiarity* predisposes us to seek free spaces of open, convivial possibilities in *whatever* might come to meet us. It allows us to go to the tropics, to look for the Greek etymology of *tropos* as "turning" and to rest assured that there is a place, here, full of possibilities, and that Cancer and Capricorn will somehow figure in all of this. This is the ontological space in which a pedagogy left in peace is cultivated. It is not a pedagogy born solely on the back of cramming ourselves full of as much as we can but a pedagogy born of letting go of such panics and resting assured that, despite the tough work ahead, the venture is there to be had, the solidarities are there to be made and re-made and set right anew. This is not the false assurance that wants to guarantee that it will happen. Distraction, circumstance, contingency, frailty, fear, and exhaustion are always afoot. But, as with all meditative practices, when we are able come back to this spot, it is right where we left it *despite* troubled surrounding circumstances, causes, and conditions.

You can start to get good at this. You can become experienced in taking up the world interpretively, meditatively. But this needs to be looped back to Hans-Georg Gadamer's words about "being experienced." Being experienced doesn't culminate in knowing more and better than anyone else (expertise). "Experience has its proper fulfillment not in definitive [amassed] knowledge but in the openness to [new] experience[s] that is made possible by experience itself" (Gadamer 1989, p. 355).

II

This is the real refuge of pedagogy left in peace. It is not a large matter of grand proportions, but *this* moment and *that*, when this fluttering open arrives. There can be joy and peace here. Comfort in these moments, when the "sickness out there" (see Chapter 4) gives way and we are invited out of our heads.

Out of our heads: a pedagogy left in peace does not arrive simply by cultivating a still inwardness (Sanskrit *Samadhi*) separate from the world. Such stillness is a *necessary condition* of our healing, but it is not *sufficient condition*. A pedagogy left in peace also invites and requires the cultivation of wisdom (Sanskrit *Vipassana*) about the world:

> There are two kinds of peacefulness. One is the peace that comes through *Samadhi*. The other is the peace that comes through Wisdom. The mind that is peaceful through Samadhi is still deluded. Such peace is dependent on the mind being separated from phenomena. When it's not experiencing any contact or activity, there is calm, and consequently you get attached to the happiness that comes with that calm state. But as soon as there is impingement through the sense, the mind gives in right away. It gets to be afraid of phenomena [and, as we've seen, then retracts inward and secures its surroundings all over again]. (Chah 2001, p. 91)
>
> . . .
>
> The peace that comes from wisdom is distinctive, because when the mind withdraws from tranquility [and moves outwards into the world], the presence of wisdom makes it unafraid. With such energy, you become fearless. Now you know phenomena as they are and are no longer afraid. (p. 93)

Letting ourselves experience the interpretability of the world and its convivial, dependent co-arisings can be *experienced*, it can be *articulated*, it can be *shared*, it can be *cultivated*, it can be *practiced*. And through shared, convivial practice, one can become increasingly familiar with this experience and, hopefully less caught by fear, more compassionate, more forgiving of ourselves and others. You start to get unanticipated e-mails. You go looking for one Earnest Haeckel reference and suddenly *Die Radiolarien (Rhizopoda Radiaria)* arrives. I still haven't sat with it carefully enough, but I know that is what it will require of me if I am to do well by it. I must shape my life in its light if I am to understand it properly.

So, this book, *Pedagogy Left in Peace*, has not been a prescription for how to cure the world—and, in particular, the world of education—of its woes and its myriad embattlements, because its focus has on what can and has arisen in schools and in the hearts and minds of teachers and students *despite* such woes. It is about some wisdom about the world and its ways into which we can invite our students and ourselves. Some sense of fearlessness. Some sense of freedom and solidarity.

Here is where I will end. When talking about these ideas with some teachers and colleagues, I've often run into a particular lament: "Yeah, sure, I've also seen some wonderful stuff in classrooms. But what about . . . ," which then leads, too often, to reiterations of our sad lot and the terrible conditions that surround us and to always imminent, always urgent, time-is-running-out plans to cure the world or complaints or laments about its terminal condition. It is right in this lingering ellipsis that lays the point of a pedagogy left in peace. When wonderful things erupt between teachers and students in the real world of schooling, it is *miraculous*—from the Latin *miraculum*, "of wonder" (On-Line Etymological Dictionary [2007])—and sloughing off, trivializing, or marginalizing these events with "it can't happen here," is ignoring the advent of the very sort of truth that might be our real refuge. Patricia Clifford, a dear friend and colleague who died on August 12, 2008, would always have a loving yet sharp-edged comeback to those who said such work in schools is not possible in "the real world." If it actually exists, it *must* be possible.

There is nothing necessary to a pedagogy left in peace and the deep pleasures of scholarship and thinking that it entails, and no amount of insistence or urgency will force its arrival. And even if all the troubled conditions of schooling were lifted, if all the "if onlys" were met, its arrival is *still* not assured. Although a bit of a rarity, however, it *is* possible. All we can do is practice and invite our students and colleagues into the rich lift of the world that comes from thinking rigorously and deeply and well.

These sorts of frail assurances might be as good as it gets in this odd profession of ours, premised as it is on the ongoing dance between the impermanence of the world and the impermanence of my self.

REFERENCES

Aaronovitch, D. (2003). Lost from the Baghdad museum: Truth. *The Guardian Unlimited*. June 10, 2003. Retrieved August 4, 2007 from www.Guardian.co.uk/Iraq.

Addy, O. (1992). From the liner notes to the Kronos Quartet's (1992). *Pieces of Africa*. Elektra/Nonesuch CD 979253-2.

al-Zubaidi cited in (n.a.), *La Convivencia*: The Peaceful and Productive Co-existence of Jews, Christians, and Muslims in Medieval Spain. Accessed on-line October 2007 at: http://www.geocities.com/Athens/Academy/8636/Convivencia.html.

Aqsa Parvez. (2010). Aqsa Parvez's father, brother get life sentences. No parole for 18 years in 'honour killing.' Accessed on-line July 18, 2010 at: http://www.cbc.ca/canada/story/2010/06/16/parvez-sentence.html.

Arab Influence in Mathematics and Hispanic Culture (2011). Accessed on-line September 3, 2011 at: http://projects.cbe.ab.ca/ict/2learn/jkshpur/redele/index.html.

Arendt, H. (1969). *Between past and future: Eight exercises in political thought*. New York: Penguin Books.

Arnaldez, R. (2006). Entry on Ibn Hazm. Retrieved September 30, 2007 from http://www.muslimphilosophy.com/hazm/ibnhazm.htm.

Arthos, J. (2000). "To be alive when something happens": Retrieving Dilthey's *Erlebnis*. *Janus Head*, (3), 1. Accessed on-line August 30, 2010 at: http://www.janushead.org/3-1/jarthos.cfm.

Ayres, L. (1909). *Laggards in our schools*. New York. A "pdf" version is available on line at: http://www.archive.org/details/laggardsinoursch00ayrerich.

—(1915). *A measuring scale for ability in spelling*. Available on line at: donpotter.net.

Bastock, M. (2005). *Suffering the image: Literacy and pedagogic imagination*. Unpublished Doctoral Dissertation, Faculty of Education, University of Calgary.

Bastock, M. and Jardine, D. (2006). Children's literacy, the Biblia Pauperum and the wiles of images. *Journal of Curriculum and Pedagogy*. 2(2), 65–9.

Benedict XVI. (2006). Faith, reason and the university: Memories and reflections. A speech by Benedict XVI, Tuesday, September 12, 2006, to the Aula Magna of the University of Regensburg. Retrieved September 22, 2007 from www.vatican.va/holy_father/benedict_xvi/speeches/2006/September.

Berry, W. (1983). *Standing by words*. San Francisco, CA: North Point Press.

—(1986). *The unsettling of America: Essays in culture and agriculture*. San Francisco, CA: Sierra Club Books.

—(1989). The profit in work's pleasure. *Harper's Magazine*, March 1989, 19–24.

Bly, R. (1988). *A Little Book on the Human Shadow*. New York: Harper and Row.

Bobbitt, F. (1918). *The curriculum*. Boston, MA: Houghton Mifflin.

—(1924). *How to make a curriculum*. Boston, MA: Houghton Mifflin.

Bordo, S. (1987). *The flight to objectivity*. Albany, NY: State University of New York Press.

Bowers, C. A. (2005). *The false promises of constructivist theories of learning: A global and ecological critique*. New York: Peter Lang Publishers.

Boyle, D. (2006). The man who made us all work like this . . . . *BBC History Magazine*, June 2003. Accessed on-line August 5, 2009 at: http://www.david-boyle.co.uk/history/frederickwinslowtaylor.html.

Braverman, H. (1998). *Labor and monopoly capital: the degradation of work in the twentieth century*. New York: Monthly Review Press.

Brown, W. (2006). *Regulating aversion: Tolerance in the age of identity and empire*. Princeton, NJ: Princeton University Press.

Bush, G. W. (2001). *Address to a Joint Session of Congress and the American People*. September 20, 2001. Accessed on-line July 14, 2008 at: http://www.whitehouse.gov/news/releases/2001/09/20010920-8.html.

Butler J. (2004). *Precarious life: The power of mourning and violence*. London, UK: Verso.

Calasso, R. (1993). *The marriage of Cadmus and Harmony*. New York: Alfred Knopf.

Callahan, R. (1964). *America, education and the cult of efficiency*. Chicago, IL: University of Chicago Press.

Campbell, D. (1998). *Writing security: United States foreign policy and the politics of identity*. Minneapolis, MN: University of Minnesota Press.

Caputo, J. (1987). *Radical hermeneutics: Repetition deconstruction and the hermeneutic project*. Bloomington, IN: Indiana University Press.

Carruthers, M. (2003). *The craft of thought: Meditation, rhetoric, and the making of images, 400–1200*. Cambridge, UK: Cambridge University Press.

—(2005). *The book of memory: A study of memory in medieval culture*. Cambridge, UK: Cambridge University Press.

Carruthers, M. and Ziolkowski, J. (2002). *The Medieval craft of memory: An anthology of texts and pictures*. Philadelphia, PA: University of Pennsylvania Press.

Chah, A. (1987). Our real home: A talk to an aging lay disciple approaching death. *Access to Insight*. Accessed on-line December 24th, 2010 at: http://www.accesstoinsight.org/lib/thai/chah/bl111.html.

—(2001). *Being Dharma: The essence of the Buddha's teachings*. Boston, MA: Shambala Press.

—(2005a). *Everything arises, everything falls away*. Boston, MA: Shambala.

—(2005b). *Food for the heart*. Somerville, MA: Wisdom Publications.

Charters, W. (1923). *Curriculum construction*. New York: Macmillan.

Clarke, J. J. (1997). *Oriental enlightenment: the encounter between Asian and Western thought*. London: Routledge.

Cleary, T. and Cleary, J. C. (1992). Introduction to *The Blue Cliff Record*. Boston, MA: Shambala Press, xvii–xxx.

Cubberley, E. P. (1922). *A brief history of education: A history of the practice and progress and organization of education*. Boston, MA: Houghton Mifflin Co.

Daly, M. (1978). *Gyn/Ecology: The Metaethics of Radical Feminism*. Boston, MA: Beacon Press.

Derrida, J. and Ferraris, M. (2001). *A Taste for the Secret*. Cambridge, UK: Polity Press.

Descartes, R. (circa 1640/1901). *Descartes Meditations: A Trilingual HTML Edition*. David B. Manley and Charles S. Taylor, eds. (Includes original Latin text of 1641, Duc de Luynes French translation of 1647, and an English Translation by John Veitch from 1901). Accessed on-line, June 22, 2008 at: http://www.wright.edu/cola/descartes/mede.html.

—(circa 1637/1955). Discourse on method. In *Descartes Selections*. New York: Charles Scribner's Sons.

Dibdin, M. (1996). On-line (unpaginated) citation from *Dead Lagoon: An Aurelio Zen Mystery*. Posted April 11, 2002. Accessed on-line July 15, 2008 at: http://www.freerepublic.com/focus/news/664292/posts.

Dressman, M. (1993). Lionizing lone wolves: The cultural Romantics of literacy Workshops. *Curriculum Inquiry*, 23, 3, (Autumn, 1993), 245–63.

Dufour, R. and Eaker, R. (1998). A New Model: The Professional Learning Community. Professional Learning Communities at Work:

Best Practices for Enhancing Student Achievement. From *A New Model: The Professional Learning Community*. The Eisenhower National Clearinghouse for Mathematics and Science Education (ENC). Accessed on-line at: http://www.myeport.com/published/t/uc/tucson73/collection/1/4/upload.doc.

Dussel, E. (1988). Was America discovered or invaded? *Concilium* (1988), pp. 126–34.

—(1995). *The invention of the Americas: Eclipse of the "other" and the myth of modernity.* New York: Continuum Books.

—(2000). Europe, modernity, and Eurocentrism. *Neplanta: Views from the South*. 1(3), 465–78.

El Akkad, O. and Bascaramurty, D. (2007). Aqsa's slaying and the religion-culture clash. Toronto's *Globe and Mail*, December 13, 2007. Accessed on-line July 15, 2008 at: http://www.theglobeandmail.com/servlet/Page/document/v5/content/

Eltahawy, M. (2008). Caught in the clash of civilizations. *International Herald Tribune. The Global Edition of the NewYork Times*. January 18, 2008. Accessed on-line July 15, 2008 at: http://www.iht.com/articles/2008/01/18/opinion/edelta.php.

English, K. (2007). Private tragedy and public issues. *Toronto Daily Star On-Line*, December 15, 2007. Accessed on-line July 15, 2008 at: http://www.thestar.com/comment/columnists/article/28579.

Feldman, L. (2003). The impact of Bush linking 9/11 and Iraq. *The Christian Science Monitor*. March 14, 2003 edition. Retrieved September 16, 2007 from http://www.csmonitor.com/2003/0314/p02s01-woiq.html.

Ferrero-Waldner, B. (2006). Clash of civilizations or dialogue of cultures: Building bridges across the Mediterranean. Bibliotheca Alexandrina and Anna Lindh Foundation Lecture, Alexandria, Egypt, 6 May 2006. Accessed on-line July 17, 2008 at: http://europa.eu/rapid/pressReleasesAction.do?reference=SPEECH/06/279&form at=HTML&aged=1&language=EN&guiLanguage=en.

Fischlin, D. and Nandorfy, M. (2002). *Eduardo Galeano: Through the looking glass*. Montreal, QC: Black Rose Books.

Fordham University (2007). *Internet Medieval sourcebook of Fordham University*. Retrieved September 22, 2007 from http://www.fordham.edu/halsall.

Friesen, S. (2010). Uncomfortable bedfellows: Discipline-based inquiry and standardized examinations. *Teacher Librarian: The Journal for School Library* Professionals. October 2010. Accessed on-line January 29, 2011 at: http://www.encyclopedia.com/Teacher+Librarian/publications.aspx?pageNumber=1.

Friesen, S. and Jardine, D. (2009). On field(ing) knowledge. In S. Goodchild and B. Sriraman, (eds), *Relatively and Philosophically E[a] rnest: Festschrifte in Honour of Paul Ernest's 65th Birthday. The Montana Mathematics Enthusiast: Monograph Series in Mathematics Education*. Charlotte, NC: Information Age Publishing, pp. 149–75.

Frum, D. and Solomon, E. (2004, January 18). Interview. On the Canadian Broadcasting Corporation television program *Sunday Morning*.

Fukyama, F. (2006). *The end of history and the last man*. New York: Free Press.

Gadamer, H.-G. (1970). Concerning empty and ful-filled time. *Southern journal of philosophy, 8*(Winter), 341–53.

—(1977). *Philosophical hermeneutics*. Berkeley, CA: University of California Press.

—(1983). *Reason in the age of science*. Cambridge, MA: MIT Press.

—(1986).The idea of the University–Yesterday, today, tomorrow. In D. Misgeld and G. Nicholson, eds. and trans. *Hans-Georg Gadamer On Education, Poetry, and History: Applied Hermeneutics*. Albany, NY: SUNY Press, pp. 47–62.

—(1989). *Truth and method*. J. Weinsheimer, Trans. New York: Continuum Books.

—(1994). *Heidegger's ways*. Boston, MA: MIT Press.

—(2001). *Gadamer in conversation: Reflections and commentary*. R. Palmer, ed. and trans. New Haven CT: Yale University Press.

—(2007a). Aesthetics and hermeneutics. In R. E. Palmer, ed. *The Gadamer reader: A Bouquet of the later writings*. Evanston IL: Northwestern University Press, pp. 124–31.

—(2007b). Classical and philosophical hermeneutics. In R. E. Palmer, ed. *The Gadamer reader: A Bouquet of the later writings*. Evanston IL: Northwestern University Press, pp. 41–71.

—(2007c). In R. Palmer, Trans. and Ed. *The Gadamer reader: A bouquet of later writings*. Evanston IL: Northwestern University Press.

—(2007d). Greek philosophy and modern thinking. In R. E. Palmer, ed. *The Gadamer reader: A Bouquet of the later writings*. Evanston IL: Northwestern University Press, pp. 266–73.

—(2007e). Hermeneutics as practical philosophy. In R. E. Palmer, ed. *The Gadamer reader: A Bouquet of the later writings*. Evanston IL: Northwestern University Press, pp. 227–45.

—(2007f). From word to concept: the task of hermeneutics as philosophy. In R. Palmer, ed. and trans. *The Gadamer reader: A Bouquet of the later writings*. Evanston IL: Northwestern University Press, pp. 108–22.

Gadamer, H. G. and Derrida, J. (1989). *Dialogue and Deconstruction: The Gadamer-Derrida encounter*. Albany, NY: State University of New York Press.

Gadamer, H. G. and Palmer, R. (2007). A look back over the collected works and their effective history. In R. E. Palmer, ed. *The Gadamer reader: A Bouquet of the later writings*. Evanston IL: Northwestern University Press, pp. 409–27.

Gatto, J. (2006). The national press attack on academic schooling. Available on-line at: http://www.rit.edu/~cma8660/mirror/www.johntaylorgatto.com/chapters/9d.htm.

Gray, J. (1995). *Enlightenment's wake*. London: Routledge.

—(2001). *False dawn: The delusions of global capitalism*. New York: The New Press.

—(2003). *Al Qaeda and what it means to be modern*. New York: The New Press.

Gruber, H. and Voneche, J. J., eds. (1977). *The essential Piaget*. New York: Basic Books.

Gyalchok, S. and Gyaltsen, K., Compilers (2006). The peacock's neutralizing of poison (attributed to Dharmaraksita). In *Mind training: The great collection*. Boston, MA: Wisdom Publications, pp. 155–70.

Haeckel, E. (1900). *Riddle of the universe at the close of the nineteenth century*. New York: Harper Brothers.

Hardon, J. (1985). *Pocket Catholic dictionary*. NewYork: Doubleday.

Heidegger, M. (1962). *Being and time*. New York: Harper and Row.

—(1968). *What is called thinking?* New York: Harper and Row.

—(1971). *Origin of the Work of Art*. New York: Harper and Row.

—(1972). *Poetry, language and thought*. New York: Harper and Row.

—(1977a). Letter on humanism. In M. Heidegger (1977). *Basic Writings*. New York: Harper and Row, pp. 189–242.

—(1977b). The essence of truth. In M. Heidegger (1977). *Basic Writings*. New York: Harper and Row, pp. 113–42.

—(1978). *The Metaphysical Foundations of Logic*. Bloomington, IL: Indiana University Press.

—(1985). *History of the Concept of Time*. Bloomington, IL: Indiana University Press.

Henry, M. and Mitchell, B. (2007). Muslim teen was abused, friends say. *The Toronto Daily Star On-Line*. December 12, 2007. Accessed on-line July 20, 2008 at: http://www.thestar.com/article/284824.

Herrin, J. (1987). *The formation of Christendom*. Princeton, NJ: Princeton University Press.

Herriot, T. (2002). *River in a Dry Land*. Toronto, ON: Macfarlane, Walter and Ross.

Hillman, J. (2005a). Notes on opportunism. In James Hillman (2005). *Senex and Puer*. Putnam, CT: Spring Publications, pp. 96–112.

—(2005b). Senex and puer: an aspect of the historical and psychological present. In James Hillman (2005). *Senex and Puer*. Putnam, CT: Spring Publications, pp. 30–70.

—(2006a). Anima Mundi: Returning the soul to the world. In James Hillman (2006). *City and soul*. Putnam, CT: Spring Publications, Inc., pp. 27–49.
—(2006b). Loving the world anyway. In James Hillman (2006). *City and soul*. Putnam, CT: Spring Publications, Inc., pp. 128–30.
Hongzhi, Z. (1991). *Cultivating the empty field: The silent illumination of Zen master Hongzhi*. San Francisco, CA: North Point Press.
Humphreys K. (2004). *Death on the Nile–Murder of Hypatia, end of Classic scholarship in Egypt*. Retrieved September 22, 2007 from http://www.jesusneverexisted.com/hypatia.html.
Huntington, S. (1993). The Clash of Civilizations? *Foreign Affairs*. Summer 1993. Accessed on-line July 17, 2008 at: http://uniset.ca/terr/news/fgnaff_huntingtonclash.html.
—(1996). The West: Unique, not universal. *Foreign Affairs*, *75*(6), 28–46.
—(2003). *The clash of civilizations and the remaking of world order*. New York: Simon and Schuster Paperbacks.
Husserl, E. (1970). *The crisis of European science and transcendental phenomenology*. Evanston, IL: Northwestern University Press.
Hyde, L. (1983). *The gift: Imagination and the erotic life of property*. New York: Vintage Books.
Illich, I. (1970). *Deschooling society*. New York: Harper and Row.
—(1980). Vernacular values. Accessed on-line, July 7, 2008 at: http://www.preservenet.com/theory/Illich/Vernacular.html#EMPIRE.
—(1992). *In the mirror of the past: addresses and lectures, 1978–1990*. New York: Marion Boyars.
—(1993). *In the vineyard of the text: A commentary on Hugh's Didascalicon*. Chicago, IL: University of Chicago Press.
—(2001a). Guarding the eye in the age of show. Accessed on-line August 31, 2011 at: http://www.davidtinapple.com/illich/.
—(2001b). The Scoptic past and the ethics of the gaze. Accessed on-line August 31, 2011 at: http://www.davidtinapple.com/illich/.
—(2005). The rivers north of the future. Toronto, ON: House of Anansi Press.
—(with Cayley, D.) (1992). *Ivan Illich in conversation*. Concord, ON: The House of Anansi Press.
Illich, I. and Sanders, B. (1988). *ABC: The alphabetization of the popular mind*. Berkeley, CA: North Point Press.
Inhelder, B. (1969). Some aspects of Piaget's genetic approach to cognition. In H. Furth ed. *Piaget and knowledge: Theoretical foundations* Englewood Cliffs, NJ: Prentice-Hall, pp. 9–23.
James, W. (1890/1981). *The Principles of psychology*. Cambridge, MA: Harvard University Press.

Jardine, D. (1992a). Reflections on hermeneutics, education and ambiguity: Hermeneutics as a restoring of life to its original difficulty. In Pinar, W. and Reynolds, W., (eds), *Understanding Curriculum as a Phenomenological and Deconstructed Text*. New York: Teacher's College Press, pp. 116–30.

—(1992b). *Speaking with a boneless tongue*. Bragg Creek, AB: Makyo Press.

—(1997). "Under the tough old stars": Pedagogical hyperactivity and the mood of environmental education. *Clearing: Environmental Education in the Pacific Northwest*. 97, April/May 1997, 20–3.

—(1998a). Awakening from Descartes' nightmare. In Jardine (1998), pp. 5–33.

—(1998b). *"To dwell with a boundless heart": On curriculum theory, hermeneutics and the ecological imagination*. New York: Peter Lang Publishers.

—(1998c). Student teaching, interpretation and the monstrous child. In Jardine (1998), pp. 123–34.

—(2000). *"Under the tough old stars": Ecopedagogical essays*. Brandon, VT: Holistic Education Press.

—(2005). *Piaget and education: A primer*. New York: Peter Lang Publishers.

—(2006a). Dreaming of a single logic. Foreword to D. Smith (2006), pp. ix–xvii.

—(2006b). On the ecologies of mathematical language and the rhythms of the earth. In D. Jardine, P. Clifford, and S. Friesen (2006). *Curriculum in abundance*. Mahwah, NJ: Lawrence Erlbaum and Associates, pp. 187–99.

—(2006c) On hermeneutics: "What happens to us over and above our wanting and doing." In K. Tobin and J. Kincheloe (eds), *Doing Educational Research: A Handbook*. Amsterdam: Sense Publishers, pp. 269–88.

—(2006d). Youth need images for their imaginations and for the formation of their memories. *Journal of Curriculum Theorizing*, *22*(4), 3–12.

—(2008a). Birding lessons and the teachings of cicadas. In Jardine, Clifford, and Friesen, pp. 153–8.

—(2008b). The stubborn particulars of grace. In Jardine, Clifford, and Friesen (2008), pp. 143–52.

—(2008c). The surroundings. In Jardine, Clifford, and Friesen (2008), pp. 159–64.

—(2008d). On the while of things. *Journal of the American Association for the Advancement of Curriculum Studies*. February 2008. Accessed at: http://www.uwstout.edu/soe/jaaacs/vol4/Jardine.htm

Jardine, D., Clifford, P., and Friesen, S. (2003). *Back to the basics of teaching and learning: "Thinking the world together."* 1st Edition. Mahwah, New Jersey: Lawrence Erlbaum and Associates.

—(2006). *Curriculum in abundance*. Mahwah, NJ: Lawrence Erlbaum and Associates.
—(2008a). *Back to the Basics of Teaching and Learning: Thinking the World Together*, 2nd Edition. New York: Routledge.
Jardine, D., Bastock, M., George, J. and Martin, J. (2008b). Cleaving with affection: On grain elevators and the cultivation of memory. In Jardine, D., Clifford, P., and Friesen, S., (2008), pp. 31–58.
Jardine, D., Clifford, P., and Friesen, S. (2008c). Introduction: An interpretive reading of "back to the basics." In Jardine, D., Clifford, P., and Friesen, S. (2008), pp. 1–10.
—(2008d). Scenes from Calypso's cave: On globalisation and the pedagogical prospects of the gift. In Jardine, D., Clifford, P., and Friesen, S. (2008), pp. 211–22.
—(2008e). "Whatever happens to him happens to us": Reading Coyote reading the world. In Jardine, D., Clifford, P., and Friesen, S. (2008), pp. 67–78.
Joffee, A. (2004). Museum madness in Baghdad. *Middle East Quarterly*. Spring 2004. Retrieved June 30, 2006 from www.meforum.org/article/609.
Johnson, B, Fawcett, L. and Jardine, D. (2006). Further thoughts on "Cutting nature's leading strings": A conversation. In Jardine, D., Friesen, S. and Clifford, P. (2006), pp. 139–48.
Kanigel, R. (2005). *The one best way: Fredrick Winslow Taylor and the enigma of efficiency*. Cambridge MT: The MIT Press.
Kant, I. (1964). *Critique of pure reason*. London: MacMillan.
—(1794/1983). What is enlightenment? In *Perpetual peace and other essays*. Indianapolis, IN: Hackett Publishing Company.
Kay, J. (2007). The true enemy: human tribalism. *National Post*, On-line edition. December 18, 2007. Accessed on-line
December 22, 1007 at: www.nationalpost.com/story-printer.html?id=175169.
Kemal, S. (2007). Entry on Avicenna. Retrieved September 16, 2007 from http://www.muslimphilosophy.com.
Kermode, F. (1980). *The Genesis of Secrecy: On the Interpretation of Narrative*. Cambridge, MA: Harvard University Press.
Kincheloe, J. (2006). How did this happen? The right-wing politics of knowledge and education. In J. Kincheloe and S. Steinberg, (eds) (2006). *What you don't know about schools*. New York: Palgrave MacMillan, pp. 31–68.
Kincheloe, J and Steinberg, S. (eds) (2006). *What you don't know about schools*. New York: Palgrave MacMillan.
Kovitz, R. (1997). *Room behaviour*. Toronto, ON: Insomniac Press.
Levering Lewis, D. (2008). *God's crucible: Islam and the making of Europe, 570–1215*. New York: W.W. Norton.

Lowney, C. (2006). *A Vanished World: Muslims, Christians, and Jews in Medieval Spain*. Oxford UK: Oxford University Press.
MacMillan, M. (2006). What would Kissinger do? In *The Globe and Mail* (Toronto, Ontario), Saturday, February 2, 2006, A12.
Makiya, K. (2003). Kanan Makiya's war diary. *The new republic online*. April 14, 2003. Retrieved September 11, 2007 from www.tnr.com/doc.mhtml?i=iraq&s=diary041403.
Malvern, S. (1994). Recapping on recapitulation: How to primitivise the child. *The Third Text, 27* (summer), 21–30.
Mann, V., Glick, T., and Dodds, J., (eds) (2007). *Convivencia: Jews, Muslims, and Christians in Medieval Spain*. New York: George Brazillier.
McMurtry, J. (1988). *Unequal freedoms: the global market as an ethical system*. Toronto, ON: Garamond Press.
Melnick, C. (1997). Review of Max Van Manen and Bas Levering's Childhood secrets: Intimacy, privacy and the self reconsidered. *Journal of Curriculum Studies*, 29(3), 370–3.
Meschonnic, H. and Bedetti, G. (1988). Rhyme and life. *Critical Inquiry*. *15*(1), (Autumn 1988), 90–107.
Miller, A. (1989). *For your own good: Hidden cruelty in child-rearing and the roots of violence*. Toronto: Collins.
Mommsen, T. E. (1942). "Petrarch's conception of the 'Dark Ages'." *Speculum*, 17(2) (April 1942), 226–42.
Moosa, E. (2005). *Ghazali and the poetics of the imagination*. Chapel Hill: The University of North Carolina Press.
Morris, M. and Weaver, J. (2002). *Difficult Memories: Talk in a (Post) Holocaust Era*. New York: Peter Lang Publishers.
Muller, J. (2008). Us and Them. In *Foreign Affairs*, March/April 2008, pp. 18–35.
Nandy, A. (1983). *The intimate enemy: Loss and recovery of self under colonialism*. Delhi: Oxford University Press.
—(1987) Cultural frames for social transformation: A Credo. *Alternatives 12*(1), 113–23.
Naqvi, R. and Prasow, C. (2007). Precarious positionings. *Journal of the American Association for the Advancement of Curriculum Studies*. (3), February 2007. Retrieved September 30, 2007 from http://www.uwstout.edu/soe/jaaacs/vol3/naqviprasow.htm.
Naqvi, R. and Jardine, D. (2008) "Some say the present age is not the time for meditation": Thoughts on things left unsaid in contemporary invocations of "traditional education." Jardine, D., Clifford, P., and Friesen, S. (2008), pp. 185–94).
Naqvi, R. and Smits, H., (eds) (2011). *Thinking about and enacting curriculum in "Frames of War."*, Landham MD: Lexington Books.

Naqvi, R., Coburn, H., Goddard, S., and Mayer, L. (2007). Speaking in tongues: what do I do when 80 percent of my students don't speak English? *The ATA [Alberta Teachers' Association] Magazine*. Summer 2007, 8–11.

Netton, I. R. (1998). Entry on Abu Nasr Muhammad ibn Muhammad ibn Tarkhan ibn Awzalagh al-Farabi. Retrieved September 16, 2007 from http://www.muslimphilosophy.com.

Nietzsche, F. (1975). *The Will To Power.* New York: Random House.

Nishitani, K. (1982). *Religion and nothingness*. Berkeley, CA: University of California Press.

Norris-Clarke, W. (1976). 'Analogy and the Meaningfulness of Language about God: A Reply to Kai Nielsen', *The Thomist, 40,* 176–98.

Offman, C. (2007). Muslim clerics denounce girl's death, but reiterate hijab's importance. *CanWest News Service; National Post.* Published:Friday, December 14, 2007. Accessed on-line July 10, 2008 at: http://www.canada.com/story.html?id=56e824c9-fd7e-401c-bf91-1a1721a37bb6&k=98221&p=2.

On-Line Etymological Dictionary (OED). Accessed on-line September 30, 2007 from www.etymology-on-line.com.

Pabongka Rinpoche (2006). *Liberation in the palm of your hands.* Boston, MA: Wisdom Publications.

Palmer, R. (2007). Introduction to Gadamer, H.G. (2007c). In R. Palmer, Trans. and ed. *The Gadamer reader: A bouquet of later writings.* , Evanston IL: Northwestern University Press, pp. 123–4.

Peterson, Roger Tory (1980). *A field guide to the birds east of the Rockies*, 4th Edition. Boston, MA: Houghton Mifflin Company.

Pezze, B. D. (2006). Heidegger on *Gelassenheit. Minerva – An Internet Journal of Philosophy.* (10), 94–122. Accessed on-line September 19, 2010 at: http://www.ul.ie/~philos/Own2.html.

Piaget, J. (1952). *Origins of intelligence in children.* New York: International Universities Press.

—(1965). *Insights and Illusions of Philosophy*. New York: Meridian Books.

—(1970). *Structuralism*. New York: Harper and Row.

—(1971a). *The construction of reality in the child*. New York: Ballantine Books.

—(1971b). *Genetic epistemology*. New York: W.W. Norton.

—(1972). *Judgment and reasoning in the child.* Totawa, NJ: Littlefield and Adams.

—(1973). *Psychology of Intelligence*. Totowa, NJ: Littlefield and Adams.

—(1974). *The child's conception of the world*. London: Paladin Books.

—(1977). The mission of the idea. In H. Gruber and J. J. Voneche, (eds), *The essential Piaget* New York: Meridian Books, pp. 26–37.

Piaget, J. and Evans. R. (1973). *Jean Piaget: the Man and his Ideas*. New York: E. P. Dutton and Co.

Pinar, W. (2006). Foreword: The lure that pulls flowerheads to the sun. In D. Jardine, S. Friesen and P. Clifford, (eds) (2006), pp. ix–xxii.

Pinar, W., Reynolds, W., Slattery, P., and Taubman, P. (1995). Understanding curriculum: An introduction to the study of historical and contemporary curriculum discourses. New York: Peter Lang Publishers.

Pinkola-Estes, C. (1996). *Women who run with the wolves*. New York: Random House.

Postel, D. and Drury, S. (2003). Noble lies and perpetual war: Leo Strauss, the Neo-Cons, and Iraq. Danny Postel interviews Shadia Drury. *Information clearing house*. October 2003. Retrieved October 1, 2007 from http://www.informationclearinghouse.info/article5010.htm.

Rasmussen, L. (2003). The everlasting covenant. Sunday, February 2nd, 2003. Retrieved October 2, 2007 from http://www.stjoan.com/homilies3/rasmussen2.02.03.htm.

Reston, J. (2005). *Dogs of God: Columbus, the Inquisition and the defeat of the Moors*. New York: Doubleday.

Robert, R. (2007). Muslim teen's death 'not about culture' relative says. *The National Post*. December 12, 2007. Accessed on-line April 4, 2008 at: http://network.nationalpost.com/np/blogs/toronto/archive/2007/12/12/aqsa-s-father-remanded-into-custody.aspx.

Ross, S. M. (2004). Gadamer's late thinking on *Verweilen*." *Minerva - An Internet Journal of Philosophy*, Vol. 8. Access on-line July 19, 2010 at: http://www.ul.ie/~philos/vol8/gadamer.html.

Ross, S. M. and Jardine, D. (2009). Won by a certain labour: A conversation on the while of things. *Journal of the American Association for the Advancement of Curriculum Studies*. Accessed on-line July 21, 2009 at: http://www.uwstout.edu/soe/jaaacs/Vol5/Ross_Jardine.htm.

Sahib, A. (2011). *Determining the Direction of the Kaaba*. Part one of six parts accessed on-line September 3, 2011 at: http://www.youtube.com/watch?v=z82C-SUcjSw).

Said, E. (2001). The clash of ignorance. *The nation*. October 22, 2001. Accessed on-line October 22, 2006 at: http://www.thenation.com/doc/20011022/said.

Sen, A. (2007). *Identity and violence: The illusion of destiny*. New York: Penguin Books Ltd.

Sendak, M. (1988). *Where the wild things are*. New York: Harper Collins.

Smith, D. G. (1999a). Brighter than a Thousand Suns: Pedagogy in the Nuclear Shadow. In David G. Smith (1999). *Pedagon: Interdisciplinary*

Essays in the Human Sciences, Pedagogy and Culture. New York: Peter Lang Publishers, pp. 127–36.
—(1999b). Children and the gods of war. In David G. Smith (1999). *Pedagon: Interdisciplinary essays in the human sciences, pedagogy and culture*. New York: Peter Lang Publishing, pp. 137–42.
—(1999c). The hermeneutic imagination and the pedagogic text. In David G. Smith (1999). *Pedagon: Interdisciplinary essays in the human sciences, pedagogy and culture*. New York: Peter Lang Publishing, pp. 27–44.
—(1999d). *Pedagon: Interdisciplinary Essays on Pedagogy and Culture*. New York: Peter Lang Publishers.
—(2006a). Enfraudening in the public sphere: The futility of empire and the future of knowledge after "America." In D. G. Smith, *Trying to teach in a season of great untruth: Globalization, empire and the crises of pedagogy* Rotterdam, NL: Sense Publishing, pp. 1–13.
—(2006b). The farthest West is but the farthest East: The long way of Oriental/Occidental engagement. In D. G. Smith, *Trying to teach in a season of great untruth: Globalization, empire and the crises of pedagogy* . Rotterdam, NL: Sense Publishing, pp. 35–58.
—(2006c). Introduction. In D. G. Smith, *Trying to teach in a season of great untruth: Globalization, empire and the crises of pedagogy* Rotterdam, NL: Sense Publishing, pp. xxi–xxvii.
—(2006d). Not rocket science. In D. G. Smith, *Trying to teach in a season of great untruth: Globalization, empire and the crises of pedagogy* Rotterdam, NL: Sense Publishing, pp. 71–80.
—(2006e). The specific challenges of globalization for teaching and vice versa. In D. G. Smith, *Trying to teach in a season of great untruth: Globalization, empire and the crises of pedagogy* Rotterdam, NL: Sense Publishing, pp. 15–34.
—(2006f). *Trying to teach in a season of great untruth: Globalization, empire and the crises of pedagogy*. Rotterdam, NL: Sense Publishing.
—(2008). From Leo Strauss to collapse theory: considering the Neoconservative attack on modernity and the work of education. *Critical Studies in Education*, 49(1), March 2008, pp. 33–48.
Snyder, G. (1980). *The real work*. New York: New Directions Books.
—(2003). The place, the region and the commons. In *The practice of the wild*. Berkley CA: Counterpoint Books, pp. 27–51.
Spanish: Real Academia Espanola de la Lengua Castellana 1714. Accessed on-line June 28, 2008 at: http://foolswisdom.com/users/sbett/acadamia-real.htm.
Spock, B., and Parker, S. (1957). *Dr. Spock's Baby and Child Care*. New York: Cardinal.

Steinberg, S., Kincheloe, J., and Stonebanks, C. (2010). *Teaching against Islamophobia*. New York: Peter Lang Publishing.

Stock, B. (1983). *The implications of literacy: Written language and models of interpretation in the eleventh and twelfth centuries*. Princeton, NJ: Princeton University Press.

Talbot, A. (2003). US government implicated in planned theft of Iraqi artistic treasures. *World Socialist Web Site*. Retrieved September 30, 2007 from http://wsw.org/articles/2003/apr2003/loot-a19.shtml.

Taylor, F. W. (1903) *Shop Management [Excerpts]*. Accessed on-line August 14, 2010 at:http://www.marxists.org/reference/subject/economics/taylor/shop-management/abstract.htm.

—(1911). *Scientific management, comprising shop management, the principles of scientific management and testimony before the special house committee*. New York: Harper and Row.

Teixeira, R. (2006). Public opinion watch. *Center for American progress*. Retrieved September 16, 2007 from http://www.americanprogress.org/issues/2006/03/b1500197.html.

Thomas Aquinas (1986). *The division and method of the sciences*. Toronto, ON: Pontifical Institute.

Thompson, W. I. (1981). *The time falling bodies take to light: Mythology, sexuality and the origin of culture*. New York: St. Martin's Press.

Trungpa. C. (2003). The myth of freedom and the way of meditation. In C. Trungpa *The collected works of Chogyam Trungpa*, Vol. 3. Boston: Shambala Press.

Tsong-Kha-Pa (2000). *The great treatise on the stages of the path to enlightenment (Lam rim chen mo)*. Vol. 1. Ithaca, NY: Snow Lion Publications.

Turner, V. (1987). Betwixt and between: The liminal period in rites of passage. In L. Mahdi, S. Foster, and M. Little, (eds), *Betwixt and between: Patterns of masculine and feminine initiation*. La Salle, IL: Open Court, pp. 3–41.

Tyler, R. W. (1949) Basic principles of curriculum and instruction. Chicago, IL: The University of Chicago Press.

Tyler, S. (1986). Post-modern ethnography: From document of the occult to occult documentation. In J. Clifford and G. Marcus, eds. (1986) *Writing culture: The poetics and politics of ethnography*. Berkeley: University of California Press, pp. 122–40.

Usher, R. and Edwards, R. (1994). *Postmodernism and education*. London: Routledge.

Vico, G. (1984). *The new science of Giambattista Vico. Unabridged translation of the Third Edition (1744)*. Ithica, NY: Cornell University Press.

Voneche, J., and Bovet, M. (1982). Training research and cognitive development: What do Piagetians want to accomplish? In S. Modgil and C. Modgil (eds), *Jean Piaget: Consensus and controversy* . London: Holt, Rinehart and Winston, pp. 83–94.

von Humbolt, Wilhelm (2000 [1793–4]). Theory of Bildung. In I. Westbury, S. Hopmann, and K. Riquarts (eds), *Teaching as a Reflective Practice: The German Didaktik Tradition* [Trans. By Gillian Horton-Kruger.] Mahwah, NJ: Lawrence Erlbaum. pp. 57–61.

Wallace, B. (1987). *The stubborn particulars of grace*. Toronto, ON: McClelland and Stewart.

Walther, I. and Metzger, R. (1997). *Vincent van Gogh: The complete paintings*. New York: Taschen.

Weinsheimer, J. (1987). *Gadamer's hermeneutics*. New Haven, CT: Yale University Press.

White, P. and Mick, H. (2007). Teen death highlights cultural tensions. *The Globe and Mail On-Line*. December 12, 2007. Accessed on-line June 22, 2008 at: http://www.theglobeandmail.com/servlet/story/RTGAM.20071212.wlfathers12/BNStory/National.

Winter, J. (2005). *The librarian of Basra: A true story from Iraq*. Toronto, ON: Harcourt Inc.

Wittgenstein, L. (1968). *Philosophical investigations*. Cambridge, UK: Blackwell's.

Wood, E. M. (2006). Democracy as ideology of empire. In C. Mooers, ed. *The new imperialists*. Oxford, UK: One World Press, pp. 9–24.

Wrege, C. D. and Greenwood, R. (1991). *Frederick W. Taylor: The Father of Scientific Management: Myth and Reality*. New York: Irwin Professional Publishing. Currently out of print. The text of *Chapter 9* is available on-line at: johntaylorgatto.com/chapters/9d.hFtm.

Yates, F. (1974). *The art of memory*. Chicago, IL: University of Chicago Press.

Yolen, J. (1992). *Encounter*. Illustrated by D. Shannon. San Diego, CA: Harcourt Brace Jovanovich.

Zahoor, A. (1997). Entry on Abul-Waleed Muhammad Ibn Rushd (L. Averroes). Retrieved September 16, 2007 from http://www.muslimphilosophy.com.

INDEX